Strategic Planning for the Family Business

To our families, who daily remind us of the
importance of balancing love and work

Also by Randel S. Carlock:

The Need for Organization Development in Successful
Entrepreneurial Firms

Also by John L. Ward:

Creating Effective Boards for Private Enterprises: Meeting the
Challenges of Continuity and Competition

Keeping the Family Business Healthy: How to Plan for Continuing
Growth, Profitability and Family Leadership

Strategic Planning
for the
Family Business

Parallel Planning to Unify
the Family and Business

Randel S. Carlock

and

John L. Ward

palgrave

First published 2001 by
PALGRAVE
Houndmills, Basingstoke, Hampshire RG21 6XS and
175 Fifth Avenue, New York, N.Y. 10010
Companies and representatives throughout the world

PALGRAVE is the new global academic imprint of
St. Martin's Press LLC Scholarly and Reference Division and
Palgrave Publishers Ltd (formerly Macmillan Press Ltd).

ISBN 0–333–94731–2 hardcover

This book is printed on paper suitable for recycling and made from fully managed and sustained forest sources.

A catalogue record for this book is available from the British Library.

Library of Congress Cataloging-in-Publication Data

Carlock, Randel S., 1948–
   Strategic planning for the family business : parallel planning to unify the family and business / Randel S. Carlock and John L. Ward.
     p. cm.
   Includes bibliographical references (p.) and index.
   ISBN 0–333–94731–2
   1. Family-owned business enterprises—Planning—Handbooks, manuals, etc. 2. Businesspeople—Family relationships—Handbooks, manuals, etc. I. Ward, John L., 1945– II. Title.
HD62.25 .C37 2000
658.4'012—dc21   00–048298

Editing and origination by
Aardvark Editorial, Mendham, Suffolk

10 9   8   7   6   5   4   3   2   1
10 09 08 07 06 05 04 03 02 01

Printed in Great Britain by
Creative Print & Design (Wales), Ebbw Vale

Contents

PART II
Planning for the Family

PART III
Planning for the Business

PART IV

Integrating Family and Business Plans

List of Figures

List of Tables

Preface

John Ward and I began discussing this new book more than two years ago. Our plan at that time was to write a second edition of *Keeping the Family Business Healthy* (Jossey-Bass, 1987). As it turned out, we came up with something we think is better.

John invited me to co-author a second edition because our decade of work together demonstrated our shared belief in the importance of planning in long-term family business success. Of course, the fact that I had been using *Keeping* in my family business courses since 1989 was also a plus. John knows that it is a good idea to keep one's best customers committed!

At first, we thought our plan to write an updated edition of *Keeping* made sense. *Keeping* was the first book to encourage strategic planning for family businesses. It was a landmark in helping to shape the field of family business as an academic discipline. And since it was a recognized classic, and the most referenced book in the field of family business, why not just improve it with current thinking and new materials?

Once the project got started, we quickly realized that we were creating a book for a new and very different family business reader. In the last 13 years, the change in family business has been startling. When *Keeping* was published in 1987, the participation of the family in the family business was acknowledged, but the focus was clearly on the owner-manager. That point of view made sense because the owner-manager was the central actor in the family business. He (most business owners at that time were male) was typically a founder or controlling owner and had been in power a long time. His values, personality and management style were the main influences on the company's culture.

That is less so today. While men still dominate as leaders of family businesses, statistics show that women are making great strides as first and subsequent generation business leaders. Approximately 40 percent of all family firms have a female family member in top management and 15 percent expect a female member of the family to be the next CEO (chief executive officer).[1] Beyond gender, though, we find that our unit of study is not only owner-managers or even sibling teams, but rather the entrepreneurial family.

What does this mean? We find that the separation of business and family issues is diminishing. As we proceeded with this project, we found we were writing about business leaders who wanted to make family an even more integral part of the business plan at an early stage. No longer are these families content to let the CEO pick the 'favorite son' – or 'favorite daughter' – to carry on the family legacy. Today's successful 'business family', two words that you will see linked throughout this book, is creating an open culture that involves as many family and non-family members as possible in the shaping and focus of the business. As publicly traded corporations have discovered the value of shattering barriers to information and idea sharing among employees, smart family leaders are doing the same.

Although the role of the senior generation is obviously still very important, we propose that the family business of the 21st century will be based on an expanded business model of shared power and ownership. The single owner-manager is being replaced by men and women from multiple generations of the extended family who benefit by working well as a team. In addition, changing social and family values are shaping new roles beyond that of the owner-manager. New social values related to gender, careers, power and pluralism require more inclusive and flexible family business structures.

A demand for increased participation has resulted in new ownership, governance, family leadership and community leadership roles beyond the traditional role of an owner-manager.

When *Keeping* was published, one of the chapters was entitled 'Ensuring Family Interest in Leading the Business'. Thirteen years ago, the idea of joining the family business was not always the next generation's first priority. A family business career was often viewed as a fall-back or an alternative to a 'real' job in a large publicly traded corporation. Since then, the value of a family business career has improved – for two very important reasons.

First, the downsizing wave within public corporations during the 1980s and 90s killed the notion of lifetime career security for most workers. Second, entrepreneurial activity became recognized as an important contributor to economic growth.

That is why the new family-owned business is no longer the chafing, limited institution it used to be. If planned and executed well, the family business can become a dream job for all who participate and a chance to better control careers and lives. We now see a younger generation that has a stronger interest in the family business because it is something that is uniquely theirs to build.

The family-owned firm is also being recognized on an international scale. A 1996 article in *The Economist* highlighted this importance of family firms to national economies:

> Family firms dominate commercial life in the emerging markets of Asia and Latin America and play a larger part than is generally acknowledged in developed economies as well. In America, Germany and Italy, such firms make an especially big cumulative contribution to jobs and exports. A lot of big companies are nowadays eager to copy the speed of decisions and the entrepreneurial flair that family ownership and control are thought to confer.[2]

During the past decade, the combination of a strong global economy, new technologies, increasing market opportunities and the participation of a new generation of family members have together contributed to the increased vitality of family businesses. Family businesses are becoming more sophisticated – not only about management but also more specifically about family business management. The recognition that a family business model is a legitimate subject of study by colleges, universities, trade associations, professional consultants and family business organizations has created an increased awareness of the challenges and opportunities that exist in business families.

For all of these reasons, we decided to write this new book with a very different version of how to keep the family business not only healthy, but thriving into the 21st century.

We are introducing a new concept to meet this challenge. We call it the Parallel Planning Process (PPP)™ – a new way to gather the personal, financial and strategic priorities of both family and business and combine them into a single planning strategy for the family business.

For years, the focus of family business planning centered on two issues – estates and management succession. Those goals are far too limited for today's family firm. Today, business families want more. The business is not only a tool for profit but for self-expression, innovation and legacy. Today's successful family business, with its more inclusive structure, can be an organic institution that changes and prospers with each generation of leadership.

We are going to introduce a number of new planning ideas with brand new names in this edition. These terms are discussed when introduced and can be found in the Glossary at the end of the book. Here is a summary of our concepts:

Parallel Planning Process (PPP): In greater detail, the PPP integrates planning for the needs and expectations of the family and the business systems. The PPP assumes that family and business systems are interdependent and that an action or an event in either system affects the other. It also proposes new processes that link the family and business systems.

Family Enterprise Continuity Plan: This aspect of the PPP is a regular review of the family's values, talents and commitment to the business. It is a plan, updated at agreed-upon intervals, to look objectively at the skills and commitment of family members to sustain and grow the business over time.

Business Strategy Plan: This element of the PPP is forged when all the best identified talent of the organization – family and non-family – gathers to review regularly the nature of the business. The questions asked in this segment of the planning process should go well beyond the simple 'Are we making money?'; it should regularly review the course and growth of the business and always ask the toughest question: Should this business continue to be family owned?

Business Analysis Tools: In this edition, we are encouraging the application of business planning tools commonly used by the most sophisticated large corporations. These include concepts such as Economic Value Added, Sustainable Growth Rate, SWOT (Strengths, Weaknesses, Opportunities and Threats) Analysis, Balanced Score Card, 7-S Analysis and Stakeholder Thinking. We will explain these concepts and their implementation within the PPP in the coming chapters.

This new emphasis on the business family, rather than just the family business, represents an important change in thinking about how families view themselves. The expansion of the family stakeholder group and the increasing number of non-business roles require recognition of this new reality. There are also many business families that are not directly involved with running a business, but rather participate in a range of enterprise activities including a family holding company, a family investment partnership, or a family foundation. All of these activities create challenges and benefits for a family.

As you read, we plan to insert exercises and real-life business examples called *Family Experiences* which give real family business examples of these concepts in action. It is one thing to introduce terms into your business vocabulary, but we think it is considerably more valuable to show you how families are using the PPP to solve problems and continually revitalize their businesses. We will also introduce the *Reardon Family Challenge*, a series of vignettes on how a single business family deals with the concepts that we introduce throughout the book. These mini-cases will help to apply the ideas developed in this book to a family situation. A sample Reardon Family Enterprise Continuity Plan and Business Strategy Plan are included in the Appendices (see Appendices E and G). *Planning Tools* will provide additional resources to better plan your family business strategy.

We also offer planning and decision-making templates that address common family business challenges. These templates should always be read as suggestions and not prescriptions. Each family needs to develop their own best practices based on their values, vision and expectations.

You will notice that this book is separated into four parts:

Part I: Understanding Family Business Planning explores the challenges of business families, discusses how families and businesses are influenced by life cycles and explains how parallel planning not only helps, but transforms the family enterprise.

Part II: Planning for the Family reinforces the theme that Family Commitment and a Shared Future Vision are essential for long-term family business success. This series of chapters explains how to plan family participation, and prepare the next generation for leadership and ownership roles.

Part III: Planning for the Business focuses on management content for the business planning process. It shows how to assess the firm's overall Strategic Potential, identify possible market strategies and closes with advice on how to finalize strategy and investment decisions. It then explains how to unite both working and non-working family members in adoption of this strategy going forward. This section addresses the important question families always have to deal with: Is it appropriate to harvest, invest, sell to or buy out family members with different agendas?

Part IV: Integrating Family and Business Plans is a summary section that shows how an effective board creates a critical link between the views of management and the family throughout the PPP.

We think this structure is a logical progression for any business family looking at formal planning for the first time, or for families interested in strengthening their existing planning process.

The beginning of the 21st century initiates a new era of opportunity for human creativity, particularly for family businesses. John and I believe that the best practices of successful family firms can serve as a model for the entire business community. All organizations can learn from successful families that develop plans based on core values, shared visions, fair process, long-term thinking, a commitment to stakeholders and steward-ship. We hope that we have captured what families and our colleagues have taught us. We also hope that we have been able to share those ideas in this book.

RANDEL S. CARLOCK
Paris, France

After reading Randy's preface you can appreciate why this partnership has been both stimulating and a joy. Randy's many years of experience leading a significant business along with all his academic and consulting exper-ience have brought a special perspective and rigor to this book.

He is the perfect partner: modest, generous, fun and dedicated to the common goal of supporting families. He has reinvented *Keeping the Family Business Healthy* by modifying its themes for a new audience while preserving its central values regarding families. We believe family businesses are a beautiful form of economic and social enterprise. We believe that business families can shape their own destiny. We believe that families can continuously grow and learn. Fundamentally, we believe in the value of planning for business families.

JOHN L. WARD
Evanston, Illinois

Acknowledgments

In undertaking this project, we have asked for and received help from a wide variety of colleagues and organizations.

We would like to thank our many friends who challenged us in our thinking: Craig Aronoff, Glenn Ayres, Christine Blondel, Léon Danco, Miguel Gallo, Tom Hubler, Ludo van der Heyden, Harry McNeely and Sidney Schoefler.

Lisa Holton and Sandra Johnson have contributed much to the final writing and editing of this book. Our colleagues have helped us to reduce our mistakes and clarify our ideas. Any confusion that remains we own. We appreciate the time and thoughts of anyone who contacts us to point out the errors we missed.

We would also like to thank all the students, families and colleagues we have worked with at the Kellogg Graduate School of Management at Northwestern University, Loyola University Chicago Family Business Center, IMD (International Institute of Management Development in Switzerland), the Division of Business and Graduate School of Business at the University of St. Thomas and INSEAD (European Institute of Business Management in France).

Finally, we would like to thank personally the families around the world who have participated in classrooms, conferences or consulting projects with us. We are deeply indebted to you for helping us to learn more about the field of family business management. This book would not have been possible without the energy and insight that comes from working with business families.

Every effort has been made to trace all the copyright holders but if any have been inadvertently overlooked the publishers will be pleased to make the necessary arrangements at the first opportunity.

Part I

Understanding Family Business Planning

1 The Importance of Planning for Business Families

In 1987, *Keeping the Family Business Healthy* opened with the statement, 'Keeping a family business alive is perhaps the toughest management job on earth.' Since that was written, family businesses have found themselves competing in a more turbulent environment driven by new technology, pluralistic social values, intensified competition, a global economy and changing politics and regulations.

Ten years ago, a family business did not have to consider the Internet, digital communications, balancing family and career demands, the growing number of women in management ranks, the impact of Asian economies, the European Union or the wholesale deregulation of the marketplace. The family business of the 1980s was much more concerned about interest rates, defending local market position and minimizing estate taxes.

THE CHALLENGES FACING FAMILY BUSINESSES

All businesses – family-owned or otherwise – find it difficult to continue long term. The evolution of the *Fortune 500* list is a case in point: since 1955, only 77 companies have stayed independent. More than 80 percent have been sold or acquired or witnessed their sales slide significantly in the past 45 years.

There are many reasons for this change: businesses mature; markets and technology change, eliminating the need for various products and services; suppliers and customers alter the rules of the game or competitors quickly copy successful strategies. Any of these changes can take a company by surprise, decreasing its sales and profits. Sometimes industry consolidation makes a strategic buyer willing to pay more to acquire the company than it is worth on a stand-alone basis. The senior generation facing retirement or other life events is unable to resist the premium and often decides to sell.

More often family businesses discover the family is the stumbling block. This can occur for many different reasons: unresolved personal conflicts, lack of trust, difficult family relationships or family demands on

3

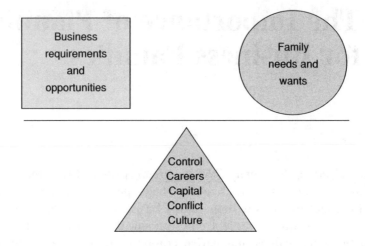

Figure 1.1   *The family business dilemma*

the business. Conflict is a natural element of human relationships. Unfortunately in some families, conflict becomes the regular pattern of interaction. Working together intensifies family interactions and can exacerbate family problems such as sibling rivalry or competition between the generations. When a family allows unresolved or recurring conflicts to diminish communication and trust in the family, it becomes difficult for family members to share ideas, discuss issues or make decisions effectively.

The friction between loved ones and business interests is what makes family business unique. The family has a deeply personal stake rooted in generations of family and business history. Figure 1.1 shows this family enterprise dilemma as a scale that needs to balance evenly family demands with the requirements of the business.

To accomplish this balance, business families need to identify plans and policies to address five pivotal variables:

1. *Control:* Establishing, in a fair way, how the family will address decision-making in the family, in management and in ownership of the business.

2. *Careers:* Making it possible for various family members to pursue rewarding careers or other roles in the business with advancement and rewards based on performance.

3. *Capital:* Creating systems and agreements so that family members can reinvest and, if necessary, harvest or sell their investment without damage to other family members' interests.

4. *Conflict:* Addressing the conflicts that business families face because their work and personal lives intersect so closely.

5. *Culture:* Using family values in developing plans and actions. Family business culture represents enacted family values.

BALANCING FAMILY AND BUSINESS DEMANDS

Freud observed that the intensity of family and work relationships is created by the conflicts between *'lieben und arbeiten'* (love and work). He suggested that love and work are the main sources of self-esteem and pleasure in life and only when both are balanced do we achieve satisfaction.[1]

So how would the average family business survive on Freud's couch? In reality, families and businesses are concerned about different goals. Figure 1.2 depicts the conflicting goals within a family enterprise. Families are concerned about emotions, they focus inward and generally they resist change. Business systems must take the opposite approach if they are to survive – accomplishing tasks, focusing outward on the external environment and looking for ways to exploit change are key success factors for business systems.[2]

Family members can be either a great strength or a potential weakness for the family business. Ignoring them, whatever their agenda, inevitably weakens the business. Family businesses that overemphasize the business system, and consequently diminish attention to the family system, often end up with families that do not relate to each other and psychologically compete with the business.

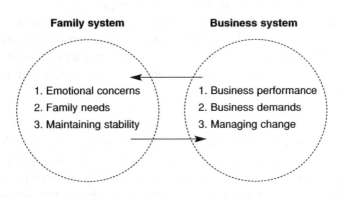

Family system	Business system
1. Emotional concerns	1. Business performance
2. Family needs	2. Business demands
3. Maintaining stability	3. Managing change

Figure 1.2   *Different goals: family system versus business system*

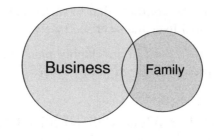

Overemphasis on   Family communications
the business erodes: Family identification
                         Family loyalty
                         Family time
                         Family emotions

Figure 1.3   *Off-balance: business first*
Source: T. Hubler and G. Ayres, University of St. Thomas:
Family Business Management Course, 1996

These families report that the business dominates all of the family's time together. Figure 1.3 shows the outcome of Business First thinking. When the business system is preeminent, family issues and needs are neglected.

Developing a Family Enterprise Continuity Plan ensures that the family's interests are considered along with those of the business. There are many benefits to a planning process for the family:

- It encourages the next generation and in-laws to learn about the family's history and values.
- It reinforces a sound family communication process.
- It supports the development of family agreements on issues such as employment or ownership before a specific decision must be made.
- It provides a fair process for the family's planning and decision-making.
- It clarifies expectations around such inherently difficult issues as money, careers and control.

On the other hand, families can also overemphasize their thinking about matters at home to the detriment of their business concerns (see Figure 1.4). Family considerations and needs become the first priority in business planning and decision-making. A desire to make everyone happy can result in unqualified family employees entering the business, threatening effective next-generation leadership. The business that places the family first

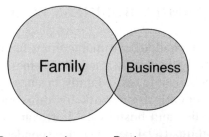

Overemphasis on
the family erodes:

Business communications
Business relations
Performance appraisals
Decision-making
Strategic options

Figure 1.4 *Off-balance: family first*
Source: T. Hubler and G. Ayres, University of St. Thomas:
Family Business Management Course, 1996

often neglects making objective performance appraisals and leadership development plans for family members.

Families who equalize family and business systems create a positive environment where the family thrives and the business performs. This type of thinking is particularly important as family businesses grow. The balanced approach to addressing these two subsystems becomes the foundation for healthy family business relationships and for the creation of a family business legacy. Figure 1.5 shows the successful balancing of family and business systems.[3]

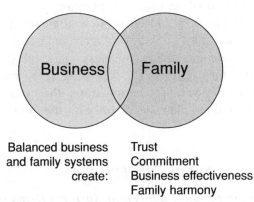

Balanced business
and family systems
create:

Trust
Commitment
Business effectiveness
Family harmony

Figure 1.5 *Successfully balancing family and business systems*
Source: T. Hubler and G. Ayres, University of St. Thomas:
Family Business Management Course, 1996

THE NEED FOR FAMILY BUSINESS PLANNING

There is another major challenge to maintaining family ownership: the ability to plan objectively the family's and the business' shared future.

Many family businesspeople resist family business planning and even fail to develop a systematic framework for thinking about the future strategy of their families and businesses. For example, recent research shows that over two-thirds (69.4 percent) of respondents to the *American Family Business Survey* reported not having a written strategic plan. The survey also said that 40 percent do not have buy–sell agreements and that almost two-thirds of CEOs aged 56 to 60 who plan to retire within the next 6–10 years have not named a successor.[4]

Interestingly, the study also found that those with a written strategic plan were more likely to have developed formal buy–sell agreements and stock redemption plans, to have held more board meetings and to have formalized family employment and succession plans. Planning supports successful management succession, ownership transition, effective governance and profitable business strategies.

A planning process to guide and coordinate both company and family actions is critical. First, a planning process will encourage the family to examine its values, needs and goals on a regularly scheduled basis. Too often, families fail to appreciate the critical role that their commitment plays in family business success and how that commitment may change. A parallel process can also set the stage for mediating conflict between family and business needs. Family business managers need to review and revise their business strategies constantly to meet increasingly dynamic marketplaces.

Second, development of an effective planning process will help the family focus on the business and create new strategies to revitalize the company and promote future growth over years and generations. Business families must appreciate and address business goals and needs. A business plan will ensure that they do this. The following case, 'Faribault Woolen Trades Stake for New Agenda', demonstrates the consequences for a family business if it fails to plan successfully for the future.

FAMILY EXPERIENCES

Planning for the Family and Business Demands

At the end of fiscal 1992, the Faribault Woolen Mills Co. completed 127 consecutive years in the black since its founding in 1865. The two families that owned the private mill on the banks of the Cannon River, south of the Twin Cities (Minneapolis-St. Paul, Minnesota, USA) – the Klemers and the Johnsons – could be forgiven their 'If it ain't broke, don't fix it' attitude.

But complacency exacts a cost. June 1997 found the company looking back at five consecutive years of red ink, with fiscal 1997 the worst.

During the 1990s the blankets and throws industry shrank as upscale customers showed a preference for down comforters and price-sensitive consumers turned to acrylic blankets. Nor did it help when a competitor of Faribault Woolen bought Faribault's acrylics supplier. The department stores – preferring to buy from companies that supply wool, cotton and acrylic blankets – reduced their orders to Faribault Woolen because it could only furnish two of the three.

'For 127 years, we were a profitable company, so nobody questioned the way things were done and people had confidence in the management,' says President Charlie Champlin. 'After five years of no profits that changed. Once that happens, unless you do something you're doomed.'

The first thing the company did was cut costs. The total number of employees went from 178 in mid-1997 to 125 by year-end and crept back up to 160. Also, early in 1998, Champlin – a 27-year veteran with Faribault Woolen – became the company's first president not to be a member of one of the owner families. For the fiscal year ended in June 1998, the company was once again profitable. That was the result of cost cutting, says Champlin. 'Sales were actually down, but that was planned as we exited lower-profit businesses. We cut out a tremendous amount of fat. Our more frugal management cut overhead that was not helping our bottom line.'

That, however, was just the curtain raiser. In April the companies announced that the families had sold an 80 percent ownership position to Business Development Group – a management consulting firm in Orono (a suburb of Minneapolis) headed by Peter Lytle – and its investors. Lytle was named chairman. 'We changed the vision for the company,' Champlin says. 'That's where Peter comes in, with the vision and the authority behind it.' Lytle says that Faribault Woolen will be able to finance a grander vision because this was an equity purchase. While some funds went to existing shareholders, most represented an equity infusion for the company. The investor group gave the company more cash for operating purposes, allowing it to grow, Lytle says. 'Often you get to the point where you can't raise the money you need to achieve your vision and you have to bring in outside partners.'

Source: S. Regan, *Faribault Woolen Trades Stake for New Agenda*, Corporate Report, **XXIX**, 9 (September 1998), pp. 30–1. Copyright 1998 by American City Business Journals. Reprinted by permission.

THE BENEFITS OF FAMILY BUSINESS PLANNING

The Faribault Woolen story clearly demonstrates many of the family business challenges that effective planning can address. The quality of Faribault's products was excellent, they had a strong market niche and state-of-the-art manufacturing technology. Unfortunately, their planning was not vision driven and failed to address the changes in their market. More importantly, their planning did not consider the family's changing expectations and reinvestment commitment. An effective family business planning process is concerned about improving business performance, addressing family expectations and sustaining trust.

Improving Business Performance

The essence of planning is setting goals and describing actions to achieve those goals. Businesses need to change and develop new strategies if they are to remain healthy and financially viable. The dynamic external environment, driven by increasingly competitive markets, makes it difficult – if not impossible – for any organization to maintain the status quo. However, planning allows management to identify new opportunities that are compatible with the business' resources and capabilities.

The planning process creates an excellent opportunity to think and reflect amid the daily pressures of business activity. Through planning – one could just as easily call it strategic thinking – the family and management can deliberate about larger, more abstract issues.[5] Planning enables a family to identify policies and programs that reflect their changing values and allow them to create a new vision of the future.

The vision could include the opportunities created by new technology or growth beyond the current local or regional market served. Through planning, they can build a common understanding of business and family goals among the key stakeholders of both systems. They can also increase the odds of persuading those key stakeholders to support each other so that everyone can achieve their mutual goals.

Addressing Family Expectation

As the family grows and matures, planning is crucial for accommodating changing family relationships and changing agendas. Negotiating life transitions in families is more difficult than managing business change.

Creating a formal structure to examine change generates new and important information and insights. Well-structured inquiries should be designed to unlock information and new ideas about how changes in the family influence the business. If families do not ask these tough questions, new alternatives might not be considered, let alone pursued.

Sustaining Trust

Trust is based on individual experiences with the family or business. A business family creates trust when it works together to plan or problem solve around tough issues. Fairly developing family rules and then applying them consistently to all family members builds trust. Each family member knows what to expect from his or her interactions with the family and business.

Trust is a special form of business capital that is a critical to all organizational relationships. The willingness to risk vulnerability and rely on another person is rare in a world dominated by cynicism.[6] The difficulty in building and maintaining trust can make it a unique competitive advantage for family firms. Figure 1.6 presents a family business balance sheet that identifies actions that build trust as assets and actions that reduce trust as liabilities. These trust-building actions (processes) will be discussed throughout the book.

Levi Strauss & Co., which remains a family controlled business, makes valuing trust and creating a trusting environment the foundation of their planning and management systems.[7] Trust is an important form of capital

Family business trust
Balance sheet (July 1, 20XX)

Assets	Liabilities
Addressing conflict	Ignoring conflict
Shared vision	Individual goals
Fair process in decisions	Unilateral decisions
Planning	Reaction
Governance structures	Family politics
Family agreements	Individual deals
Institutional trust	Lack of trust

Figure 1.6   *Building trust as family business capital*

that can be created by the planning process and used like financial capital to build a competitive advantage. Trust facilitates effective decision-making because stakeholders are less concerned about defending positions or protecting personal interests. It also reduces the risk in investments and creates stronger owner–management relationships. The structures and systems created by planning build new levels of trust and stronger relationships among all the stakeholders.

To support a successful planning process, business families must use an organized framework of systematic inquiry to help direct and control the destiny of both company and family. Parallel planning means that both family and management are simultaneously exploring critical questions from their distinct perspectives.

THE PARALLEL PLANNING PROCESS

This book proposes a Parallel Planning Process (PPP) that expands on the traditional model of family business planning. The development of a viable business strategy is still the outcome, but it is an outcome shaped by the concerns of the family. The PPP becomes a tool for integrating and balancing family and business thinking and action. The parallel approach is founded on four premises (see Figure 1.7).

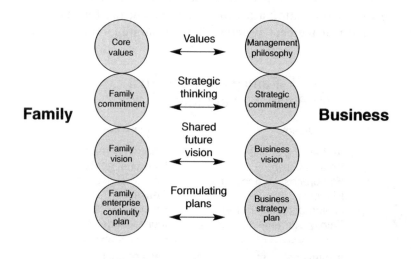

Figure 1.7   *The parallel planning process*

1. Family values and business philosophy are the foundation for the planning process.
2. Strategic thinking has implications for the family as well as for the management team.
3. Successful families and businesses are driven by a Shared Future Vision.
4. Long-term family business success requires formulating family and business plans.

Using the Parallel Planning Process

The goal of the PPP is to identify family and business plans that are mutually supportive of the other's needs and goals. This is accomplished by considering business strategies in the context of both the family and business expectations. The ultimate goal of the business plan remains the development of strategies that create long-term economic value for the stakeholders.

The PPP uses a series of planning and programming activities that lead the family and management to a business strategy that matches the family's interests and the business' potential. Strategic thinking by the family and management teams leads to their mutual commitment to a Shared Future Vision. Based on this shared vision, both systems begin their respective planning activities leading to the development of the Family Enterprise Continuity Plan and Business Strategy Plan. The final choice of business strategy reflects the family owners' reinvestment decision.

Figure 1.8 suggests how the PPP would look if it could be drawn as a logical sequence of activities. Unfortunately, family business planning is too complex, and in practice represents an iterative process, to reach the final choice of business strategy.

Possible strategy alternatives are subject to three decision screens that the PPP creates. The Vision Fit reflects the interaction of the Family Commitment and management's Strategic Commitment; the Strategic Fit is based on the Business Strategy Plan and the Family Enterprise Continuity Plan; and the Family Fit reflects the Family's Reinvestment Decision.

The three screens ensure that a business strategy is aligned with the overall goals of the family. The first screen focuses on the shared vision. At this point the question is: Does the possible business strategy support both the family's and management's Shared Future Vision? This first screen will sift out many of the options because they simply do not lead to

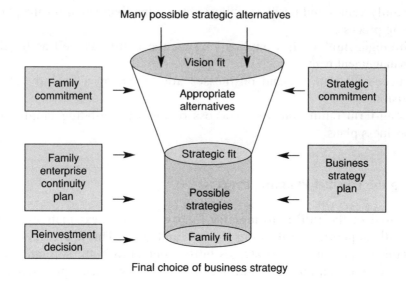

Figure 1.8   *Selecting a business strategy*

the vision espoused by the family and management. These concepts are discussed in Chapters 2 and 3.

The second screen focuses on the Strategic Fit of the possible alternatives based on family and business planning. The Family Enterprise Continuity Plan looks at family participation (Chapter 4), management and leadership development (Chapter 5) and ownership (Chapter 6). The Business Strategy Plan considers the internal and external environments, the firm's Strategic Potential (Chapter 7) and which strategies best match with the firm's Strategic Potential (Chapter 8).

As the strategic decision process continues there should now probably be only a few possible strategic alternatives under consideration. It is possible that all these alternatives would support the first two screens for the Vision and Strategic Fits. However, the third screen ensures that the final strategy best fits the family. The alternatives that are appropriate in terms of the Vision and Strategic Fits may require very different levels of investment. The final strategy and investment choice will be decided by family considerations (Chapter 9).

Family Business Planning Questions

The PPP proposes that family members as well as the management team are simultaneously exploring the family and business systems. This collaborative process not only yields new ideas, but also establishes a shared understanding of the family business' values, goals, strengths, weaknesses, threats and potential opportunities. Yet the real value of planning does not lie within the creation of planning documents. It lies within the group's discussion and thinking – sometimes the first discussion of its kind in many family businesses.

The following list of family planning questions demonstrates a balanced approach to family and business planning:

- What are the family's core values?
- What is the family's vision of their relationship to each other and the business?
- What is the Family Business Philosophy?
- What is the family's level of commitment to business ownership?
- Is the family willing to participate actively in supporting the business?
- How will the family prepare family members for management and leadership roles?
- Who will own the business in the future?

The answers to these questions will shape the Family Enterprise Continuity Plan.

As the family centers on a framework for discussion, management addresses specific questions about the business:

- What is management's business philosophy?
- What are management's long-term goals?
- What is management's vision of the business?
- What is the Strategic Potential of the business?
- What are the possible business strategies?
- What is the business strategy and required level of investment?

The answers to these questions frame the Business Strategy Plan.

Table 1.1 summarizes the goals of the family and business planning actions proposed in this book.

Table 1.1 *Goals of the parallel planning process*

The Family Enterprise Continuity Plan

Securing Family Commitment

- Help the family to explore their level of commitment to the business.
- Identify core family values.
- Agree on a Family Business Philosophy.
- Develop a Family Vision.

Encouraging Family Participation

- Appreciate the nature and sources of conflict and a model for improving family fairness.
- Understand the importance of family meetings and the development of family agreements.

Preparing the Next Generation of Family Managers and Leaders

- Recognize how life cycle influences careers and management transitions.
- Appreciate the challenges of preparing the next generation of family members for business and family leadership roles.
- Develop systems to support meaningful family career experiences.

Developing Effective Owners

- Recognize how life cycle influences ownership transitions.
- Consider the choice of future ownership structures.
- Develop systems to support the development of capable owners.
- Prepare estate plans that address financial needs, estate taxes and future ownership considerations.
- Develop an effective family and business governance system.

The Business Strategy Plan

Assessing the Firm's Strategic Potential

- Assess the firm's internal capabilities in finance, marketing and organization.
- Understand the external environmental forces that will influence future opportunities and threats.
- Analyze the firm's industry and markets.
- Determine the firm's Strategic Potential.

Exploring Possible Business Strategies

- Explore whether to renew, reformulate or regenerate the business.
- Assess possible business strategies for the firm.
- Recognize the factors that influence the choice of a business strategy.
- Utilize the unique strengths of family businesses in developing a business strategy.

Finalizing Strategic and Reinvestment Decisions

- Apply the Family Business Reinvestment Matrix to identify planning overlaps.
- Balance business and family demands in making investment decisions.
- Appreciate the impact of the family's commitment on investment decisions.

THE OBSTACLES TO FAMILY BUSINESS PLANNING

Planning plays a critical role in a family business, but many obstacles can get in the way. For example, formal or even informal attempts at planning are often perceived as a threat by the senior generation of family leaders. Many senior family executives view planning as a straitjacket that will constrain instinctive survival skills and limit business flexibility.[8]

Some senior family members, however, may feel that exploring family topics interferes with what should be a natural process. They feel that a family's involvement should simply happen. They resist the idea of formal planning because it is time consuming, seems to involve too many unknowns and it may expose conflict by initiating discussion of sensitive topics. They often fail to see the need for developing family plans because it was not part of their own experience or past success.

The nature of any formal planning process requires that these independent-minded business leaders share decisions – and private financial statements – with others in the family and company. For many senior family members, this means sharing power and information that they would rather keep to themselves. Others object to planning because they think the future is too full of uncertainties to make the effort worthwhile. Businesses risk being hurt by rapidly changing markets, an unpredictable economy and the next generation's unclear interests if there is no reliable planning process.

Many times, the president or senior family members are blamed for the lack of planning for any of the above reasons. However, this type of thinking fails to recognize that all family and non-family stakeholders play a role in family business decision-making and action taking. They also create obstacles to planning.

Often, members of the next generation who support transferring ownership and leadership simply do not know what the family expects from them. Their family's expectations can overwhelm them with self-doubt about their capability to lead the family enterprise to its next level. Sharing power with their siblings or cousins, or differences in individual's goals can also block the first stages of any planning process.

Families also fail to calculate the impact that the spouses of the senior generation may have on the business and the planning process. If a spouse has developed a comfortable lifestyle based on the CEO's full engagement in the business, a CEO's retirement may create friction for the family and the business if specific payment and consulting agreements are not spelled out. For example, if a CEO retires and still controls most of the stock, families have to address whether that ownership will grant him or her continued leadership responsibility within the company. In other words, has the family spelled out whether the founder will let go or continue to consult for the business once he or she completes a career?

There are also issues regarding the spouse's role and status within the family. Often, the female spouse may raise issues about her financial security since statistically she stands to live longer than her husband does. Unless her claim to the assets of the company – and the voting power those assets contain – is spelled out, the family risks friction that could threaten both their personal relationships and the business.

Non-family employees and other stakeholders such as professionals and service providers may also have a personal stake in maintaining the status quo if they perceive a threat from the planning process. These groups have an established relationship with current management and shareholders and have confidence in their predictable actions. The transition to new leadership and ownership may raise doubts for them about the financial stability of the business and a fear of losing personal relationships.

Identifying specific obstacles to family business planning will enable the family to explore what planning means to stakeholders in the family enterprise and that process will stimulate ideas for actions to help overcome the obstacles.[9] The following table shows examples of obstacles and possible actions.

Table 1.2   *Planning obstacles and suggested actions*

	Obstacles	**Suggested action steps**
Senior generation	Doubts regarding younger generation's capabilities	Create meaningful career opportunities
	Loss of enjoyment from day-to-day operations	Identify a future role that contributes to the firm
	Resistance to change in business direction or strategy	Participate in Strategic Planning
Successors	Concern about family expectations	Support family meetings to explore commitment and vision
	Self-doubt about capabilities	Engage in management development activities
	Sharing power and multiple shareholders	Create family and business governance structures
Spouse	Impact on marital relationship	Develop a future lifestyle plan
	Concerns regarding financial security	Create personal estate and financial plans
Other stakeholders	Loss of personal relationships	Phase down involvement over time
	Concerns over financial stability	Show confidence in successor

Allowing any of these obstacles to block the planning process creates the potential for lost opportunities, reduced trust and less chance of a successful transition to a new generation of family ownership and management.

On the other hand, when the family identifies the obstacles and takes on the planning process, there are many potential benefits.

THE CHALLENGE OF CREATING A FAMILY BUSINESS LEGACY

When companies are founded, they are rarely conceived of as a family business. Instead, they are typically viewed as the product of an entrepreneur's need for achievement and self-expression. He or she views it as 'my business' or 'my company'. Even though the family is a source of social and financial support – and often employees – it remains in the background. Yet eventually there comes a time when these successful entrepreneurs need to harvest their life's work. Typically, this occurs in one of three ways: selling the business, taking it public or transferring ownership to the family.

Usually, an entrepreneur's interest in family succession is first stimulated when sons and daughters enter their teenage years and start asking questions about the business. Perhaps they begin to work in it part time. The option of family continuity becomes more compelling as the business owner matures and realizes that selling or taking the business public is risky and threatens his or her role.

The idea of keeping it in the family has many benefits: economic advantages, the possibility to enjoy family relationships and the opportunity for an entrepreneur to keep his or her hand in the business. The *American Family Business Survey* reported that over 90 percent of the respondents believe that the same family or families will control their businesses in five years.[10]

Why do business owners eventually yearn to pass on the family business? Results from a survey of 75 family business owners and spouses who were working diligently to ensure family perpetuation of their businesses offer some insights. Many stated that owning a family business benefits the family. Founders stated that their children, by entering the business, could enjoy the same opportunity for freedom and growth as they enjoyed. They also saw the business as a way to perpetuate the family's tradition and business heritage. Keeping the family together, generating wealth and ensuring their own secure retirement were also cited.[11]

Family succession is a hot issue. Businesses founded in the 1950s and 60s are now facing their second family transition; businesses founded in the 1970s and 80s are preparing for their first. All this is happening as a new generation is considering entrepreneurial careers more challenging than working for someone else.

PLANNING TOOLS

How Does Your Business Stack Up?

At this point, many readers are asking themselves: How does our family compare? Do we have the capabilities to succeed as a family owned and managed business? This book includes a Family Business Assessment (see Appendix A) as a tool families can use to explore their family business situation. Many families report that the checklist is an excellent tool for beginning the planning process because it identifies critical issues. Identifying, discussing and addressing topics critical to a family business is the foundation for a successful planning outcome.

Should the Family Business Continue?

This question is among the toughest that the family must answer in the PPP, but it might be the most important. In reality, it might not be best for a family business to continue in the family. There are many circumstances that, alone or in combination, make it unwise for the family to maintain the family business. Sometimes, family members' life and career interests do not include the business. There may be an unwillingness to make a personal or investment commitment to support the business' long-term growth. A long history of conflicted family relationships can also indicate that working together may not be the healthiest course.

In many ways, this thinking runs counter to an early premise of the family business field; that is, that success equals succession to the next generation. More careful thinking suggests that success is doing what is best for the family and for all those who depend on the family business. The following *Family Experiences* points to that exact issue.

When the Successor No Longer Wants the Throne

So what happens when an heir apparent decides the kingdom is no longer worth running?

A successor who had all the preparation and the flawless support of her family was quite distressed because she realized she really wanted to leave the family business. This came after she and her family spent years of planning for her move to the top job – a plan that included her working outside the family firm for five years for a large public company, and her completion of an MBA degree.

When she returned to the family firm, she held sales, operations and management positions, always demonstrating excellent performance. Her father had designated her as his successor and was broadening her exposure to all aspects of the business. He had even begun to step away from the daily operations so that his daughter and the non-family managers on her team could run the business.

This family was a textbook case of family business success – except that the successor found she was not satisfied with her career choice. She finally shared her uncertainty with her father, who demonstrated unlimited support for her best interests and suggested that she take some time to consider her options. He also encouraged her to get some outside advice. Advisors challenged her about balancing her responsibilities to family against her own career interests. She had decided that she liked business and management, but not the nature and characteristics of her family business. She admitted that she didn't feel that running the family business was a rewarding, long-term career goal and that she experienced little satisfaction from her job.

The father was disappointed but felt more concern for his daughter's happiness and personal fulfillment. Over the next few months, they decided to sell the business to the management group. She moved to New York and now works for a large public corporation and is well on her way to a senior management position.

Source: R.S. Carlock, Center for Family Enterprise, Graduate School of Business, University of St. Thomas, Minneapolis, MN, (1995).

The above story recognizes the importance of considering the individual needs of family members, not just the business demands. This case, from a family business perspective, was rather unexceptional because there were no negative family business factors or special challenges. Rather, there was a loving founder who recognized the importance of supporting his talented daughter's need for personal autonomy and self-actualization. His ability to balance family and business concerns is the essence of the PPP. That in itself was the exceptional factor in this situation.

What is Family Business Success?

Kenneth Kaye, a psychologist and family business consultant, offered four points to define long-term family business success, which captures much of the *Family Experiences* described above.

A family business is successful if:

- Both generations believe the successors have contributed to the business success.
- They either transferred the business to the next generation or they worked together to sell it.
- The experience was rewarding for individuals and the family.
- There were no personal casualties along the way.[12]

SUMMARY

Family business planning involves more than just a thoughtful review of business challenges and opportunities and the family's exploration of its expectations and talents. It is a way of learning and thinking about the possibilities for both the family and the business systems. Over the past 30 years, academics, consultants and researchers have developed valuable insights into what planning actually involves and the ways in which it leads to business success. Their insights offer guidance to family businesses on how to think about their challenges.

Those insights are summarized in the following five propositions about the performance of families and businesses:

- Businesses and families follow predictable, evolutionary life cycles that create transitions and new challenges.[13]
- It is possible to learn from one's own experiences and from the experiences of others.[14]
- The family's values, culture and goals influence the achievements of the business far more than any other factor.[15]
- External forces will influence the future performance and long-term viability of the business.[16]
- The firm's capabilities are a critical influence on business strategy.[17]

These insights support the family business planning challenge: keeping the business healthy and thriving into the next generation and beyond, while maintaining the family's commitment and support. Chapter 2 will explore the Parallel Planning Process. Many business families believe that their issues and challenges are unique. Typically though, they experience predictable patterns of growth and similar life transitions.

The discussion of the PPP will identify and demonstrate the critical activities of family business planning. Understanding a process for planning growth and change is an important factor in family business continuity. When business families discuss the strategic plans for their firms, they should first look at the interaction and relationships between the family and business systems.

2 The Parallel Planning Process

Planning together helps family members and management understand the critical factors for long-term business growth and helps to build long-term Family Commitment.[1] It also provides a foundation for coordinating, directing and controlling the activities of the business. These goals have special meaning for a business family concerned about the additional challenges of management and ownership succession while maintaining family relationships.

Adopting the Parallel Planning Process (PPP) is a chance to address expectations, change and conflict. These are three elements present in all family relationships. Many family businesses are driven by an expanded set of goals related to family stewardship and legacy. They recognize planning's contribution to meeting the challenge that Léon Danco, the founder of family business consulting, identified as creating a 'business that shall last forever'.[2]

This chapter begins with a brief overview of the influence of life cycles on family business planning. The interest in family business planning is usually triggered by a family or business life cycle event such as a next-generation family member graduating from university and joining the firm or stagnant sales created by a mature market. Studying the life cycle patterns of markets, organizations, families and individuals will help to explain the challenges ahead and the planning that is required to address those challenges. Chapters 4–7 include further discussion of life cycle influences on planning.

THE INFLUENCE OF LIFE CYCLES ON FAMILY BUSINESSES

Planning for business growth while transferring ownership and management across generations presents many challenges in today's complex business environment. Family businesses must cope with endless industry-related and organizational decisions while simultaneously planning for the

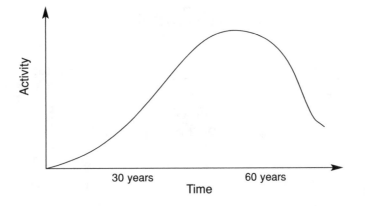

Figure 2.1 *The human life cycle: the biological imperative*

Source: N.C. Churchill and K.J. Hatten 'Non-market-based Transfers of Wealth and Power: A Research Framework for Family Business', *Family Business Review*, **10**(1), 1997, 53–67. Copyright 1997 by the Family Firm Institue. Reprinted by permission.

management and ownership transitions driven by individual and family life cycles. These challenges are not unique to a particular family enterprise. Rather, they are related to predictable transitions that occur as both families and businesses grow and mature.

Families and their businesses must address life cycle change because it is a biological inevitability.[3] Figure 2.1 depicts the human life cycle from birth, through growth and development, to the highly productive adult years and then phase-down. In a family business, managers and owners have the most influence during their adult years, from around age 30 until they peak in their 60s or 70s.

All businesses face challenges created by industry and organizational life cycles. The addition of the individual and family life cycle forces is what makes family business planning unique (see Figure 2.2). Because family members are intimately involved as employees and owners, their life cycles also have an impact on the business. The combination of continuous life transitions and events within the family and business systems makes it imperative to understand the planning challenges driven by family and business life cycles. These forces can be as complex as those in Figure 2.2.

Life cycle models are used in the field of family business to explore planning and organizational issues. For example, Gersick et al. proposed a family business developmental model that includes three overlapping subsystems: business, ownership and family. Their model recognizes the

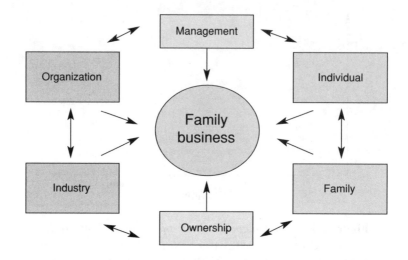

Figure 2.2   *Four life cycle forces influencing family business planning*

interrelationship of these three subsystems and presents three developmental stages for each.[4]

The framework proposed in this book takes a slightly different perspective. Ownership is not a life cycle, but rather an Ownership Configuration influenced by life cycle forces and family decisions. This model proposes that family business can be structured with six Ownership Configurations that result from life cycle forces and family decisions:

- Entrepreneurship
- Owner-managed
- Family Partnership
- Sibling Partnership
- Cousins' Collaboration
- Family Syndicate.

The planning implications for these different Ownership Configurations are discussed in Chapter 6. Figure 2.3 elaborates on the four life cycle forces that create the unique challenges of family enterprises. This framework integrates industry, organization, family and individual life cycle forces to demonstrate their combined impact on the family business Ownership Configurations.

Applying life cycle thinking to human and business development is a challenge. Human life cycle events follow a life pattern that evolves over

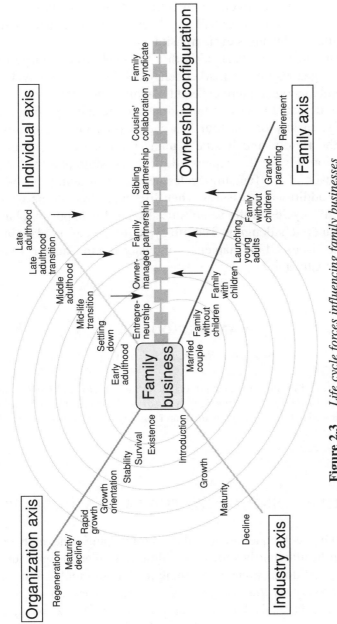

Figure 2.3 *Life cycle forces influencing family businesses*

Adapted from: R.S. Carlock, *Family Business Management Course Materials*, University of St. Thomas, 1995; C.K. Sigelman and D.R. Shaffer, *Life-span Development*, Belmont, CA: Brooks/Cole Publishing, 1991; D.J. Levinson, *The Season of a Man's Life*, New York: Balantine Books, 1978; J.H. Eggers, K.T. Leahy, and N.C. Churchill, 'Stages of Small Business Growth Revisisted: Insights into Growth Path and Leadership/Management Skills in Low and High Growth Companies', in W.D. Bygrave, S. Birely, N.C. Churchill, E. Gatewood, F. Hoy, and W.E. Wetzel (eds) *Frontiers of Entrepreneurship Research*, Boston: Babson College, 1994, 131–44.

an average of 70–80 years. Industry and even organizational life cycles are much less predictable. A new computer software product may move through the industry life cycle from introduction to decline in a few months. For these reasons, there will not always be clear linkages between the different life and business cycle transitions.

What is important to understand is that life cycle forces shape individual, family, organization and market behaviors. Different life cycle situations and combinations require different planning and strategies.

Actual or anticipated life cycle transitions are the starting point for the PPP. A change in any of the four life cycles presented in Figure 2.3 means that the family and business plans require new thinking and possibly revision. Figure 2.3 depicts all of the possible phases that may occur within each of the four life cycles operating in family businesses. Families face additional pressures when life cycle transitions occur in two or more life cycles at the same time. When this happens, planning also becomes more challenging. The life cycle influences on planning for careers will be discussed in Chapter 5, for ownership in Chapter 6 and for the business in Chapter 7.

PLANNING TOOLS

For Your Business Library

Readers interested in more information on life cycles should read *Generation to Generation: Life Cycles of the Family Business* by Kelin Gersick, John Davis, Marion McCollom Hampton and Ivan Lansberg (Boston: Harvard Business School Press, 1997).

STRATEGIC PLANNING AND THE FAMILY BUSINESS

Strategic planning techniques are useful tools for helping to develop a long-term approach to utilizing business capabilities and market opportunities. Unfortunately, traditional strategic planning models and tools are designed to focus exclusively on the business and its needs. They do not address family challenges that make family businesses unique. The expanded scope of family business requires a very different planning framework.

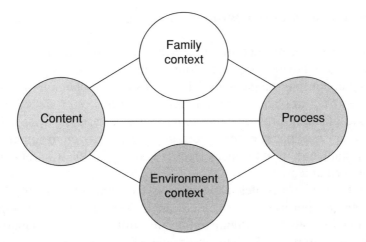

Figure 2.4   *Planning considerations created by family business ownership*

The Expanded Scope of Family Business Planning

All organizations that engage in strategic planning are concerned about three variables:

1. *Content:* What they plan.
2. *Process:* How they work together.
3. *Context:* Where the planning takes place.

It is obvious that the content, process and context will vary among organizations, but a family business must include another consideration in its planning process – the Family Context. This means that family needs, expectations and relationships must be considered as a part of the planning process. Figure 2.4 illustrates the expanded set of planning considerations created by family business ownership.

In addition to the expanded context, the process for planning is a more important consideration in family business planning, because family membership is a lifetime relationship. In most business or other organizational planning, relationships are temporal. The dynamics of most organizations allow an individual to be involved in multiple personal, superior–subordinate and team relationships during a career. In a family business, this is usually not true. A family business owned and managed by a family will produce lifetime work relationships. For this reason, families have to focus much more on process – that is, how they do things. The ways in which the family learns to work together may well be the critical factor in family harmony and ownership continuity.

Understanding Strategic Business Planning

It is assumed that readers are already budgeting within their companies, that they are developing operating plans and that they have begun thinking about long-range goals. The term strategic planning refers to the processes used to plan for the long-term performance of an organization. Strategic planning provides a systematic way to ask key business questions. It creates insights into the company and its environment. Such inquiry challenges past business practices and opens the way for exploring new opportunities.

This book views strategic planning as the foundation of the Strategic Management approach to business. Strategic Management is a comprehensive model of business administration that fully integrates planning with action (see Figure 2.5). This planning and action process creates a systemic way to recognize opportunities (strategic thinking), make decisions (strategic formulation), take action (strategic implementation) and improve performance (strategic reformulation). Strategic Management becomes a way of managing the firm, actually ingrained in the management process.

The questions asked in the strategic planning process become an integral part of how managers think. These questions perpetually challenge basic assumptions and identify new market opportunities. Managers experiment by putting new ideas into action and become planners for the future. Figure 2.5 demonstrates that thinking is a continuous process that influences all phases of the management process. When this business plan-

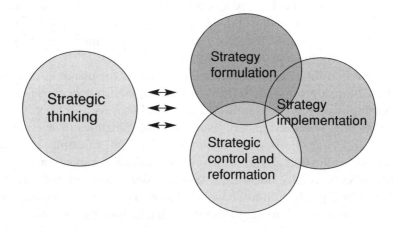

Figure 2.5   *A strategic management approach to business*

ning process becomes second nature to managers, the firm is practicing Strategic Management. At that point, business planning and action are integrated into a unified framework for linking the firm's daily operations with its long-term goals.

Strategic Planning and the Parallel Planning Process

Strategic planning using the Parallel Planning Process is a very different activity because of the integration of the family system. The scope of the planning process is broadened to consider the interaction and mutual influence of the family and business systems. This parallel process is recommended because it links family and business planning so that the values and goals of both the family and the business are fully considered. In the ultimate choice of business strategy, the plan must reflect family considerations, especially the family's values and vision for the future.

The first phase of the strategic planning process is strategic thinking. The goal of this phase is to identify planning options that are appropriate for both the family and the business. The family explores core values, family business philosophies and a Family Vision. The management team explores the management's business philosophy, a Business Vision and its long-term goals. The outcome of this strategic thinking phase is determining Family Commitment and clarifying management's Strategic Commitment.

During the second phase of the planning process, strategy formulation, the Family Enterprise Continuity Plan and the Business Strategy Plan are developed. The family considers family participation, leadership and ownership while management explores the firm's strategic potential, possible strategies and finalizes strategy and investment decisions. These plans detail the family and the business' activities, tactics and programs designed to meet their goals and support the achievement of their Shared Future Vision.

This book concentrates on exploring the planning phases of Strategic Management: strategic thinking and strategy formulation. In some cases, actions or activities related to implementation and reformulation are also addressed, when they overlap with planning. For example, when discussing the development of plans for developing family management, one of the activities addressed will be performance review – an important tool in strategic reformulation.

PARALLEL PLANNING FOR THE FAMILY AND BUSINESS SYSTEMS

Parallel planning for the family and business systems represents a special challenge for the family business. Unfortunately, the development of these two plans cannot always proceed in lock-step fashion due to different time requirements of the family and business systems. The development of a Business Strategy Plan, when identified as a high priority, can be completed in a relatively short period. Families, on the other hand, will require a much longer period to address the highly emotional tasks that are involved in securing Family Commitment and developing the Family Enterprise Continuity Plan.

There is no single path to follow in order to accomplish this. It may take several years for the family and business plans to fully interconnect and for the goals of each to become fully harmonious. However, the principle remains clear. Planning for the future of the business and for the future of the family is a continuous process that is affected by changes and events that influence each system. The *Reardon Family Challenge* demonstrates many of the issues that make the PPP valuable to family firms.

The *Reardon Family Challenge* is introduced here to provide the reader with a case example to think about as the planning process develops. The Reardon family's issues will be explored in each chapter resulting in the development of a Family Enterprise Continuity Plan and a Business Strategy Plan (see Appendices E and G).

REARDON FAMILY CHALLENGE

The Reardon Technology Case

Bob and Steve Reardon are frustrated with their siblings' behavior. Their business has accumulated cash for expansion that Bob and Steve believed would strengthen the company's growth and competitive position, but their siblings are requesting a large dividend for themselves instead.

Reardon Technology is a $100 million-a-year manufacturer of electronics products owned equally by the six Reardon siblings and their father. Their father, who was Reardon's founder and chief engineer, retired nine years ago. He lives out of state and limits his company participation to chairing two board meetings a year. Bob, who is 49 and the third oldest sibling, has worked at Reardon for 19 years, serving as CEO since his dad retired. He has done a superlative job, increasing revenue fourfold by acquiring a competitor and entering new markets for Internet electronic components.

Reardon is an industry leader, has no debt and is a strong niche market player, but its growth rate is slowing. Competitors (no longer local companies but national and international conglomerates) are squeezing margins and more of its customers are purchasing overseas. Running at full capacity, it needs extensive capital expenditures to increase manufacturing capability, fund new product development and increase marketing efforts.

Bob and his older brother Steve, who serves as an engineer in Reardon's design department, are the only family members actively involved with the company. The other siblings, who are settled in outside careers, have recently shared an interest in becoming more active. They have also expressed concerns about the company's lack of liquidity. Some seem to resent Bob's high salary, although they are all very glad to have such a capable CEO. Their father, who loved inventing, never seemed able to capitalize on his good ideas.

In particular, Bob's 57-year-old sister Nancy believes her brother is overpaid. Her husband Phil is division president in a public company. Although Phil's company dwarfs Reardon in sales, Bob earns more than Phil does. Nancy also has a daughter with a master's degree in electrical engineering and she would like to work at Reardon. Bob has resisted the idea of any of the third-generation members joining the firm because he is not sure he likes the idea of 'becoming a family business'.

THE PARALLEL PLANNING PROCESS FOR THE FAMILY

The Reardon case demonstrates the need for a planning process that considers the expectations and demands of the family system. Traditionally, strategic planning focuses on the business and its goals and performance. Bob has done a superior job of strategically positioning Reardon Technology into high-growth markets, but this is not enough if he wants to maintain the support of the family shareholders that is critical to continued growth.

He has demonstrated his management acumen by dramatically growing the firm. His family recognizes and appreciates his business efforts. Unfortunately for Bob and his family, superior business performance is not enough because they have failed to develop any plans to address the family's needs. This is creating frustrations for Bob and his co-worker brother and their sibling shareholders, who feel trapped by their ownership in the firm.

There appears to be a widening gap between the 'insiders' who want to invest heavily for the future and the 'outsiders' who want more control of their ownership and an expanded role for the family. Additionally, issues of management compensation and career opportunities for the next generation need to be addressed. Bob's uncertainty about 'becoming a family business' demonstrates his belief that Reardon Technology is 'not a family business' despite two and possibly three generations of family involvement. Bob's comments suggest that he and his siblings do not have a shared vision of the future business or the family's relationship to the business.

The importance of building Family Commitment and developing a Shared Future Vision of both the family and business cannot be overestimated. This book argues that exploring, identifying and articulating a future vision for both the family and business is fundamental to the family business planning process.

The process of aligning a vision for these two systems is the basis for the PPP. The family business, with its two competing systems, demands a clear agreement on what 'we want to become' both as a family and as a business if creativity, talent and resources are to be efficiently and effectively utilized. The Reardon family demonstrates the need for developing a Shared Future Vision of the family and business.

While both groups want Reardon to succeed, their definitions and timing for success are very different. The Reardon family is experiencing conflict because of a lack of agreed commitment and different future visions of their business and family. Exploring Family Commitment is the first step for the development of mutually supportive visions.

Exploring Family Commitment

The process for exploring Family Commitment requires the family to consider two questions. First, does the family have an interest in remaining family business owners based on the financial and social benefits that they will receive? Second, is the family willing and able to accept the responsibilities of ownership? Family Commitment requires a 'yes' response to both these questions. It is possible that a family can maintain ownership and neglect its obligations as responsible owners. Unfortunately, research indicates that a lack of active ownership in areas such as effective governance does result in reduced financial performance.[5]

Exploring Family Commitment becomes an important issue as the family matures and new family members are available. During the Entrepreneurship and Owner-managed Phases continued ownership is a given. As the expanding family becomes involved, it is useful to work together so that all family members, including in-laws and the next generation, can

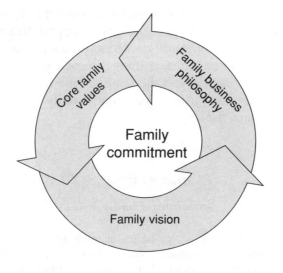

Figure 2.6   *Thinking about family commitment*

appreciate what the family's commitment to the business means. This book offers a template for exploring Family Commitment based on three elements: the family's core values, its Family Business Philosophy and its Family Vision (see Figure 2.6). As the figure shows, these three are not static. They are continually influenced by family and business changes.

The family's consensus on these three ideas forms the basis for making a decision on a long-term commitment to family business ownership. The following is a brief overview of Family Commitment to support thinking about the larger PPP. Chapter 3 explores the activities required to secure Family Commitment in more detail.

Determining Core Values

The first family planning activity is to explore its core values to determine beliefs about the family and the business. The family's commitment and vision of itself are shaped by what the family holds as important. The principles relating to how employees and customers are treated and how the family defines its responsibilities to its members and other stakeholders will guide the development of business plans, policies and family agreements. For these reasons, core family values are the basis for developing a commitment to the business.

Many family businesses attempt planning without fully recognizing the importance of identifying their core values to support decision-making on issues such as investment, family careers, product quality and wealth. Family values can mean different things to each family. The following story of L.L. Bean demonstrates the power of the family's core values in driving both family and business planning. Family values are discussed more extensively in Chapter 3.

FAMILY EXPERIENCES

Sustaining Family Values

Catalog retailer L.L. Bean Inc. has been a mainstay for lovers of the outdoors since 1912. Still family controlled, the company has prospered and grown through Leon Leonwood Bean's version of the Golden Rule: 'Sell good merchandise at a reasonable profit, treat your customers like human beings and they will always come back for more.'

Bean's Golden Rule represented more than the founder's personal values – it proved to be an effective management tool and the backbone of the L.L. Bean culture. First, Bean defined good merchandise as goods that he would wear and enjoy – so he tested products himself. That singular philosophy has grown into Bean's worldwide network of product testers who climb mountains, bike, ski or hike to test the new products and suggest improvements when necessary.

Second, the treating customers as human beings component made Bean the first proponent of the 100% Guarantee on all merchandise. While thousands of other retailers have duplicated the Bean promise in the last century, Bean's promise hasn't been altered: 'Our products are guaranteed to give 100 percent satisfaction in every way. Return anything purchased from us at any time if it proves otherwise.' It also offers perpetual replacement of the rubber soles of its well-known Maine Hunting Shoe.

Today, the Freeport, Me.-based company publishes 50 catalogs a year and operates its flagship retail store on Main Street in Freeport (which attracts 3.5 million visitors annually and is open 24 hours a day, 365 days a year). It also sells its wares through 10 outlet stores in the United States, 20-plus stores in Japan and through its Web site. The company offers more than 16,000 items ranging from outdoor apparel to sporting goods to household furnishings, most of which carry the L.L. Bean label. It makes more than 300 of its products (such as shoes, tote bags, luggage) in Maine.

Leon Gorman, L.L. Bean's grandson, relied on the family's core value of outstanding customer service when he introduced Total Quality Management (TQM) and a flat organizational architecture. The TQM program redefined the role of management as managers took on the role of a coach and developer.

And as the company refined its management system to allow speedier customer response, employees were empowered to serve customers better.

Note: Information from Hoovers Online (www.Hoovers.com) and P. Kepos (ed.) *International Directory of Company Histories*, 10 (Detroit: St. James Press, 1995), pp. 388–90.

Many long-lived family companies use core values as a basis for their family relationships to the business. As the case of L.L. Bean demonstrates, the founder's core values can help the family to make decisions about the business. Achieving a unity of purpose, based on family values, serves both the family and the business.

Discussing and negotiating an understanding of core values are particularly important activities when multiple generations of family or in-laws become involved with the business. All will have different experiences and agendas, hence potentially different values than the current senior generation.

If the family does not share a set of beliefs about what the business means to the family and what the family's responsibilities are to the business, there will be unproductive conflict. Therefore, gaining family consensus on core values is critical to the planning process.

What Is Our Family Business Philosophy?

This discussion explores the issues raised in Chapter 1 about balancing business and family relationships. Discussing a Family Business Philosophy can stimulate strong feelings about whether the needs of the business or the family should come first. Some family members will argue that the family must be willing to sacrifice for the good of the business.

Others may see the business as serving the needs of the family. Exploring how to balance the needs of the family and business allows the family to develop agreement on topics such as compensation, ownership, family responsibilities, employment, family behavior, governance and management succession. For each of the topics the Family Business Philosophy defines a relationship between the family and their business.

Creating a Family Vision

The final family action is developing a vision of the family in relationship to each other and the business. It is important that the family work together to clarify their future expectations. It is critical to understand what each family member can and will contribute and, eventually, what the business will be able to return to the family. This is a good discussion topic for all families, even those with an unqualified long-term commitment to business. It challenges everyone to consider under what circumstances or contingencies the family would consider a sale or harvest. Other typical topics for the Family Vision include the following:

■ Desired business accomplishments (innovation, growth, service).
■ Possible family legacies (five generations of family ownership, socially responsible firm).
■ Benefits for the family (wealth, recognition, meaningful careers).
■ Responsibilities to the business (investment, governance, philanthropy).
■ Responsibilities to other stakeholders (employees, customers, suppliers, communities).

The Challenges of Securing Family Commitment

The family's commitment is the foundation for creating unity of purpose and maintaining family harmony. The format, or even the content, of these actions is not as important as the process for developing them. Whatever their format, securing and maintaining Family Commitment is a demanding process. It requires each family member to freely discuss his or her values, goals and expectations.

At least one person needs to take the lead in coordinating the drafting of a Statement of Family Commitment. The effort requires a careful process of discussion and consensus building. It often represents a commitment from several family members to work on these activities initially over a period of years and then on an ongoing basis as part of the family participation activities. Each new generation must explore their commitment and the family should reconfirm its commitment as part of the annual family meeting.

Maintaining the family's commitment to the business is an ongoing work in progress. The preliminary commitment may change during later stages of the planning process, based on new business information or changes in the family's goals, but it is important that the family have at least a basic agreement.

THE PARALLEL PLANNING PROCESS FOR THE BUSINESS

While the PPP adds the family dimension, planning for the business is still a fundamental activity. The first step in this process is for management to ascertain its willingness to lead a strategic change effort. This section will fully explore management's preparatory steps so that Chapter 7 can begin development of the Business Strategy Plan.

Zeroing in on Management's Strategic Commitment

While the family is working to illustrate their commitment to the business, the management team needs to identify what they believe the business can become. This process includes refining management's business philosophy, exploring a Business Vision, and setting long-term goals (see Figure 2.7). The Strategic Commitment is an interactive process influenced by the organization and industry life cycles, and obviously changes in the family. The Strategic Commitment process enables management to clarify their thinking and develop a vision of the business.

Figure 2.7   *Thinking about strategic commitment*

Creating a Management Business Philosophy

Management has to build a business philosophy around its values and beliefs. How do they see this business competing? What are they willing to commit to the business? Management must clarify their comfort with risk, growth, innovation and development of the organization. A final question that will shape all aspects of the business strategy is management's relationship to the family. As in the previous discussion, if the management team's philosophy is not compatible with the family's expectations, it will be very difficult to develop a Shared Future Vision that will support the family's participation and a viable business strategy.

Defining a Business Vision

James Collins and Jerry Porras, in their best selling book *Built to Last: Successful Habits of Visionary Companies*, demonstrate that companies with strong values, goals and future visions outperform comparable companies that are not vision driven. They propose that a strong vision of the future enables a company to endure beyond the tenure of powerful managers, through significant market changes and despite challenging economic periods.[6]

Sony Corp. fits their example of being values and vision driven. Sony's founder, Akio Morita, described Sony as: 'A pioneer (that) never intends to follow others' progress as it serves "the whole world."'[7] This vision, created 50 years ago when Sony was a small company struggling to survive in postwar Japan, focused Sony on innovation and world markets from its beginnings. This vision was vivid to all of Sony's employees and stakeholders.

James Collins and Jerry Porras use the term 'envisioned future' to describe thinking about how the firm will look in the future. They see the vision as having two parts: first, a BHAG ('bee-hag' or Big, Hairy, Audacious Goal) and second, a vivid description of what the future will mean to the organization.[8] Long-term visions by definition should focus 10 or more years into the future and stretch the organization's imagination beyond its current thinking.

Sam Walton's vision for Wal-Mart motivated his entire organization. The idea that Wal-Mart could build stores in small rural towns skipping the major cities and overtaking Sears within 30 years was truly audacious. Believing in this vision allowed the entire organization to consider the implications of being the largest US retailer on their planning and decision-making for the future.[9]

The management team can begin its exploration of a Business Vision by discussing ideas such as the following questions. Ten years from now:

■ How big will the business be (sales, profits, markets and employees)?
■ What will this vision require of the organization?
■ What markets or industry will offer us an opportunity for growth and value creation?
■ What does everyone say is impossible for this organization to accomplish?
■ Does the Business Vision support the family's core values?
■ What will customers expect in 10 years?

Identifying Goals and a Possible Business Vision

The final task for management is to answer the question 'How do we achieve our vision?' They need to brainstorm and explore possible scenarios about what management actions are required. This type of thinking challenges management to forget a continuation of the existing strategy and consider new possibilities. 'What if we sold part of the core business and reinvested in a high growth market that is currently only 20 percent of our sales?' These qualitative discussions about possible scenarios and the Business Vision help the management team clarify their thinking and develop long-term goals.

Long-term goals serve several purposes. First, goals direct the firm to its new vision. An organization with a goal of 20 percent annual sales growth will look very different in five years than a firm with 5 percent sales growth. Second, they provide a framework for unifying the planning process. In all organizations employees need to know what is expected of them. In a family firm goals allow the family shareholders to understand and support management's plans. Third, goals provide a basis for evaluating management's performance and making decisions about future investment. A family business needs objective criteria for assessing family or non-family management performance.

The work of the management team in creating a business philosophy, setting goals and exploring a Business Vision creates their statement of Strategic Commitment. The Family Vision, from the Family Commitment, and the Business Vision, from the Strategic Commitment, form the basis for the Shared Future Vision. Figure 2.8 shows the symbiotic relationship between the family and business planning processes.

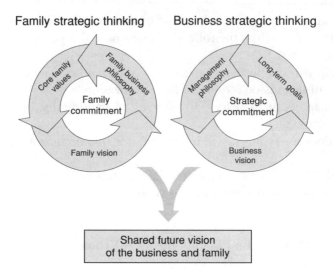

Figure 2.8 *Family and business strategic thinking supports the development of a shared vision*

THE SHARED FUTURE VISION OF THE FAMILY AND BUSINESS

Shared Future Vision is a powerful concept for planning because it focuses thinking on values and future goals rather than on current issues or problems. For family businesses, the Shared Future Vision of the family and business is a linkage between the systems, which expresses their mutual interdependence and the power of their combined efforts. The Shared Future Vision can serve many different functions:

■ Educational, providing new information about future direction.
■ Motivational, providing meaning for the planning process.
■ Strategic, providing clear direction for decision-making.

Securing Agreement on the Shared Future Vision

The Shared Future Vision of the family and business evolves from two different processes. Typically the overlap in the family and business systems and the influence of the family's values will create Family and

Business Vision statements that are mutually supportive. Most families and management teams engaged in long-term planning recognize and appreciate the advantage of understanding each other's needs and expectations. A management team, especially one with family executives, should have a reasonable idea of the family's concern for risk or expected rate of return.

The business plans they propose should reflect these family expectations if they want to keep the family's long-term support. As was suggested earlier, the family can contribute by inviting the management team to share their thinking at the family's planning sessions.

Unfortunately, family business planning processes are not always as rational or intuitive as they could be. As the family grows and matures and the number of individuals in ownership or management roles increases, it will become necessary to organize formal planning sessions among key family members and senior management to develop a mutually supported Shared Future Vision. The senior management team, board of directors and family must engage in a process to negotiate complementary shared visions for the family and business. If formal planning begins in the Family or Sibling Partnership Phases, management and family task forces may need to be created to facilitate the visioning process. Families in a later developmental phase or those who have created a governance structure that includes a board of directors and a family council often include an annual review of the vision as part of the formal planning process. Some families include a review and discussion of the Shared Future Vision as a part of the family's annual meeting.

Based on this Shared Future Vision, the family builds its Family Enterprise Continuity Plan and the management team crafts its Business Strategy Plan. There is direct interaction between these two planning processes, and changes in either will affect the other. As stated earlier, this planning process is interactive and it is not a linear series of events. The power of parallel planning comes from developing understanding and agreement throughout the process. A family business in which family and management are strongly aligned around the future is positioned to develop a clearer strategic direction and mutually supportive goals.

The Shared Future Vision, based on the combined Family Commitment and Strategic Commitment, provides a good opening for announcing to employees that the planning process is proceeding.

Many families might wish to keep the planning process private until they are ready to share its results with non-family managers, employees and other stakeholders. Yet encouraging ongoing communication has many benefits. Employees in a family business, for example, expect to see family considerations affect the direction of the business. They watch for

Figure 2.9   *The family enterprise continuity plan*

Figure 2.10   *The business strategy plan*

signals of the family's plans and they speculate about what is happening in family discussions. It adds up to a tremendous amount of wasted productivity. It is better for the result of these ongoing discussions to be shared so that people can get back to their jobs.

Formulating Family and Business Plans

Once the initial agreement on a Shared Future Vision of the business and the family is confirmed, the rest of the planning process will flow from it. The Shared Future Vision creates momentum for developing the Family Enterprise Continuity Plan and the Business Strategy Plan. During this formulation stage, plans and actions for the family and business systems are developed. In the family arena, this includes the creation of a Family Enterprise Continuity Plan (see Figure 2.9). This plan describes how the family will develop and maintain a long-term and mutually supportive relationship with the business. The essential family topics include participation, management and leadership development and ownership. Plans and actions for each of these important topics must complement efforts to achieve the family's Shared Future Vision.

The counterpart of the family planning process is the Business Strategy Plan (see Figure 2.10). This plan typically covers a wide range of topics that describe how the business will compete. The critical components of that plan include assessing the firm's potential, exploring business strategies and finalizing strategy and investment decisions. Formulating plans and tactics in these three areas is the foundation of the business' strategy.

The final two steps in the strategic management process, implementation and reformulation, relate to taking action on the firm's plans and revising the plans after the results are known. These two important steps of the management process are not discussed in this book, which focuses on the planning aspects (thinking and formulation) of strategic management. Figure 2.11, however, identifies the implementation and reformulation phases because they are important to understanding the larger strategic management process.

A critical task for all organizations is learning. Organizational learning occurs as the firm identifies personal and interpersonal skills that are needed for successful interaction with the external environment.[10] The dotted lines in Figure 2.11 represent feedback to both the family and business planning systems based on actual results. Effective organizations use feedback from actual results for improving their plans and the organization's performance. Becoming a learning family and a learning business are essential for the long-term success of the family business.

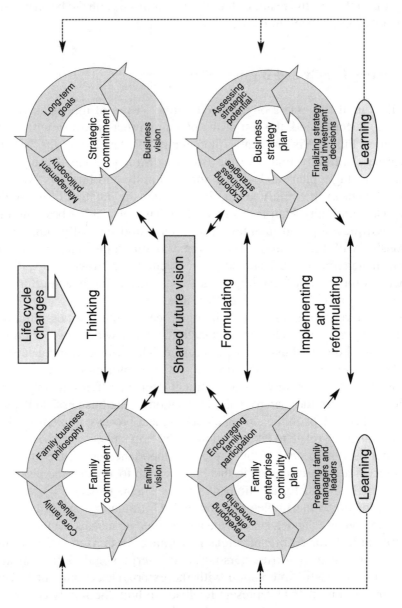

Figure 2.11 *Parallel family and business planning*

Understanding the PPP can help families and management work together to coordinate activities and support the development of each other's plan. Figure 2.11 shows how the PPP actions are complementary because the information developed by the family's planning serves as input for the business' planning and vice versa.

For example, a family that is interested in a long-term return from a high potential venture could share this goal with the management and be informed that the current family business does not have a market opportunity or the competitive strength to achieve this goal. This information would help the family to make a better decision about its long-term commitment, which may include divesting itself of some or all of the current family business and/or repositioning into a new market.

SUMMARY

For many family businesses, developing a family and business planning process has substantial value. It is a powerful tool for addressing change and transitions in the family and business systems. For businesses that have become stagnant over the years, strategic business planning discussions can revitalize operations. For a family challenged by transitions in ownership or control, it begins a process of creating new understandings and agreements. When a family faces seemingly insurmountable conflicts, planning creates a vehicle to reconnect with values and relationships.

The PPP proposed in this book requires the participation of the family and management team in developing a Family Enterprise Continuity Plan that complements the Business Strategy Plan. The PPP challenges both the family and the business systems. The family must explore its values, Family Business Philosophy and Family Vision to assess its commitment to the business. Simultaneously, it challenges the management team to consider its management philosophy, the firm's goals and a Business Vision in developing its Strategic Commitment.

The interaction and relationship of the family's and management's commitment drive the planning process for family enterprises. These two interdependent factors must be compatible and support each other in order to develop a Shared Future Vision of the family and business. For example, if a family decides to limit its commitment to the business by reducing investments in capital expenditures and increasing the dividends, it would be very difficult for management to develop an aggressive growth strategy.

The next four chapters explore the elements of the Family Enterprise Continuity Plan. Chapter 3 addresses securing Family Commitment, Chapter 4, encouraging family participation, Chapter 5, preparing family managers and leaders and, Chapter 6, developing effective ownership. These topics are essential activities designed to support a positive family business relationship.

Part II

Planning for the Family

3 Securing Family Commitment

Family Commitment is what makes a family business – a family business. Without the family's commitment, there can be no Parallel Planning Process. If the family cannot develop a shared commitment to invest and participate in the business, then it is time to sell or liquidate.

So the first step is to explore what the family wants its future relationship with the business to be. Assessing the family's commitment to the business and its willingness to work together is also a necessary for family harmony and individual satisfaction.

The process of considering the family's Statement of Commitment confirms that business ownership is not preordained. The family's review of its commitment to the business is a strong demonstration that family values and goals determine whether continued ownership is the right course of action.

As discussed in Chapter 2, the process for exploring Family Commitment requires the family to consider two questions. First, does the family have an interest in maintaining ownership based on the financial and social benefits they will receive? Second, is the family willing and able to accept the responsibilities of active ownership? This book argues that Family Commitment requires a 'yes' answer to both these questions if there is to be an optimization of business performance and family harmony.

The second question is especially important because the next generation must have a realistic picture of the challenges created by family business ownership. Too often the incoming generation or in-laws do not appreciate the increasing demands that an expanding business family can create. Active participation is hard work – developing family programs, monitoring business performance, serving on the board or family council – and sometimes conflicts with careers and marital/family demands. If the next generations are unwilling to take on the responsibility now, it might be best to consider alternatives for the business.

Chapters 4 and 6 discuss some of the responsibilities that family business ownership creates. The discussion of Family Commitment can create several possible outcomes. There may be a family, investment or business issue that motivates the entire family to agree to keep or sell the business. Relatives who cannot make peace or who are interested in only a passive investment might consider selling to new owners. Likewise, families may discover their multi-generation firm is waging a losing war against a declining market and it might finally be time to let go.

At the same time, these meetings might uncover a surprising amount of leadership within the family that gives new life to the business. These new leaders may either get the entire family behind their strategy or work out a plan to buy the shares of less interested relations.

Whatever the decision, it is important to respect the wishes of all members related to commitment. The worst possible scenario for the family is not to recognize and address individual needs or demands. Forcing individuals into relationships that they do not want only creates the potential for increased future conflict. It may not be possible to immediately redeem certain family members' shares because of business or financial demands, but a long-term plan should be developed to redeem the shares of those interested in selling as soon as it is feasible.

This chapter reviews in detail the process for exploring Family Commitment. The family's goal after completing the discussion of core values, Family Business Philosophy and Future Vision is to write a preliminary Statement of Commitment that forms the basis for continuing the planning process. The family's or individual member's commitment may change as the planning process proceeds and new information is explored. After a preliminary commitment is shared with management and a Shared Future Vision of the family and business is agreed to, the next phase of the family planning process can proceed.

That step is encouraging family participation in formulating a Family Enterprise Continuity Plan that is meaningful to the family (see Figure 3.1).

UNDERSTANDING FAMILY COMMITMENT

Commitment is an important variable in understanding individual behavior and organizational relationships. Commitment to an organization is based on at least three factors:

1. A personal belief and support of the organization's goals and visions.
2. A willingness to contribute to the organization.
3. A desire for a relationship with the organization.

The authors of a comprehensive study of commitment describe it as follows:

> Commitment supposes something beyond mere passing loyalty to an organization. It involves active relationship with the organization such that individuals are willing to give something of themselves in order to contribute to the organization's well being.[1]

This definition suggests that a critical element of commitment is behavior supportive of the business, not just passing loyalty. Commitment that reflects the following themes can help to focus a family's discussions on positive behaviors that meet both individual and family needs:

- Loyalty and pride
- Shared values and goals
- Positive personal experience
- Personal connection with the firm's future vision.

REARDON FAMILY CHALLENGE

How Does a Business Build Family Commitment?

Bob and Steve Reardon, the only Reardon family members employed or even actively involved in the business, are at odds with siblings who are objecting to their limited voice in the company. On one hand, Bob and Steve want everyone to commit to continued investment in the business so they can make it grow. The non-employee family members, on the other hand, have an equally valid concern that they have no say in the business and they are not receiving a reasonable return on their investment.

How can the Reardon family explore these widely divergent views? Some questions:

- Bob made the comment that Reardon Technology isn't really a family business. Is this a family business?

- What are the family's core values?

- Do their family goals support long-term growth and ownership of the business?

- How many personal agendas are out there? Can they be identified and discussed by the family?

PLANNING TOOLS

Family Business Commitment Questionnaire

The series of statements below represent possible feelings that individuals might have about their family business. Based on your own feelings about your family business, please indicate the degree of your agreement or disagreement with each statement by using one of the five responses below to rate each statement. The individual responses create material for a family discussion about the differences in individual commitment and why those differences occur.

Response choices:

1. Strongly Disagree
2. Moderately Disagree
3. Neither Agree Nor Disagree
4. Moderately Agree
5. Strongly Agree

For each of the following statements, choose the number that best describes your situation:

_____1. I am willing to put in a great deal of effort beyond that normally expected in order to help the family business be successful.

_____2. I support the family business in discussions with friends, employees and other family members.

_____3. I feel loyalty to the family business.

_____4. I find that my values are compatible with the business' values.

_____5. I am proud to tell others that I am part of the family business.

_____6. There is much to be gained by participating with the family business on a long-term basis.

_____7. I agree with the family business' goals, plans and policies.

_____8. I really care about the fate of the family business.

_____9. Deciding to be involved with the family business has had a positive influence on my life.

_____10. I understand and support my family's decisions regarding the future of the family business.

_____ **Total points**

Scoring: Divide the total points by 10 to calculate the average score.

Adapted from: R.T. Mowday, R.M. Steers and L.W. Porter, 'The Measurement of Organizational Commitment', *Journal of Vocational Behavior*, **14** (1979), 224–47. Modified by R.S. Carlock, Family Enterprise Center, Graduate School of Business, University of St. Thomas, Minneapolis, MN, (1999).

The organizational commitment questionnaire (shown opposite) may support exploration of individual and family feelings about commitment to the family business. The responses to the questionnaire can be explored during the discussion of core values, Family Business Philosophy and Family Vision (see Figure 2.6). These statements are intended to demonstrate values and behaviors that are associated with high levels of commitment to a family business.

Many families that are concerned about balancing personal autonomy and Family Commitment include this topic as an agenda item for their family meetings and family education programs (both topics are discussed in Chapter 4).

Family Commitment is not a difficult issue to understand or discuss, but the decision regarding commitment can create individual uncertainty and stress. Family members usually feel a psychological ownership of the business. Growing up with a family business can create strong bonds that are difficult to break. Family members choosing not to commit to the family business may sense that they are losing their family connections. If an individual's strongest link to their family is through the business, they might be reluctant to terminate that relationship even if it is not in their best long-term interest. That is why it is important for family members in the family business to assure family members outside the business that they are still very much a part of the family.

EXPLORING FAMILY COMMITMENT

Family Commitment is a priority discussion for the family because it supports the development of the Shared Future Vision and the Family Enterprise Continuity Plan. Simply, a family that plans its future together can build stronger family relationships and new opportunities for family participation and achievement.[2] This statement should describe in detail the family's commitment to the business and explain how the family's talents and resources will contribute to perpetuating family ownership. Such statements might also include the following:

- A summary of family values, goals and priorities.
- A list of the strengths that the family can contribute to the business.
- An outline of what the business needs from the family.

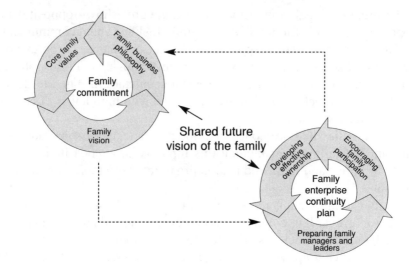

Figure 3.1   *The relationship of family commitment
to the family enterprise continuity plan*

The following are examples of family business issues that are typically addressed:

- What career qualifications are required to work for the business?
- How are financial rewards shared?
- How should ownership be distributed?
- What returns does ownership receive?
- Who has what leadership responsibilities?
- How are family and business decisions balanced?
- What roles should the family and business play in the community?
- What non-career roles (governance, or family leadership) does the family need to play?

The discussion of Family Commitment usually requires a series of meetings that include a complete discussion of critical issues the family will face regarding core values, the Family Business Philosophy and a Family Vision. Often the discussion may shift to specific issues such as investment, governance, ownership, careers and financial goals. It is usually helpful at this stage to attempt to focus first on the larger issues of core values and Family Business Philosophy.

DISCUSSING CORE FAMILY VALUES

The ultimate question that the family needs to discuss is, 'Should the family work together to perpetuate ownership in this business?' Unfortunately for most families this question cannot be asked directly because many members of the family will not have given the idea sufficient thought to make an informed response. It is also possible that there will not be a level of trust that allows people to feel they can answer candidly. For these reasons, the family should begin their discussions by exploring personal and family values that will shape the decision on Family Commitment.

Examining and documenting the values that the family shares is important in helping individual family members to relate to the family group and develop a sense of shared purpose. This is especially true in multi-generation families with in-laws or cousins participating in the business. The interdependent nature of a family system means that the beliefs and actions of each individual influence all other members of the system. Understanding the family's values is an important foundation for building a long-term commitment.

The perceived benefits of maintaining a business that is family owned and managed may vary widely among family members. One may see it as a source of family careers; others, as an opportunity to create wealth. Others may see it as a source of pride based on a family's legacy of achievement. Still more family members may view the business as a drain on family energy and resources or as a source of constant conflict.

The goal for this discussion is to begin the process of sharing ideas and exploring the core values that will influence the decision on making a commitment to the family business. A good starting point for sharing family values is a discussion of the following open-ended statements based on the family's experience:

- Successful families always…
- Our family legacy is…
- Our most important priority as a family is…
- Someone who wants to be influential in our family must…
- Balancing my personal life and career will…
- Our family has a responsibility to ensure that…
- When faced with conflict, our family…
- Our family is blessed with success because…

One simple way to begin is to ask each family member to complete these generic questions around family business values. Their shared answers will stimulate meaningful, and possibly even heated, discussions. Talking about values is important because a family's core values are the foundation of meaningful family and business plans. It is important to allow sufficient time for family members to share their ideas and have others respond. It may be necessary to identify core values that the family agrees on and identify other values for future agenda items at regular family meetings.

Some families find that discussing values is too difficult, and instead find it helpful to discuss real issues and then identify their underlying family values. Table 3.1 summarizes a list of family business issues in question form that can help the family start to think about the challenges they need to address as family business owners. These questions are also useful in outlining topics for inclusion in the discussion of Family Agreements coming up in the next chapter.

The intention of the discussion is not to solve these potential issues, but rather to understand the family values that will drive a solution. These meetings are not likely to be a pleasant, polite process. But if the family takes its job seriously, this will be an honest process that reveals the strength and maturity of the family.

Table 3.1   *Family business issues for discussion*

Managing Succession

- How to identify the next president?
- When does the presidential transition take place (timing)?
- How do the current CEO and successor share planning and decision-making responsibilities during the transition?
- How to evaluate the next president's performance and plan for his or her replacement?
- What non-business interests will keep the senior generation fulfilled during retirement?

Family Business Careers

- How to decide which family members can join the family business?
- How to plan management development experiences?
- What preparation or experience, if any, is required?
- How to evaluate performance and reward achievement?
- What if a family employee does not perform?
- How to encourage the contributions of non-family employees?
- What if a family member chooses to leave the business?
- Whether to permit spouses, partners or other non-blood relatives to work full or part time in the business?
- Whether to allow the next generation's children to enter the business? Under what circumstances?

(cont'd)

Table 3.1 *(cont'd)*

Compensation

- How to evaluate and compensate family members?
- How are bonuses determined?
- Who participates in stock option programs?

Ownership and Governance

- How to assure the senior generation of financial security?
- Who can own stock in the business?
- What returns and rewards do shareholders get?
- Whether to pay dividends?
- How to redeem stock to provide liquidity for shareholders?
- Does all stock have the same voting rights?
- How are members of the board of directors selected?

Family Relationships

- How to deal with conflicts between generations?
- How to deal with sibling or cousin conflict?
- How to teach young members and in-laws the business and also family traditions?
- How to share the family activities and customs with the next generation?
- How to develop and revise family agreements?
- How are family meetings and activities planned?
- How to create a process for family planning and decision-making?
- When to formalize the family governance by organizing a family council?

Responsibility and Code of Conduct

- How to help family members with financial, personal, or career difficulties?
- What responsibilities does one family member have to the others?
- What if there is a divorce?
- What if a family member breaks the law or acts in a seriously irresponsible manner?
- How much financial information to share with whom?
- How to support family members' new business venture ideas?
- How to cope with the visibility and the public's expectations of successful families?
- What responsibility does the family have to the community?
- How to share credit for family achievements?

IDENTIFYING A FAMILY BUSINESS PHILOSOPHY

An agreement on a Family Business Philosophy is closely related to the family's core values. Often during a discussion of family values and the related issues identified in Table 3.1, family members will recognize a consistent pattern of responses from themselves or others. Any business family has three generic choices for its philosophical orientation to family business ownership.

Business First

This decision is to support what will be best for the company, including its customers, employees and shareholders. The family selects professional business principles to govern such matters as compensation, hiring and promotion. They reason that such principles are fair and thus constitute excellent criteria by which to make the tough decisions that will affect the entire family. They are willing to abide by these principles even if they lead to unequal treatment of family members or, ultimately, to selling the business.

Family First

This belief is that the family's happiness and sense of togetherness should come before everything else. Family business decisions will favor family equality and unity, even if they come at some expense to the company's future. The practical result of this philosophy is that differences in the quality and degree of family members' contributions to the business will not be fully recognized. Such families will allow almost everyone to enter the business and will pay everyone more equally. It is rare that a family member would ever be fired. These families believe that these principles are important, even if they cause financial harm or fail to optimize the company's performance. They feel that the business cannot stay healthy in the long term, unless the family is happy and united.

Family Enterprise Approach

The feeling here is that there should be a balance between the Business First and the Family First camps. This philosophy holds that any decision must provide for both the satisfaction of the family and the economic health of the business. Only under such conditions can a company stay in the family well into the future. Only a good compromise will win the commitment of the family and support for the business. Family members who hold this view believe that abusing the needs of either family or business will damage the future. This philosophy is one that promotes the Family Enterprise Approach. It implies a long-term commitment to the future of the business and the family and it requires the family to creatively resolve conflicts between the two interests.

On monetary matters – compensation, dividends and stock ownership – the family would work to keep personal financial expectations in line with business reality. Additionally, the family would also work to share many of the benefits of business success with all family members.

Table 3.2, which outlines ways to resolve difficult family business decisions, details how different business philosophies affect decisions common to all family businesses. For example, when deciding who will and who will not be allowed to enter the family business, families would select only those offspring who could actually contribute to the business. But the family would also work diligently to make certain that others had suitable career opportunities outside the business.

As noted, the choice of the family's philosophy helps to resolve the very decisions most likely to arouse conflict. While every family must decide what is best for it, families concerned about long-term family ownership generally use the Family Enterprise Approach.

FAMILY EXPERIENCES

Maintaining Family Commitment

Keeping family dedicated to the business through generations is the most difficult family business success factor to achieve and maintain. It requires the collaboration of the entire family. It also becomes progressively more challenging as the family grows and expands and family members become more removed from the founder and the business.

The Ford family represents an excellent model of strong commitment to the business that bears their family name. Henry Ford created the modern automobile industry and the Ford Motor Co. has grown to an international giant with plants and employees all over the world. Despite this dramatic growth and their position as the world's second largest industrial corporation, the Ford family has maintained a 40 percent share of the voting stock, more than enough to ensure their control of this giant public corporation.

In 1999, William Clay Ford Jr. became the first family member in over 30 years to assume the chairmanship of the family firm. However, Ford was named chairman not only for his family's significant control of voting shares. He played a key role in the restructuring of the Ford Motor Co. during the 1980s and 1990s as chairman of the company's finance committee. Before that, he had been General Manager of Ford Switzerland and Vice President of the Commercial Truck Center.

William Ford earned his way to the chairmanship through a strong commitment to the family business. In the spring of 1999, shortly after being named chairman, Ford Motor Co.'s giant and historic River Rouge plant was badly

Table 3.2 *Family philosophy's impact on business decisions*

Business Decision	Business First	Family First	Family Enterprise Spirit
Entry rules	Specific job, if qualified	All welcome	Opportunities will be developed for all individuals in the business, based on business needs
Compensation	Based on job description and market conditions	Equal pay for family members of same generation	Acceptable family standard of living assured for everyone
Stock ownership	Chief executive or family managers receive stock according to contribution or possibly among non-family employees	Equal by branch of family	Equal values for all – some in business stock, others in passive investments or entrepreneurial opportunities
Dividends	None	Stable, fair return to capital	Variable, modest return to capital
Titles and authority	Based on merit in a business hierarchy where each person has only one boss	Equal titles for all members of same generations and role in decision-making for all shareholders	Equal roles for all those with high degree of competence
Governance	Board of outside directors	Broad family consensus	Board of directors and representative Family Council
Role in community	Leadership	Voluntary	Active according to family needs and individual interests

damaged by explosions and fire. As one of the first executives on the scene, William Ford described the fire as one of the saddest days ever for his family.

Like his great-grandfather who founded the company, Ford recognizes the unique challenges he will face. He currently drives a prototype electric truck being tested by the company, which he projects will be in production early in the 21st century. When named chairman, he articulated his personal commitment to the family firm by saying, 'I want to serve this company to the best of my ability. The Ford Motor Co. is my heritage and has always been a part of my life.'

Note: Information from 'William Ford Aims to Show He's in the Driving Seat', *The Times*, (UK) (29 January 1999), 33.

Influences on the Choice of a Family Business Philosophy

Family members may disagree about which philosophy suits their family. But understanding values and assumptions that underlie such disagreements will make discussion valuable to family planning. The family and business circumstances will influence the debate: the nature of the family, the nature of the business and the family's core values.

The size of the family, the size of the business, the number of family members in and out of the business and the nature of the business itself will all shape the choice of philosophy. For example, if a small number of offspring are running a mid-sized business in an efficient way, the family choosing a Family First philosophy – based on equal partners – works

Table 3.3   *Influences on the choice of family business philosophy*

Health and magnitude of the business	Number of family members in leadership generation		
	1 to 2	**3 to 5**	**6 or more**
Weak and small	No debate: business survival	No debate: business first	No debate: business first
Modest	No problem: family first	Conflict resolution critical	Conflict resolution critical
Large (probably partially publicly held or external financing)	No problem: business first	Conflict resolution critical	No problem: business first

Note: The majority of family businesses are in the conflict resolution critical stage due to typical family and business size. Those cases require deliberate planning and effort to develop the family's philosophy and vision.

well. If there are numerous offspring in a small business (or offspring with expensive lifestyles in a larger business), the result may create anarchy.

To improve effectiveness, the family would need to 'prune the family tree', in other words, agree on who will actively be involved in the business and buy the others out. Table 3.3 provides a summary of these views. A family with a large number of offspring working in a big business with many non-employed family shareholders will probably lean toward the Business First philosophy. The family's philosophy of organizing needs to be revisited as a part of the annual planning process. Changes in the family or business may lead to a modification of the family's original principles.

Articulating a Family Business Philosophy

As noted earlier, families have three generic approaches to a Family Business Philosophy; generally put the business before the family (Business First), favor the family over the business (Family First) or work to generate a solution that meets the needs of both (Family Enterprise Approach).

For many, circumstances make the choice between family, business, or family enterprise. Thus, if the family is large and the business is small, there is usually no room to support family interests at the expense of the business. Business survival is paramount. In the case of a small family and a prosperous business, however, there is little penalty in serving family needs first. The business can readily afford it.

The choice grows difficult only when the business has limited resources and the family is large enough to spawn conflicting career and financial goals among members. The choice is also difficult in a business of any size when ownership is shared among several relatives, some of who are active in the business while others are not. In such circumstances, developing a Family Business Philosophy is critical.

PLANNING TOOLS

What is Your Family/Business Balance?

Are you wondering how to rank family issues against business issues? See Appendix C. The Exploring Family Business Philosophy Questionnaire will provide a score sheet to evaluate how your family views these issues.

Each family member will develop his or her own reasons for selecting one philosophy over another. When the process ends, the reasons are likely to cluster around a dominant set of values. The question that best reveals such overriding family values is: What do family members think holds the family together? Wealth? Shared ownership? Working together? Family gatherings? Fun and social activities? New opportunities? Success? Hard work? Individual achievement?

The more the family leans toward sharing ownership as the 'familial glue', the more Family First the philosophy will become. The more the family members lean toward hard work, shared success and social activities, however, the more likely that families will choose a Family Enterprise philosophy. A family that is driven by growth and individual opportunities to achieve tends to favor Business First.

FAMILY VISION

The discussion of the family's vision of itself is the last activity in exploring the development of Family Commitment. Visions are a powerful tool for creating a unity of purpose and focusing the attention of the family. Here is a list of benefits that a vision can provide a business family:

- Provides a guiding 'star' for family decisions.
- Describes how the family can contribute to the business' success.
- Requires working as a family team.
- Helps the family to move beyond the entrepreneur's original Business Vision.
- Provides a rationale for the family's commitment to the business.
- Describes what is special about the family.
- Builds on the family's values, rituals and traditions.

A Family Vision is an attempt to describe a desired future state for the family and its relationship to the business. A vision statement usually stipulates a time frame and includes a vivid description of the positive outcomes the family seeks. The Family Business Philosophy and core values both shape the development of the family's vision.

Families should consider the following criteria when exploring their vision:

- Based on the family's core values, is it meaningful or compelling?
- Does it represent the family's collective commitment to each other?

■ Does it force the family to develop a future focus or direction?
■ Does it encourage actions and thinking that optimize business resources and opportunities?

Using the criteria above should help the family to create a vision that answers the following:

Ten years from now....

■ What will be the family's strengths?
■ How will the family contribute to the business?
■ What will be the family's legacy?
■ What will the business provide for the family?
■ Who will own the family business?

While the family is discussing its vision they need to consider the possible business scenarios (Business Vision) that the management team is discussing and explore how these possibilities will affect the family. It is critical for the family to have realistic expectations of the business and the demands that the business may make on them.

The family may want to invite a few senior family or non-family executives to a family meeting to share management's current thinking about the future of the business. This sharing of perspectives begins the process of developing a Shared Future Vision of the business and family. Meaningful family discussions are needed so that family members who expect a passive investment can reconcile their views with others who want a high potential business demanding the active involvement of everyone.

The importance of a Family Vision cannot be overestimated, especially to a family that is financially successful. Families need some ideal to stimulate their collective spirit and think beyond the day-to-day tasks of managing a business to create more wealth.

Humans experience meaning in their lives when they are challenged to contribute to something larger than meeting their own needs and wants. They look for something in their work that offers a psychological or spiritual reward. A vision of what the family can become creates a purpose that reduces rivalries, empowers individuals and overcomes life's obstacles. A commitment decision based on core values, a Family Business Philosophy and a Family Vision creates the emotional energy required to drive the family planning process.

FAMILY EXPERIENCES

A Sample Family Business Vision Statement (Partial Excerpt)

Our Vision for the Family's Enterprise

Our dream is a dynamic, long-lasting, family owned company.

We define success as a healthy business owned and guided by a harmonious family. We hope to serve as a positive example to other families in business.

We are committed as a family to running our businesses based on sound business principles. Creating long-term shareholder value for future generations is the focus of our efforts. Building a valuable and durable company culture based on distinct family values will powerfully strengthen our enterprise. Assessing everyone, particularly family members, on merit assures a fair and productive organization.

We believe these principles are not only good business, but good for the family. A model business is a source of pride for all family. A strong business culture reinforces our family's values. Personnel decisions based on merit provide family members with an honest mirror and create an environment for personal growth and development. Such an environment also attracts the most talented non-family executives.

We hope our business interests attract keen interest and involvement by family members. Responsible family governance and widespread family visibility add special value to the businesses. Clear, united ownership commitment releases tremendous organizational energy to produce long-term value and enhances the business' culture. Therefore, family participation in the business' management and governance must satisfy family member goals and aspirations.

Despite these great mutual strengths of family with business, a threat must be vigilantly in mind. The natural competition and stresses of business life can create a battleground where family conflicts and rivalries are fought. A divided, unhappy family will not only destroy our dream for long-term family unity, but will also destroy the business and harm the lives of many who are dependent on the business.

We envision a portfolio of business interests diverse enough to attract talented family members to business leadership positions and extensive enough to provide important leadership opportunities for accomplished, ambitious, non-family executives. We know that our mix of businesses will change as surely as the competitive business environment will change.

We envision a global enterprise to better relate to the new business landscape as well as to broaden the family's horizons. We envision staying focused on the food products industry as that industry provides us with the opportunity to build our portfolio on common strengths and shared learning, and allows for many different ventures and divisions.

Source: J.L. Ward, Family Business Consulting Group, Evanston, IL, (1998).

PLANNING TOOLS

For Your Business Library

Readers interested in more information on how families develop their collec-
tive vision based on understanding their shared dreams should read *Succeeding
Generations: Realizing the Dreams of Families in Business* by Ivan Lánsberg
(Boston: Harvard Business School Press, 1999).

STATEMENT OF FAMILY COMMITMENT

Once family members begin to reach preliminary consensus on core values,
Family Business Philosophy and Family Vision, they can draft a preliminary Statement of Family Commitment. This typically occurs after a series
of family meetings reveals a broad base of support for continuing as a
family-owned company.

Some families ask each member to prepare in advance his or her personal
beliefs on the pros and cons of perpetuating the family business. These would
be shared in a family meeting, then recorded as part of the meeting summary.
Whatever method is used, once the themes are identified, various members
may propose 'family beliefs' as guidelines for resolving them. These beliefs –
call them propositions – can then be summarized and distributed among
family members for acceptance, revision, or rejection. A team of family
members can then use the family 'beliefs' to draft a proposed Statement of
Family Commitment for continued discussion at the next family meeting.

This draft – one sentence up to a paragraph – clarifies the family's
expectations from and obligations to the business. A short statement of
intent is all that is required at this stage. For example, either 'XYZ Corp.
will remain a family-owned and managed business' or 'Our family is dedicated to the long-term success of this business' is adequate. However, a
better starting point is: 'We believe that XYZ Corp., with family management and participation, can grow at a 20 percent annual rate and expand to
a number-one market share position in the southwestern US by 2004.' The
wording does not have to be elaborate. The important outcome is that the
family agrees to a written preliminary Statement of Commitment.

After the agreement on a preliminary Statement of Commitment, the
family needs a series of family meetings to expand their thinking and create
a full Statement of Commitment. Again, a smaller family group may be
employed to draft this document for the family's review and approval. It is
important to remember that the final format or title of this statement is unim-
portant. The objective is to integrate the ideas on the family's values, vision

and commitment in a written document. The *Family Experiences* presented in this chapter contain all of these elements. They confirm the family's commitment and explain what that commitment means to the family.

An excerpt of a Statement of Family Commitment that integrates supporting shareholder goals is shown below.

This commitment statement clearly articulates the family's contributions to the business and their expectations for themselves. The McNeely family

---

FAMILY EXPERIENCES

Statement of Family Commitment (Partial Excerpt)

McNeely family shareholders will act from a multigenerational perspective. We will empower the board of directors to grow the company by managing, acquiring and developing assets while maintaining a conservative financial posture. The board will shape the company's vision, policies and goals. We want the board and management to create an environment that fosters ethical and dedicated employees who are rewarded for entrepreneurial achievement and for providing exceptional customer service. The company will promote the professional development of its employees through ongoing training and education. McNeely shareholders will continue to give a portion of the company's earnings to charity.

Family Shareholder Goals

1. To critically review our vision and goals from a multigenerational perspective.

2. To make our board active in its oversight and decision-making abilities and to participate on the company's board.

3. To elect a majority of non-family members to the company's board and to populate the board through the activities of a nominating committee which will include a family, non-family and management board member.

4. Family board representatives have a duty to present family decisions to the board in an objective manner.

5. Shareholders agree to be bound by their majority.

6. Shareholders have a duty to be informed and objective.

7. Shareholders personally agree to be financially responsible to help ensure perpetuation of the company. This responsibility includes executing comprehensive personal financial planning.

Revised: March, 1998
December, 1996
April, 1994.

Source: The McNeely Family. Harry McNeely, Jr, Chairman of Meritex Enterprises. Mr McNeely also serves as Chair of the Advisory Board for the Center for Family Enterprise, University of St. Thomas, Minneapolis, MN. Used with permission.

goals clarify their responsibilities to their family business and each other. Their statement strongly emphasizes the role of the board of directors because their family values a strong governance structure. Four of their goals relate to governance issues, including a stipulation that a majority of board members will be outside directors. The statement also articulates the family's responsibilities to a 'multi-generational perspective... [being] informed and objective ...[and] fiscally responsible'.

Family Commitment Statements will vary in their topics and scope of actions based on each individual family's circumstances. The McNeely Family Commitment Statement is for a mature business with a non-family senior management team (one family member from the next generation is involved in management). It is also interesting to note that this statement has been revised by the family three times in the last six years to reflect changes in the family and business.

Typically, Statements of Family Commitment will answer the basic question: 'How does the family support the business?' The resolution of this issue will shape a consistent response to matters such as investment, business participation, ownership distribution and governance. It also supports a Family Business Philosophy that can be communicated throughout the family, which family members can understand and use when addressing difficult family business decisions such as how to handle non-performance by a family member employee.

SUMMARY

This chapter has proposed a process for considering Family Commitment based on exploring core values, clarifying a Family Business Philosophy and creating a future vision of the family. There are two equally important elements in the commitment decision: maintaining ownership and the willingness to participate and accept the responsibilities of active ownership. The outcome of these discussions is a decision to either explore selling the business or a Statement of Family Commitment.

The next chapter addresses family participation, the first component of the Family Enterprise Continuity Plan. The concept of family participation includes the family's active involvement with the business based on a shared decision-making process. Family conflict and fairness are reviewed to develop an understanding of two influences on family relationships that must be addressed to encourage participation. Family meetings and Family Agreements, tools that enable family participation and support positive family relationships, will be explained further.

4 Encouraging Family Participation

In a family business, the family is a source of employees, owners, managers and directors. In committed families, everyone contributes to the goals of the Parallel Planning Process and to the success of the business family. Managers often lead the business planning process to identify new opportunities for continued growth. The family's active participation is a powerful and constant influence on the planning processes discussed throughout this book.

Family participation is a tangible demonstration of the family's commitment to the business. But it is also an important tool for maintaining Family Commitment. If everyone is positively involved with the business, the business has achieved Family Commitment.

Ownership continuity and successful business performance both require Family Commitment over the long haul. Figure 4.1 summarizes possible opportunities for involvement in both the family and the business. As Figure 4.1 demonstrates, there are plenty of meaningful roles in the family and business systems. However, what often happens is that family members are unwilling to participate because the environment is unsupportive or worse, hostile.

An organization's style is important only to the degree that it helps people to experience satisfaction while maximizing their contribution to the organization's goals. The positive organizational effect of participa-

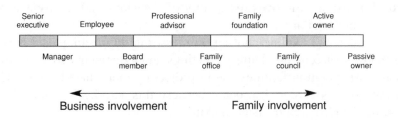

Figure 4.1   *Possible family business participation*

tion and empowerment are fundamental concepts in the management literature. Organizations that encourage appropriate participation make better decisions and the decisions receive greater support.[1] Yet leaders have to realize that the social and political change of the last 30 years has inspired individuals to continually seek more influence over the decisions that affect their lives. The traditional organizational model that saw power and decision-making as vested at the top of the hierarchy is a thing of the past.[2]

Today, this change applies equally to families and their businesses. For the business, the benefit of increasing participation is that empowerment creates opportunities for the next generation's contribution and fulfillment. Simply put, it keeps the talent at home. Opening up participation for family members helps strengthen commitment and reduces the powerlessness that so many next-generation family business members experience. Encouraging participation with the family business may assure its very survival.

This book defines family participation in two dimensions: active involvement in the family or business system and shared decision-making. The first dimension of participation is getting more family members involved in contributing to the future of the family business. As Figure 4.1 demonstrates this means that the next generation or in-laws begin business involvement as employees or family involvement in family roles. Family participation in any capacity increases a sense of ownership and helps individuals to learn more about how the family and business operate.

The second dimension of participation is expanding the family's role in the decision-making process. This action involves sharing power and responsibility for making decisions on family, ownership, governance and business issues. Reviewing and proposing revisions to the Family Agreements would be an example of an activity where the family can share responsibility. While active involvement is the first step to family participation, it is shared decision-making that creates the positive energy for the business family. Developing programs to support the family's participation in both dimensions improves the quality of decisions and family acceptance of group decisions.

This chapter will explore conflict, fairness, family meetings and developing Family Agreements. Family meetings and agreements are tools that many multi-generation families use in protecting their shared future. The family meeting is explored in detail because this activity facilitates both involvement and shared decision-making.

CREATING AN ENVIRONMENT THAT
SUPPORTS PARTICIPATION

An important issue in all families is understanding the impact of family relationships and conflict on family participation. Too often families fail to recognize that family business conflict results from a lack of participation and limited opportunities for the family to constructively explore individual differences related to values, goals and vision.[3]

Encouraging the family's participation becomes more challenging as the family grows and multiple generations have a stake in the business. Older family members have an easier experience since they typically have a closer link to the founder. They had an opportunity to learn about the business from the start; generally they share the founder's early vision.

In later generations, family members who work in the business or own stock tend to be motivated more by personal concerns. To keep the older and younger groups from splitting apart, they must be encouraged to learn about the family business, explore their possible involvement and consider the contribution they can make to the family's and the business' future success.

Unfortunately, this may not happen if the family does not create an environment that encourages exploration and participation. The following discussion of family conflict and Fair Process provides some important thinking about what families must do to create an environment that facilitates, rather than freezes out, participation.

UNDERSTANDING FAMILY CONFLICT

All families experience conflict and relationship problems as the family moves through its life cycle. Business families face bigger problems because they work so closely together.[4] This proximity often means that family disputes overshadow work, even though the company continues to function normally.[5] However, it is worth considering what a new system for reconciling business and family problems could do for the productivity of that business and the health of the family.

Many families are afraid to encourage participation because they fear that simmering conflicts may explode. They avoid honest and sometimes painful communication about the reality of their situation in the interest of maintaining the 'myth' of familial harmony.[6] There is no question that maintaining harmony is important, but conflict and change are crucial to the growth of individuals, family relationships and the company.

Children are taught not to 'rock the boat', which then prevents them from finding their own way or differentiating.[7] By silencing the younger generation and other family members who are not directly involved in the business, the family can create a false sense of itself, built on denial and idealization. When this false connection blocks the airing of differences and grievances, family relationships are not real.[8]

Many business families have recognized the value of using the planning process to create structures and systems that address family conflicts or relationship problems. Families that directly address conflict build the trust that is essential to breaking the cycle of conflict. They have learned that the most effective way to keep a family functioning is to work as a group. Families that have avoided conflict or have had difficulty with confronting issues will find that the planning process is an opportunity to begin building the family trust that will serve them not only during the planning process, but also in their ongoing family and business relationships.

Involving the family may be a challenge for some family businesses, particularly those with a tradition of highly controlling leaders and rigid hierarchies. However, many senior family members recognize how important this process can be.

PLANNING TOOLS

Is Your Family Ready to Communicate?

The Family Business Communications Questionnaire (see Appendix B) is designed to explore topics for discussion about family communication. In many ways, planning for the family's participation is a form of discovery because it challenges all family members to reflect on their interpersonal relationships, explore who has power and learn new patterns of interacting with each other. These families may need to explore their decision-making processes and develop new agreements about planning and decision-making.

THE IMPORTANCE OF ADDRESSING CONFLICT IN FAMILY RELATIONSHIPS

The cost of avoiding conflict is high. Honest relationships and trust are repressed. The family loses the healthy tension needed for personal growth and change, and they begin to experience the unhealthy kind of tension that stems from limiting individual expression. Spouses who have heard only complaints from their husbands or wives, and who are often all too willing to take sides, can heighten such tension.[9] Families need to realize that working together and preparing a family and business for the future require uncomfortable changes, mistakes and confronting conflict.

Before a family can encourage the participation of new family members, the family must have some basis for a personal relationship. Siblings, cousins or in-laws with conflicted relationships may have been always kept at bay by the senior generation. If these relationships cannot be changed or repaired, it is time for senior management to make a thoughtful decision about the family's future relationship to the business.

It is easy to deny that a problem exists by rationalizing about 'everyone pulling together' in the future or working as a 'part of the family team'. Unfortunately, it is highly unlikely that this will ever happen. Manfred Kets de Vries, a psychoanalyst and management consultant, concludes that the long-term consequences of unresolved conflict are clear:

> In normal circumstances, siblings eventually separate and choose their own course in life. With time and geographical distance, residual child-hood irritants and resentments are less likely to flare up; vindictive triumph becomes less of a burning passion. Joining the family firm, however, makes this resolution more difficult. Continuing closeness aggravates the situation, while the presence of the parents in the business may rub additional salt in never-healed wounds. Old feelings of envy and jealousy cannot be put to rest because all the actors in the play are still present. The family members may end up in a vicious circle of endlessly repeating conflicts – a continuation of the old emotional 'games' of childhood.[10]

Developing Family Agreements, business policies, career and succession programs will help to prevent unnecessary structural conflicts. Unfortunately, this may not be an adequate solution for the internal strife experienced by some siblings and cousins.

When family rivalry or competitiveness becomes the dominant pattern, it may be necessary for senior family members or the family council to resolve the problem. This may mean terminating one or more family members from the business, splitting the firm into separate operating companies or perhaps even selling the business. Senior family members have a responsibility as stewards of the business to resolve any situation that could result in long-term conflict and destruction of the business. If they do not take action, the situation will probably never be resolved. In this situation, it is unlikely that the family business will be seen as a desirable opportunity by many members of the next generation.

Encouraging Family Participation

One of the most difficult challenges for multi-generation business families is maintaining the active participation of the family. As families grow and mature through the life cycle, the family's relationship to the business weakens. The vision and values of the founder are only a memory, the firm employs a smaller percentage of the family and the ownership is dissipated over a larger pool of heirs.

The 200-member Ahlström family of Finland confronted this issue when they faced a decision of divesting the company's traditional business to improve profitability. Krister Ahlström, the fourth-generation CEO, had proposed a well-conceived strategy to sell the company's money-losing paper mill. The plan was opposed by the family and rejected by a board of directors that in Ahlström's words, 'Were too upset at the time to listen to the facts. It was dominated then by third-generation thinking.'

A year later after the business situation continued to deteriorate, Ahlström's plan was finally approved and the sale completed. At that time he and some of his generation realized that the family's problems were not just in revitalizing the business but also in improving the quality of the family's participation. As Ahlström describes it, 'There was a huge gap between the perceptions of the owners (family) and the business realities.' Ahlström and members of the younger generations decided that many of the company's problems stemmed from a lack of information and participation by the family.

The family eventually developed several mechanisms to improve the interaction with each other and the business. A Family Assembly was created to encourage social relationships among the far-flung family members as well as facilitate open discussion of business issues and the company's strategic plans. A family council was established to strengthen the family's link with the board and CEO – it also created a family governance function. This representative five-member body was charged with organizing the Family Assembly meetings, drafting family agreements and nominating candidates for the board of directors.

One of the first major tasks that the family council tackled was defining a Shared Future Vision – exploring what the family wanted and expected from the business. The council also investigated key family values that would influence future policymaking efforts. The outcome of these activities was the development of the Ahlström Family Values and Policies. Another important result was defining the family members' participation as 'enlightened owners.'

The family also created a training program for the incoming fifth generation. Krister Ahlström summarized the training as teaching the 'Younger generation what it means to be an owner. What happens inside the company? How is strategy formulated? How are the company's values put into practice? How does the company budget its resources? What accounting principles does an owner need to master? What questions should an owner ask?'

The new family plan has educated every Ahlström relative on what it means to be a great industrial family. As Krister Ahlström states, 'There is a feeling of carrying on a great tradition. Usually families put up with a lot of hardship to see their companies survive. Most find it very hard to give up because they think my forefathers have handed this down to me and I'm supposed to take care of it. What drives most families to sell out is not a lack of interest among family members but rather an inability to resolve some difficulty.'

Source: J. Magretta, 'Governing the family-owned enterprise: An interview with Finland's Krister Ahlström', *Harvard Business Review*, **76**(1): 112–23, (January–February, 1998).[11]

FAMILY FAIRNESS

Family businesses with a goal of long-term Family Commitment struggle with defining fairness, then creating practices that reinforce it.

The fairness dilemmas that many families have are a residual effect of the parent–child relationship. A behavior pattern evolves as parents exercise control over their children's lives to ensure their safety and development. Even after the children mature, this parental role remains part of the family's structure and the next generation continues as 'children' as long as their parents are alive.

Businesses are also organized on a hierarchy based on roles and authority. The management and shareholders make decisions that direct the business and its strategy. Successful performance reinforces this structure and its decision-making processes, but sometimes to the detriment of the next generation. Such a rigid structure means younger family members cannot express new ideas or aspirations without challenging management's proven formula for success. This limits their participation and personal autonomy.

The adolescent and young adult years are known for conflicts and struggles between parents and their children. Parents want control; children, independence. As families evolve from parent–child to parent–adult relationships, it is important for the older generation to introduce the family business to the children with fairness and mutual respect.

This can be tough because the younger generation has already waged rebellion at home. Why? First, families and businesses are not inherently fair. Second, the younger generation family members often see themselves as powerless and unworthy. Their family's wealth and status have shaped their lives, but they were not part of its creation.

It is often difficult for the senior generation, especially if they were the entrepreneur or significant force in building the business, to recognize the expectations and burdens that are created by birth into a successful family. John D. Rockefeller Jr. spent his entire life attempting to meet the ideals that he felt his father exhibited in building a business empire and philanthropic endeavors. Junior's inherited personal wealth and power were always a source of discomfort for him. As Ron Chernow describes in *Titan: The Life of John D. Rockefeller Sr.*:

> Nobody was more daunted by his prospect than Junior himself, who felt trapped in the iron cage of dynastic expectation. Never sure of himself, Junior plodded ahead, always wondering where he was heading.[12]

One solution to this dilemma is to create families and businesses that institutionalize fairness by empowering the next generation as soon as possible to participate in decisions that affect the family. This meaningful participation is the basis for a planning and decision-making concept called Fair Process. Applying Fair Process to the family business context addresses the issues of family justice and helps to maintain the support and participation of all family members. Christine Blondel and Ludo Van der Heyden of the Family Firms Program at INSEAD (European Institute of Business Management) suggest that Fair Process contributes to improving family business performance by creating a vehicle for 'listening to the next generation' on topics such as ownership, policies, career management and values.[13]

Creating Fair Process in Families

The essence of Fair Process is this: 'Individuals are most likely to trust and cooperate freely with systems – whether they themselves win or lose by those systems – when Fair Process is observed.'[14] The concept of Fair Process is built on three principles: engagement, explanation and expectation (Figure 4.2).

Engagement

A core activity for improving family relationships is involving the family in discussions about family issues, plans and decisions that affect them. The family meeting discussed in this chapter is a critical tool for engaging

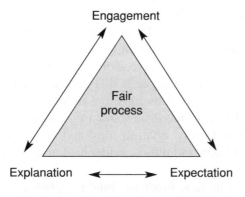

Figure 4.2 *The elements of fair process*

the family in meaningful exchanges about their assumptions and ideas regarding the family and the business. Inviting participation in a family meeting demonstrates the senior generation's commitment to creating a role for the next generation. The family's participation in the planning and decision-making process improves support and personal ownership for the final actions.

Explanation

Understanding what is happening is critical in family businesses because of the changing nature of relationships as both family and business mature. Traditionally, family business planning and decision-making were the responsibility of senior management and owners. They usually did not feel the need to discuss or explain their decisions or actions to family members or in-laws who were not owners or senior employees. However, the introduction of the next generation, especially at the cousins' level, requires new approaches because there are now family members without senior management roles or current ownership.

Expectations

Clarifying everyone's expectations, whether for careers or ownership, improves family and business relationships. Business families more often face conflict over expectations than over decision-making or planning. In the family system, failure to discuss expectations and spell them out in writing is frequently a source of family misunderstandings.

Fair Process acknowledges that families and businesses are not democracies and that certain members have more influence and control over the final decisions than others. It suggests that the entrepreneur who wants his oldest son to succeed him does have the authority to name his son as successor. Yet it also says that if he wants to maximize family support for his son, strengthen family relationships and make the best possible decision, he should listen and fully consider his family's ideas and concerns along with his own.

After accepting this new input he should explain his decision and his expectations to the family. This is often a difficult change in behavior for family and business leaders, but it is a critical step for ensuring the contribution of the family's emotional and intellectual talent to support the family business. A family working together on the development of a Family Enterprise Continuity Plan is improving their family fairness and empowering the next generation.

FAMILY MEETINGS AS A TOOL FOR ENABLING FAMILY PARTICIPATION

The starting point for working and planning as a family is the family meeting. All families can benefit from family meetings, even if they are only to plan family vacations or budget family resources. The family meeting serves an important function in helping the family to accomplish its tasks and maintain social relationships. It is the mechanism to encourage family participation, shared planning and decision-making and the resolution of family conflicts. A family that does not meet together outside the business has no opportunity to focus its attention on family issues or encourage full family participation.

Why is something as simple as a meeting so important? First, if the family is unwilling or unable to participate together, it is a clear signal that the family faces challenges in working together. If they cannot agree to regular meetings, it is unlikely they will have the skills to work together if a conflict arises. If the family cannot organize an effective meeting, it might be best to bring in a family business or organizational consultant to get the ball rolling. Multi-generation families who have never tried meetings before often find it toughest to start the process simply due to the many different perspectives within the group. But when families make a serious commitment to start this process, the meetings create their own rewards and motivations. Disputes are aired, new ideas surface and families are often surprised to find the amount of unmined talent it has in every generation.

Goals of Family Meetings

The main purpose for developing an ongoing family meeting program is to establish a structure that encourages family participation in planning, problem-solving and decision-making. All family businesses face the challenge of sharing and resolving family members' different needs and expectations. This is true whether the family business is making a transition from the first to the second generation or moving into a Family Syndicate Phase with multiple generations.

The family meeting, or a representative family council as the number of family members grows, is an effective vehicle for decision-making and gaining consensus on critical family business issues. It allows communication on any topic of general concern and eventually the unspoken family issues. It is also important to consider how family meetings can provide support for family members. These meetings are part of the family system and should reflect the family's concern for everyone's well-being. It is the balance of tasks and social interactions that make family meetings meaningful.

Long before formal written agreements are developed or major decisions are addressed, these meetings may be used to help educate the family. They may be organized like family 'seminars', including future leadership skills required and possible family roles. Informal conversation on these and other subjects can provide a solid foundation for later formal family planning and decision-making.

Evolution of Family Meetings

Some families hold meetings with their young children and adolescents, typically discussing family matters only. They talk about the assignment of chores, household rules or vacation plans. They hear each other's complaints and suggestions and learn how to negotiate conflicts through discussion. Craig Aronoff and John L. Ward, based on their work as family business consultants, suggest that such family meetings teach communication skills, encourage independence and build self-esteem. The family also learns the value of well-run meetings, planning agendas or topics, listening carefully and following up on results. Such habits lay the groundwork for sharing business decisions, an important element in perpetuating family businesses.[15]

Families that begin meeting when their offspring are teenagers and old enough to work in the business have different and expanded agendas. They tend to discuss the history and nature of the business. In these conversations, parents may comment with pride on the family's heritage and achievements. These family narratives may demonstrate the values of family behaviors that contribute to the business' success.[16] Like the meetings with younger children, these meetings establish a valuable forum for the mutual exchange of views and values. At this stage of the family's development, the topics are education and values, not formal planning. Meetings are usually casual, perhaps held at the dinner table or at an agreed-upon location and time.

As offspring become adults, however, the nature and purpose of these meetings change. First, the 'children' are actively considering their careers and their possible commitment to the family business. As young adults begin to express interest in the family business, many family business parents begin to consider holding formal family meetings for that purpose. Additionally, the family meeting can help the family 'grow up', as it becomes a family of adults. Learning to work as a family of autonomous adults is an important step toward improving family functioning.[17]

Deciding who should attend these family meetings can help the family recognize their new roles and relationships. A family meeting held by parents for their children living at home has a very different set of issues than does a family meeting held with adult children who may have spouses, partners or children of their own. The process of defining who should attend the family meeting is in itself an important step toward developing agreements about family participation and working relationships.

Who Should Attend Family Meetings

Two schools of thought govern this question. One says that only those who are adults and blood relatives should participate. The reasoning here is that sensitive family matters should have only a limited audience because it is then easier to maintain confidentiality. The other perspective maintains that all family members, including teenagers, spouses and partners, should be welcome. These people should be included because the family business affects them.

Most family business experts recommend that all family members should attend family meetings for the following reasons:

- In-laws and partners that learn about family plans and issues first hand have a more realistic picture of the family business.

- Attending meetings helps to expose everyone to the family's traditions and processes and it acquaints them with the family's shared vision and its commitment to the business.

- The next generation and in-laws can make valuable contributions by providing new perspectives. If the mood of the meeting is right, younger family members may also begin to articulate their own values and intentions regarding the business. Their participation is vital for the family's future and the future of the business.[18]

For many families, the issue of who attends these meetings will settle itself over time. When first holding family meetings, sometimes it is wise to hold a planning session with only the adult, blood-family members. This allows the family to establish some ground rules and saves the embarrassment of exposing in-laws and younger family members to a difficult or disorganized meeting that could discourage their long-term participation.

Who Should Conduct Family Meetings

Readers may assume that the natural leader of these meetings is the business president or a senior family member. Yet family meetings provide the perfect opportunity to broaden the family leadership base. With this in mind, the job of organizing and chairing the meeting should rotate among different members. This will provide leadership skills training for the next generation. At the same time, it offers the family members an opportunity to recognize which offspring might later lead the business or lead the family. Rotating leadership roles means that the leader of the business and the leader of the family do not necessarily have to be the same person.

Sometimes it may be helpful to use a consultant or professional to facilitate family meetings. They are trained in communication techniques that can help to create a more shared and balanced discussion. Some families, for example, bring in a family business consultant to begin the process and outline the issues. This removes the burden from any one family member and also encourages questions from the entire group. Whatever the means, the goal is to open up a broad range of topics and concerns where family members can begin to develop philosophies and agreements that define the family's future relationship with the business.

Agenda

A well-planned meeting agenda supports effective family communication and encourages participation. Development of the agenda requires a demo-cratic process that allows controversial or sensitive items to be addressed. The effectiveness of the family meeting is not necessarily measured by the content of the meeting, but rather by how well power is shared and partic-ipation is encouraged. Two or three family members working together should solicit agenda items or issues of mutual interest to the family group. This process should create structure and ensure that significant topics are addressed.

When a family is just beginning family meetings, there is a significant amount of material to address. After the family has finalized a Statement of Family Commitment it is usually helpful for the family to identify one or two topics that involve decision-making or family action. The topics described in Table 3.1 require anywhere from a few meetings to meetings over many years, depending on the pace at which the family chooses to proceed.

After the family has conducted several meetings, the agenda will begin to include more tasks or issues related to the business and managing family relationships. The agenda will now include topics related to reviewing the company's performance, exploring governance structures, contributing to the Business Strategy Plan, assessing the family's plan and updating personal activities and goals. Some families use these meetings to develop committees, elect members to various positions and share infor-mation about financial investments.

Reviewing the Business Strategy Plan and Family Enterprise Continuity Plans is also a specific agenda item for most family meetings. In fact, working on aspects of these plans is often a significant purpose of family meetings or family councils.

Planning a Series of Family Meetings

The mechanics of organizing a family meeting are fairly simple, provided the family has addressed the issues discussed earlier in this chapter. Figure 4.3 identifies a five-step model for planning, conducting and following up on a family meeting. As the five steps demonstrate, the overriding goal of the family meeting is professionalism and participation. There must be an agreement that the meeting will be conducted in a professional manner with an agenda, chairperson and minutes. Preparing a professional and well-planned meeting creates expectations of professional conduct, provides structure for the discussions and improves outcomes.

As discussed briefly in Chapter 3, the first meeting should center on an overview of the family and the business: who founded the business, why certain family members joined and when. Here, the eldest family members have a chance to share special stories. So do other family members who have taken key roles in the company's development. Photographs, films and videos, scrapbooks, business mementos and product catalogs may all be part of this presentation. One outcome of this first meeting should be the entire family's improved understanding of the values and experiences that shaped this family business.

In the second meeting, the focus can be on operations. Family members should be given an overview of the company's financial history, complete with summaries of sales and profit comparisons to its peer group and an overview of the current business strategies. There should also be a reinvestment discussion, particularly when growth or acquisitions are being considered. Here, presentations by non-family managers in charge of various operations can be valuable.

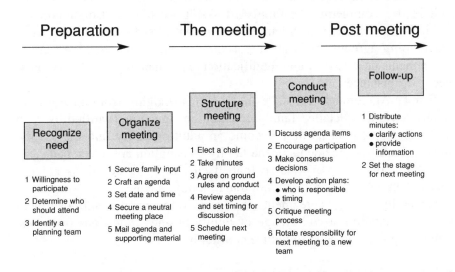

Figure 4.3   *Preparing effective family meetings*

Adapted from: Road Map for Entrepreneurial Families Program (Participant Workbook).
Copyright 1999 by the Business Families Foundation. Reprinted by permission.

Both the family and the business benefit from having non-family managers contribute to the family meeting. Non-family managers get an opportunity to meet the next generation of shareholders and begin to develop relationships that will be mutually supportive. One of the biggest concerns of non-family managers in a family business is the uncertainty of their relationship with the owners. This is an opportunity to help non-family managers develop a better understanding of the family's commitment to the business. For these first two meetings, it is important to leave a significant portion of the meeting open for questions and discussion. It is important to be sensitive to the fact that some questions may be naïve, as not all family members have strong business backgrounds.

Family Participation Agreements

Family meetings should identify issues and topics related to the family and the business that require formal processes or understandings. After the family has made a positive commitment decision, the focus of family meetings changes from 'What should we do' to 'How do we do it.'

There are several benefits to using formal Family Agreements. First, they encourage consistency based on general rules; second, they support family harmony; and third, they increase family effectiveness in achieving its Shared Future Vision. In business terms, Family Agreements create the policies for completing the family's tasks. They should also support the family's movement from reliance on personal trust to institutional trust. Developing agreements is an important first step, but effective Family Agreements need review and modification to fit changing family and business circumstances.

Family Agreements can take many forms, ranging from an informal family letter to a detailed family constitution signed and ratified by each new family member as they become an adult or marry into the family. Ideally, Family Agreements or the family constitution are developed early in the life of the enterprise so that discussions and decisions are not focused on the situation of an individual family member.

Generally, Family Agreements are designed to clarify a family's procedures for handling a wide range of family business questions or issues. Family Agreements tend to reduce conflict if:

■ They are based on family consensus.
■ They are communicated to all family members.
■ They are applied consistently.

■ The family has a mechanism for modifying the agreement based on changing conditions.

Table 3.1 (Family Business Issues for Discussion) summarizes many topics that are frequently included. The next section reviews the essential topics that should be addressed in all Family Agreements: family behavior, conflict resolution, family education, family unity and family performance.

Family Behavior

The personal behavior of individual family members in relation to the business, its employees or other important stakeholders (for example customers, suppliers) or in relation to their dealings with other family members is often a source of conflict. Personal conduct of the family members is an important issue because it can have serious legal and public relations consequences for the business. It can also be a threat to the morale of the business' employees. Family members who find them-selves constantly arguing with one another, confronting each other in the workplace, or making disrespectful remarks about one another in public are undermining the family's commitment to a shared vision for the business. This type of conflicted personal behavior can threaten family relationships and send a very negative signal to employees and other stakeholders.

Conflict Resolution

No matter how well they plan, most business families will face serious conflicts over personal relationships, business actions or future plans that the involved family members cannot resolve. Emotions will run high and differences will seem to become irreconcilable. At such points, a program for promptly addressing conflict is absolutely necessary. A family that does not address conflicts encourages a family dynamic wherein members are not open and honest with each other.

When family members feel that their disagreements over expectations or responsibilities are not being addressed, tension builds up until the emotional pressure becomes too much and it explodes. Addressing conflicts in the family or business is always a difficult task, because most people do not enjoy confronting others.

Constructively confronting each other is a skill that needs to be learned and practiced because it is not typically part of most families' behavior. Each family needs to think about their particular family values and culture as they develop programs to address conflict. Some cultures openly encourage conflict. Family members say what is on their minds with no hesitation. Others are more reticent in addressing disagreements or criticizing another family member. This is unfortunate because as family members join the business from the sibling and cousin generations, learning to constructively disagree and resolve those disagreements becomes an important factor in family business success.

It is important to remember that the starting point for any resolution must be a face-to-face dialogue between the parties, focusing clearly on the problem or decision. Family business conflicts need to be addressed like any other interpersonal problem. Simple problem-solving techniques can often be applied. First, a problem or decision statement needs to be clearly defined so that thinking and action can be focused. This step requires that participants identify the root causes for the problem, or generate alternative scenarios for the decision. This encourages the development of a shared understanding and a possible agreement. Too often, families will forget the current topic and focus instead on old experiences or hurts. This eventually results in personalizing the discussion, which reduces the probability of developing a solution or agreement.

Sometimes it is not possible for family members to resolve a conflict. In this case, the family should have other alternatives for conflict resolution, such as presenting the issue to the family council or to senior family members (that is, a council of elders) for a decision. Alternatively, the issue or disagreement should be added to the agenda for a family meeting and then the meeting should be used as a problem-solving session. If the problem is related to a business issue, asking the board of directors to review the situation and suggest a workable resolution is another possibility. It is important to remember that the goal should be to develop a resolution that is acceptable to disputing parties and compatible with the family's values and vision.

Some families actually invest time in learning conflict-resolution skills. Others depend on mediating mechanisms, such as a family council or board of directors. They often defer certain decisions to those groups. Others employ a professional to help the business family. They might choose to bring in an expert in organizational development, a trained mediator or a family business consultant to guide them through difficult decisions.

A certain amount of family meeting time should be spent in discussing the family's methods for resolving predictable future conflicts before these issues become personal. Once the family has some experience in applying its skills and techniques, the lessons and precedents need to be promoted broadly. Such shared experience will make future conflict resolution easier for all family members.

A good plan for conflict resolution includes anticipation of sensitive issues, agreed-upon conflict-resolution mechanisms and an appreciation of the importance of addressing conflict to build trusting relationships. There is a popular myth about family communication that if something is not talked about, the family relationship will be stronger because there are no fights. However, the reality is that when families have the ability to disagree about important issues and the mechanisms to resolve their conflict, they develop more trusting relationships.

REARDON FAMILY CHALLENGE

Encouraging Family Participation

As the Reardon family continues its soul-searching about its business, it needs to examine the opportunities for family participation. This will help to answer whether the business will continue as family owned in the future.

In fact, the Reardons have many opportunities for family participation. Two family members are already employed in the business and a niece has shown an interest in coming on board. Nancy and her other siblings are voicing the need for greater influence and they want to position their children for future roles in the business. Their interest may indicate an opportunity for increasing family participation. Questions that might be asked include:

- Does the family feel a connection to the business?

- Does the family feel that their ideas are welcome?

- How does the family share information and decisions about the business?

- What can the family do to involve non-employed family members in the family business?

- How does the family determine an agenda for family meetings?

Family Education

An important success factor for business families is a commitment to the education and personal development of family members. Many successful families believe that a knowledgeable and well-informed family group is an asset that contributes to the family's effectiveness and ability to work together. Some families hold regular educational activities as part of their family meetings. Other families attend business seminars that highlight such topics. Each year, family business seminars are offered at over 80 colleges and universities to help hundreds of families understand and work on family business issues such as communication, planning and succession.[19] Trade associations, lawyers, accountants, banks and the Young Presidents' Organization also offer workshops.

Some families even put together their own seminars, inviting other local families that own companies to present ideas and solutions at a panel discussion or business roundtable. One advantage of these seminars is that they provide social support and shared learning for families confronting the same challenges and they depersonalize the issues. In many families, these educational efforts are begun before the family member is involved in decision-making or planning. In other cases, they become natural extensions of family and business planning. Chapter 6 discusses several topics that are appropriate for owner education seminars.

Family Unity

Perpetuating a successful business family is not all work. It allows for fun, too. Enjoying social or recreational activities together builds rapport, friendship and ease of communication among family members. All families should spend some social time together. It is best to leave business concerns totally out of these occasions. It helps to create effective boundaries between the family and business, which is very important for strengthening family relationships. Family members, particularly those who are not employed by the family business, can feel that they are on equal ground with and a full member of the family, if business is not continually included as a topic.

Many families formalize 'fun times' through regular vacations or by purchasing a farm, summer cottage or resort condominium for family use. Some families include a formal statement in their family agreements that family holidays, vacations and religious celebrations will be exclusively centered on family experiences and will not include discussions of the business or its issues.

Family Performance

Implementing the Family Enterprise Continuity Plan and developing the supporting programs may take several years, depending on the size and complexity of the family and the business. As part of the implementation process, the family may identify specific activities as priorities for their efforts during the current year. Identifying their priorities is the family's final task in the planning process. These priorities are established after the final review of the Family's Enterprise Continuity Plan and they include the assignment of responsibilities for action and the procurement of necessary resources.

For example, a family might choose to establish a formal family meeting schedule or form a committee to develop a proposed code of conduct or develop an educational program. The possibilities are endless, depending on each family's situation. Each year, the family will probably single out several main activities to pursue. The entire family should agree upon these activities. Progress in completing them should be carefully monitored and then reviewed at subsequent family meetings.

SUMMARY

Most successful business families consciously work to overcome the problems inherent in perpetuating the family's participation in the business. Experience suggests that however casual these families may appear, their family programs and action plans deliberately promote such seeming intangibles as commitment, vision and family participation. These intangibles provide specific solutions to challenges and determine how the family interacts with the business. They shape the roles family members play in the company's future.

No particular family formula is best. Many patterns are apparent in various successful family firms. However, four principles do appear regularly across the board:

- A shared commitment to the future of the family and business.
- Meeting together to address conflicts and maintain communication.
- Family agreements to support Fair Process in family dealings.
- Conscientious and ongoing planning.

Family meetings are the appropriate vehicles to establish and practice these principles. At family meetings, a wide range of techniques and activities can be developed to encourage these principles. They range from formal meeting agendas that lead to the drafting of the Statement of Family Commitment and other Family Agreements to enjoyable family educational seminars.

The next chapter addresses the issues of developing family members for management and leadership roles. This topic provides an important linkage between the Family Enterprise Continuity Plan and the Business Strategy Plan. This linkage exists because the development of the family's talent is central to both plans.

5 Preparing the Next Generation of Family Managers and Leaders

It is not an easy task to raise children who are truly interested in the family business. It is an even tougher job to prepare them for management and leadership roles that contribute to the growth of the business. The focus of these discussions will be directed at management development for several reasons. First, an overriding family concern is meaningful careers for the next generation. Second, family members can be an important source of talent for the business.

Effective family leaders and capable managers are critical to successful family business planning. The Parallel Planning Process identifies the complementary nature of family members and business leaders and their shared role in formulating business strategy.

Family and management teams have to devise training and development activities to support the family members who may want next-generation leadership of the family or business. Thinking about this idea early in their lives will support meaningful careers for the next generation and capable leaders to support the family legacy.

This chapter will suggest several plans to do this. Chapter 4 presented the process for encouraging the family participation required for family business continuity. Here, the next step is how to plan activities that will strengthen the talents and leadership skills of the next generation. Successful families know that developing programs and agreements about careers before the next generation joins the business creates stronger companies, smoother management transitions and healthier family relationships. This chapter begins with a review of the influence of the family life cycle on family business careers.

THE INFLUENCE OF LIFE CYCLE ON FAMILY BUSINESS CAREERS

It is important to understand the implications of the family life cycle on family careers for two reasons. First, it is a force that shapes all aspects of family business careers. The birth of a child creates a potential employee, senior adulthood signals retirement and death, which is a guaranteed triggering event for management succession. Second, families often have great difficulty negotiating transitions created by the family's life events. For example, fathers and sons who fail to resolve their differences from the son's rebellious teen years often find that they carry these unresolved conflicts into the family business.

One challenge all business families face is planning for management succession when the family members are experiencing reciprocal life cycle transitions.[1] The senior generation is facing the uncertainties of retirement, their children are entering middle life and the grandchildren are entering young adulthood. The three generations are all struggling with a big question: 'Who am I and what does the family business mean in my

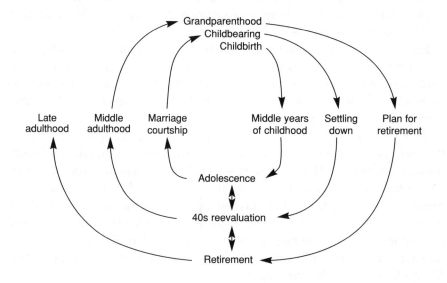

Figure 5.1   *The family life cycle spiral*

Source: L. Combrinck-Graham, 'The Development Model of Family
Systems', (June, 1985), *Family Process*, **24**: 139–50. Copyright 1985 by
Family Process. Reprinted by permission.

life?' Figure 5.1 demonstrates the conflicts that occur when different family members experience life transitions at the same time.

To add to the potential for conflict, family members are executives, shareholders and board members in their businesses for a very long time. The average tenure of the president in a closely held company is likely to be two to three times longer than that of his or her counterpart in a publicly traded company. Consequently, the family business will be deeply influenced by the senior manager's personal development over the years. As senior managers mature, their personal management skills, leadership styles and their own personal motivations will influence their companies.

A management transition for the senior and successor generations has significant implications for the family firm. Figure 5.2 presents the overlapping life cycles of two generations in a family business. The senior generation must move through several phases: planning the strategy, growing the business, mentoring the successor, letting go of control and supporting the transition. Each of these phases creates the potential for conflict and blocked careers if either generation stops or delays the process.

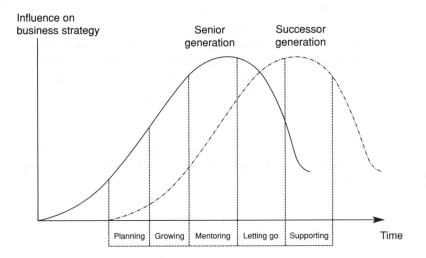

Figure 5.2   *Individual life cycle influences on family business transitions*

Adapted from: N.C. Churchill and K.J. Hatten, 'Non-market-based transfers of
wealth and power: a research framework of family business',
Family Business Review, **10**(1): 53–67. Copyright 1997 by the
Family Firm Institute. Reprinted by permission.

UNDERSTANDING THE BUSINESS' FUTURE MANAGEMENT NEEDS

The next generation of management will lead an organization that is very different from that of any previous generation. The maturation of the family firm, dynamic market conditions, and growth of the family creates a new set of demands on managers. Management skills and styles that were successful in the past may prove ineffective today because of global markets, new employee values, changes in technology or intensified competition. Too often, family businesses just replicate the skills and practices of the past without concern for these external changes.

Incoming CEOs in family firms must also deal with the influence of the family on their role. Marilyn Carlson Nelson, successor to her father as CEO at Carlson Companies (Regent and Radisson Hotels, TGI Fridays, Seven Seas Cruises and Carlson Wagonlit Travel Agencies), felt the responsibility of having to satisfy her family investors in a way her father never did. She said:

> I have to be steward of the Carlson Companies to continue to earn the support of the rest of the family and our employees who are the key stakeholders. Because I am not the founder, I must work with the family group to insure [that] they receive economic and psychological value from the company that is equal or better than what they will get in alternative investments. So we must be prepared for challenging years. I doubt if the family will tolerate maybe more than a couple of years of less-than-market performance. Hopefully, they will tolerate that if they have to.[2]

When planning the succession process, it is important to understand objectively the responsibilities of senior managers and family leaders and how those responsibilities will change in the future.

Required Management Skills

One planning idea that can be valuable to family firms is to identify what management tasks the business will need to emphasize in the future. Henry Mintzberg, a leading management thinker, has developed one of the most widely used descriptions of the manager's job.[3] Adapting this model for family businesses provides a template for thinking about the management processes that will be required of the next generation of family managers.

Table 5.1   *Family business management and leadership activities*

Interpersonal roles	Family business context
Figurehead	■ Ceremonial 'head' of the business and family
Leader	■ Organizing and staffing management ■ Motivating family and non-family employees ■ Working with board and family council
Liaison	■ Building family commitment to the business ■ Working within organization ■ Linking different family groups ■ Building relationships with outside stakeholders
Informational roles	
Monitor	■ Scanning external environment ■ Maintaining personal contacts with family members ■ Monitoring employees
Disseminator	■ Disseminating business information ■ Clarifying family information ■ Reinforcing family values and vision
Spokesperson	■ Representing business with family and family with business
Decisional roles	
Entrepreneur	■ Strategic thinking and formulation ■ Business regeneration during generational transitions
Disturbance handler	■ Dealing with conflicts or business problems ■ Reformulating business plans
Resource allocator	■ Allocating resources especially compensation, dividends, and investments
Negotiator	■ Negotiating family consensus ■ Bridging family and business conflicts

This is more helpful than identifying functional skills like marketing or accounting that will not be critical to senior management roles.

Mintzberg describes three primary roles that top management serves: interpersonal, informational and decision-making. Table 5.1 uses Mintzberg's framework for large corporations, adapted to the family business context, to demonstrate the possible management tasks facing the next generation of family CEOs. It is important to note that in many family firms a team of successors may share the senior management function, in these cases the team would need to develop the required skills.

Considering required future management competencies and the next generation's capabilities is important for the successor generation, and the Business Strategy Plan. It will help the next generation to create a realistic personal development plan that is not simply a replication of existing management practices and experience. It supports management's thinking about the types of organizational skills needed and the possibility of family members filling senior management roles.

This analysis is also useful in a larger family business with many potential successors because it can help to identify a successor team with the complementary skills that are required for leadership positions throughout the firm. Over time, the family will be able to make career decisions based on skills, creating successor competencies that will cut destructive competition and add value to the business in the future.

REARDON FAMILY CHALLENGE

Preparing the Next Generation of Family Members

Career opportunities for the next generation of the family are an important issue for the Reardon family. Only two members of the second generation joined the Reardon family business, but in the third, the growth of the business has created more opportunities. The Reardons have to plan for that. They have a niece with a graduate degree in electrical engineering who has an interest in coming on board and now they need to consider the implications of more family members working in the family business. Some questions to ask include:

- If the business proceeds with new family employees, what structures or systems will be required?

- What agreements does the family want to make regarding family business careers?

- How does the family set standards for business experience, education and the procedure for offering a family member a job?

- How does the family identify and harness the best leadership energy within the family?

Family Leadership Roles

As business families mature and their numbers increase, they often need to fashion more formal methods for selecting family leaders and fulfilling family roles. These methods will vary widely among individual families. In many families, the CEO of the business also serves as the family's chief arbiter. This arrangement is often effective, especially in first-generation entrepreneurial firms. Historically, the father has assumed the role of family decision-maker. Therefore, the mother has often assumed the implicit and invaluable role of the family's Chief Emotional Officer. She works, usually quietly, at the critical tasks of family leadership. She interprets the behavior of one family member to another, keeps communications open, makes sure that feelings are considered and plans special family functions.

Finding a successor for the family leader is equally as important to the long-term health of the family business as is finding a successor for the chief executive. As a result, some families deliberately groom a leader who will cultivate family unity and see that everyone feels appreciated in his or her individual roles. In some cases, this is the oldest son or daughter not employed by the business or another family member with special skills in human behavior. In others, it might be the spouse of the successor. Occasionally, a younger sibling of either gender takes the role. With more women leading family businesses as chief executives, the pool of applicants for the role of the family's emotional leader should expand and is likely to include males more often than in the past. In large families, members of the family council often take on aspects of the family leadership role.

FAMILY EXPERIENCES

Supporting Family Careers

Yocum Oil is a family-owned oil distribution and real estate company based in Minneapolis, Minnesota (USA). Tony Yocum IV, the current CEO, is working with his family to support transferring both management and ownership to the next generation.

He knows the challenges this requires: 'I was fortunate to have the opportunity to work with my father and mother in the family business and also having the learning experience of transferring the business and working to manage and grow the business with my parents.' Tony and his wife Ruth told their children that the goal was not necessarily to have them all join the family business. 'They needed to have the education, freedom of choice and the ability to learn.'

The Yocum sons took different paths to a family business career. Tony V, the oldest son, always saw the family business as an opportunity because he wanted to be a part of 'the big picture' early in his career. After college, he took an opportunity to join a real estate firm and gain experience outside of Yocum Oil. 'It was insightful,' he said. 'To experience the political and mechanical infrastructure of a different firm, yet my entrepreneurial drive demanded more information and control.' A year later, he came back to the family business where he felt he was 'gaining knowledge and experience at a far more rapid pace.'

After graduating from college, his brother Jon worked part-time at the family firm while trying careers from art to computers. 'I never thought that I would be interested in joining the business,' he states. After working as a computer consultant in another firm, his thinking began to change. 'If I was going to work this hard, I thought, maybe it should be in a firm where I already had an investment.' As much as he enjoyed the computer industry, the family business continued to 'pull on him.' After joining the family firm full-time, he can now explain his motivation as driven by a 'sense of ownership, of being a part of something that was started by my grandparents and continued by my parents. Once I knew that I deserved a chance to be part of that, it felt great to go back.'

Another son, Tim, joined the family firm to apply the real estate skills he learned outside the family firm. He talks about the benefit of joining a well-managed firm. 'By having the right infrastructure in place, I have been able to learn the operations aspect at an accelerated rate yet be responsible for site acquisition and construction. My father has trusted me with a large dose of responsibility, he has provided the right amount of guidance and stepped back when I needed to learn on my own.'

Father and sons now work side by side, sharing business responsibilities. The father, looking ahead to the future, is developing a new role for himself that he describes as, 'Father, trainer, partner and mentor.' He also works to encourage family communication with weekly meetings that address individual agendas, frustrations, problems and future plans. The sons are earning the opportunity to run the business while their dad works to insure their continued interest based on praise, rewards, personal development and honest feedback. Creating an inviting environment and making the family business an option, not an expectation, has had much to do with achieving active participation from the next generation.

Note: Information from *Entrepreneurial Notes* (The John M. Morrison Center for Entrepreneurship, University of St. Thomas, Minneapolis: Minnesota, May, 1999).

It is also important to recognize that there are specific leadership roles within the family system. Sometimes these roles go unnoticed, but as the family matures and grows into the siblings or cousins phase, it is important that these roles are discussed as a part of the family planning process. Examples of family leadership roles that many families find important include the following:

- *Communicator:* disseminating information to the family.
- *Harmonizer:* tending to the emotions of the family.
- *Socializer:* planning fun as part of the family's activities.
- *Facilitator:* addressing conflict and helping reach consensus decisions.

- *Steward:* ensuring the family remains sensitive to ethical issues and its core values.
- *Convener:* organizing meetings and family events.

If these roles are filled, it not only helps the family members in the business, but family members who are outside the business. It keeps the entire family on a level playing field for access to information about the family and the business, which cuts down on tension and alienation. And keeping family members who are not working in the business involved encourages them to make a contribution to the business in the future.

FAMILY BUSINESS AS CAREER

Family business careers provide a special set of opportunities, rewards and challenges. Most people never see their family members at work or directly share their career accomplishments. Working side by side with a parent, sibling or cousin, sharing success and overcoming challenges builds a special emotional bond. There is also a special psychological reward in being a part of something that is important to the family. Creating careers that provide opportunities to experience personal satisfaction requires careful planning that begins at home with the family. The next section explores planning as a tool for supporting meaningful family business career experiences.

It Starts Young

Children learn by example, from the basic lessons of honesty, responsibility, work ethic and integrity that their parents teach. There is no reason for the parents' philosophy to change as they begin to prepare their children for entry into the family business. The ethics of childhood should comfortably extend into the ethics of owning and managing a business. The only change here is how the senior generation wants to structure an effective training program to bring the best out of the younger generation so that they can put their own mark of success on the family legacy.

Well-managed businesses and healthy families do share many positive, constructive traits:

- They make decisions by consensus.
- They function more smoothly by using teamwork built on trust.

■ They address change by working together to identify new goals and re-deploying their energies and resources.

These shared characteristics should not be surprising since families and businesses are both social systems. Both are based on commitment to shared goals, whether it is marketing products or raising good children. Both work especially well when their members are autonomous but also offer one another mutual support. Leaders who convey a vision and empower the entire system head the most successful families and businesses.

Business and family principles are so similar. Parents can work to teach their children the very qualities that will help them in their careers and simultaneously make the family run more smoothly. Good financial management, for example, allows children to learn how small sacrifices can lead to great rewards later.[4] Parents can teach these values by actively involving children in discussions about how to finance things that the entire family really wants, from special vacations to college educations. At a certain point, these 'tabletop discussions' become a child's first lesson in group consensus and change management skills that will give him or her the greatest insight when it is time to manage the family business.

Thomas Hirschfeld, a venture capitalist and author, suggests that children need to develop their economic literacy at three levels: being intelligent consumers, managing personal finance and understanding business and economics.[5]

He suggests that parents can plan life experiences for their children that will help them to learn important financial concepts such as comparison shopping, scarce resources, budgeting, investment and even making a profit at the lemonade stand. Appreciating the value of money, but also understanding that wealth does not create happiness, are important lessons that children need to learn from their early family experiences.

Approaching routine childhood activities as an opportunity to develop capable children will serve a dual purpose if they wish to join the family business someday. Teaching and modeling positive characteristics will enhance the natural fit between the family and the business.

Exposing Family Members to the Business

Generally, perpetuating the business is a goal most everyone in the family shares. The majority of parents who own a business want to pass it on to their offspring for reasons highlighted in Chapter 1. Similarly, a study by

Teresa Covin, a management professor, indicated that the majority of college business students would prefer to work for a family business if their family owns it.[6] The fact that many traditional professions such as medicine and law do not offer the opportunities they once did makes the family business look even more attractive to these students. In addition, a certain prestige has come to surround entrepreneurship and self-employment.[7]

This is no guarantee, however, that the next generation will actually enter a career in the family business. There are many obstacles to overcome, including the ambivalent feelings of the parents. Parents have their own internal battle about their children joining the family business. They want to pass along their creation to their children, but they also do not want to trap them. They worry about conflicts among their children or with themselves and they are rightfully concerned that hiring their children will drive away valuable non-family managers.

Some parents may also suffer from generation envy, an unconscious fear that their child threatens their position in the company, possibly as a competitor to surpass their business achievements.[8]

The next generation faces its own demons about going into the family business. They compare themselves to their parents or other family members and find it difficult to believe that they could meet their family's expectations. They may also have had difficult relationships with parents or siblings. They are anxious that the problems they had with their parents or brother and sister as they were growing up may be translated into problems in the family business. There is also a strong fear of failure, compounded by the fact that a failure in the family business is shared with the entire family. Such ambivalence creates an atmosphere in which misunderstandings magnify fears and may ruin an offspring's chances for succession. If parents fail to communicate clearly their desire to have their children in the business, for example, it is easy for those children to back away from the business into another career because they assume they are unwanted.

Family Employment Agreements

These problems may be compounded by vague 'rules' for entering the family business. Such rules, often unspoken and unshared with potential successors, emerge when an overt action demands a response. Similar misunderstandings occur when a child tries to return to the business after leaving it, or if he or she tries to join the business without first finishing his or her education. Daughters in the family business often face challenges around the mixed messages about opportunities available to them in the family firm.[9] They are encouraged to participate, but often in secondary roles to their brothers. Many offspring see these obstacles and walk away.

PLANNING TOOLS

Supporting Family Business Careers

Parents who wish to bring children successfully into the family business should consider the following steps:

1. Make it clear to children that they are welcome to join the company. This must be a low-key effort, without imposing any obligation. Key ideas to convey are the following: the child is welcome; his or her participation in the business is voluntary; the decision will be supported no matter what the choice; and joining the business carries no guarantees or promises.

2. Granting offspring the freedom to take the business or leave it – to make up their own minds, without obligation – is important. Children must differentiate from their parents to develop as separate and distinct individuals.[10] Without that freedom, offspring who do enter the business are likely to feel their creativity and growth stifled.[11] They will rarely demonstrate the drive and enthusiasm necessary for success in business.

3. Present the business as a special, exciting place. Parents who wish their children to join their business need to express why they like the work and the industry. At home, they should discuss the joys, accomplishments and fulfillment of work. At first they may include their young children on work visits to 'play' at the office. As the children enter their teenage years they may do projects, work on a part-time basis, or, in summer, have internship experiences. It is important that these experiences provide the children with a balanced picture and an opportunity to see the career potentials the family business offers.

4. Clarify Family Agreements about career opportunities early, before any of the next generation is ready to enter the family firm. The rules themselves are not as important as having a shared understanding of those rules among all family members, and applying them fairly.

Family Employment Agreements lie at the heart of successful family business relationships. They are as important as written contracts and their terms should be handled in a similar way. If the rules change, everyone needs to be told what the new rules are, as well as why the old ones were changed. They should also understand what the new rules mean to them and to their individual circumstances. Surprise or betrayal in this regard may undermine trust in the entire family enterprise.

Family agreements about employment should cover at the minimum the following list of topics:

- When and under what circumstances are children welcome to enter the business? This includes how much education and previous work experience will be required of them and whether they must fill a vacant post or one created for them.

- At what age is it no longer possible to join the firm? At age 30? 40? Should there be a limit at all?

- Can a family member reenter the family business after a voluntary or involuntary departure? Scenarios in this case would include leaving for child rearing, graduate school, or a serious disagreement with other family members. It is important to spell out these conditions.

- Is part-time work permitted?

- Are in-laws welcome to join the company and, if so, in what capacities?

LAUNCHING A FAMILY BUSINESS CAREER

Once the invitation to join the company has been issued and accepted, two questions need attention:

1. How should the family member's entry into the business be structured?

2. What is the best career path to develop the family member's talent and capabilities for general management and ownership? Work experiences, training and personal goals should prepare these individuals to meet these needs.

The first phase of entering the company should be a probationary or testing phase. This time is designed to allow the new employee to develop a realistic picture of the family business and to assess working relationships. The following three suggestions might form a basis for the basic rules of entry into a family firm:

1. The family employee should bring meaningful work experience from outside the family business.
2. The family member should enter the business with a specific entry-level job that the organization clearly needs.

3. He or she should be assigned a mentor – someone other than a parent – for early teaching and coaching on the job.

The Importance of Outside Experience

Work experience outside the family business has advantages for both the business and the individual. Family members should consider working in another company immediately after completing their education. Such experience builds on their formal education by providing them with an opportunity to test their skills, seek a promotion or raise and work with bosses who are not subject to family influences. They should stay long enough to receive one or more promotions, work for two or more bosses and reach a point of sufficient responsibility to implement their own ideas on a particular project. This development may take anywhere from two to five years.

What the job actually entails is not critical. A professional position in sales, production, operations, market research or human resources will deliver useful skills to the family company. Also, it is not important whether the job is in the same industry as the family business or not. There are benefits on either side. Experience in a company in the same industry, for example, makes the lessons and ideas learned more readily applicable, but experience outside the industry broadens perspectives and provides new ways of thinking about business opportunities and problems.

There are also these benefits for the potential successor who decides to work for someone else:

■ Learning their true market value as measured in salary and benefits.
■ Establishing a professional identity apart from the family business.
■ Getting the chance to make their 'youthful' mistakes away from the watchful eyes of their future colleagues.
■ Developing expertise and self-assurance in the marketplace.
■ Being evaluated, promoted or demoted exclusively on their own merits.
■ Most importantly, learning that the grass is not necessarily greener outside the family firm, or vice versa.

Holding off on joining the family business to get a degree is not a bad idea either. Steven Goldberg, in his research on family succession, found that a college education offers many of the same developmental opportunities as working outside the family business.[12] Typically, potential successors learn various management systems and practices that may be of value to the family company. They expand their personal network, meeting people who may later be important contacts or even candidates for employment in the family business. These experiences broaden their view of the world and better enable them to identify new business opportunities.

All in all, gaining experience outside the business is one of the strongest recommendations that can be made for successors. Few who have worked outside the family business regret doing so; many who did not wish that they had.[13]

Starting with the Right Job

Once the offspring have returned to the business, they will need appropriate training positions. Line positions in sales, field service or operations positions that ultimately lead to supervisory management work well in this regard. Staff positions or 'assistant to the president' posts work less well because they frequently do not offer clear responsibility and accountability. Whatever the job, it should be one that the organization needs, not one that is created to provide a family member with a job.

Later, family employees should earn some organizational autonomy of their own by opening up a new territory, starting a new store or running a plant. Such projects help to develop managerial talent and depth. They also serve to keep siblings apart and therefore dampen potential rivalry. Projects on which offspring work together as a team are still necessary, however, as that is the only setting that will reveal and develop their future family leadership skills – an important prelude to selecting a successor.

Developing Multiple Mentoring Relationships

Mentoring has long been recommended for executives aspiring to senior positions in large public corporations. Research on effective family business successors found that 'virtually all of the effective successors benefited from multiple mentoring relationships'.[14]

A well-chosen mentor outside the family with broad business experience can support young adults as they learn about running a business. Ideally, the mentor would also be the business owner's complement – a key manager who is deeply trusted and is responsible for core business activities outside the president's direct purview. Since the mentor is a trusted, senior manager, his or her job security is solid. That is a necessary condition if he or she is to be an honest and effective teacher and coach.

Through these mentoring relationships, family employees will learn how to manage people and time, as well as gain valuable business principles. Such teaching usually occurs over a period of a few years. After that, however, the mentor relationship tends to lose its effectiveness, because the protégé has developed new concerns or more senior responsibilities. When this occurs, it is important for the successor to develop his or her own network of personal advisors. These trusted advisors can be family members, other executives, board members or professionals serving the firm.

Planning Personal Development

A well-conceived career and personal development program provides the necessary experience and tests to help everyone to develop a realistic understanding of individual family members' management potential. Creating a personal development program helps a successor to take additional responsibility for his or her own growth. It also provides opportunities for a successor to develop an appreciation of his or her personal interests and career potential. Such a plan encourages achievement and prepares the successor for leadership, thus smoothing the shift of power from one generation to the next.[15] It can also provide personal motivation by helping the successor to focus on long-term goals when faced with short-term challenges.

An effective career plan for successors must:

- Develop the knowledge and skills they will need to lead the company.
- Allow them to develop their own leadership style by progressively gaining managerial responsibility.
- Expand their strategic vision of the firm instead of duplicating a view of the past.

Ideally, it will also provide for outside evaluation or clear accountability. The plan must take the successor through various responsibilities he or she must know to lead the firm in the future. For example, a successor should lead a profit center, build an organization and set goals, preferably with outside review. The successor should also receive some sort of continuing professional education or actively participate in support groups that will build their skills and perspective. Successors can undertake many of these initiatives on their own, but for the heavier operational responsibilities, they will need the support of the senior generation.

PLANNING A MEANINGFUL CAREER

The time line of career development illustrated in Table 5.2 summarizes a successor's possible career path. The table shows that after family socialization in business values, successors typically spend the next ten years attending college and gaining outside work experience as they develop their personal capabilities and self-confidence. They will perhaps join the family business full time in their mid-to-late twenties and, during the next five years or so, they will gain functional expertise and experience in making decisions. This stage blends with that of the heir apparent. Now they are ready to take responsibility for one or more profit centers in order to acquire general management skills. Beyond this, they must begin to explore outside resources that will allow them to continue their professional development.

Of course, this is a goal, not reality. A successor's development will not always follow such a smooth course. For some successors, the sudden death, disability, or retirement of the parent rushes their development. Because they have not yet acquired the proper skills, these young heirs are forced to act more like entrepreneurs than like professional managers. They learn to do what is necessary through instinct and the sheer need to survive.

Table 5.2 also shows the final two stages of a family business career, which includes being appointed CEO and ends with the position of chairperson. The most important long-term consideration for successors planning a family executive career is the focus on continuous learning and personal development. As successors fulfill the role of CEO and, later, of chairpersons, they will encounter new challenges in addition to the functional and general management skills they mastered earlier in their career.

Giving Successors the Feedback They Need

Ultimately each individual must be responsible for their career and personal development. Successors are often challenged by their inability to get meaningful feedback on their preparation and job performance in the family business. It is always tough for successors to get objective feedback from family members and non-family employees who are reluctant to be candid. One helpful exercise is the Successor's Career Assessment (see Appendix D). It provides an excellent template for assessing individual management potential and personal development needs. The assessment's design and the successor's control of the process eliminate some of the

Table 5.2 *Successor's career development time line*

Successor's role	Child at home: growing up	Young adult: learning outside the family business	Professional manager: mentored within the business	Successor: designated as heir apparent. Mentored by senior executive or board members	Leader: CEO or member of the senior management team	Chairperson: leads the board and supports the CEO
Age	**0–18**	**18–28**	**25–35**	**30–40**	**35–65**	**55–70**
Developmental goals	Positive attitude toward the business, basic education, skill development and positive work habits	Higher education: develop self-confidence and organizational skills and begin career exploration	Functional expertise and planning, coaching, decision-making and problem-solving skills	General management and profit center responsibility	Executive development: personal growth, self-awareness, and continuing education	Life planning: exploring other interests and opportunities

Note: The age ranges overlap because timing can vary based on specific situation. The ages suggested are intended to support the development of the model. They are not intended as recommendations.

Adapted from: Keeping the Family Business Healthy, J.L. Ward (1987). Copyright 1997 by the Business Owner Resources. Reprinted by permission.

fears associated with assessments or other evaluations that are used for career or promotion decisions.

The process begins with the successor completing a self-assessment using the assessment forms. After completing this phase, the successor asks three or four other trusted colleagues or supervisors to use the assessment form to report their observations on the successor's performance and managerial capabilities.

After receiving the feedback the successor can then review the responses and make comparisons; exploring significant differences between her or his self-assessment and other managers' responses. Reviewing the feedback forms with a mentor is a useful activity to fully understand the responses and identify personal development actions.

The successor can explore the following questions as preparation for discussing the data with others:

- How does my self-assessment compare with the assessments from others in the family business?
- Do I feel that they have an accurate perception of my management strengths and weaknesses?
- How can I influence and monitor their feedback in the future?
- Do I have a realistic understanding of the future management skills needed by my family business?
- What development actions do I feel would improve my performance and potential for additional responsibilities?

Many of the assessment questions are objective and help to identify skills that can be developed or relationships that can be built. On the other hand, some of the assessment questions are more subjective, relating to the successor's personal commitment to the business, concern for ethics and understanding of the 'big picture'. Even though some questions are subjective, they represent an important source of information for the successor. If, for example, the feedback from other managers identifies a lack of commitment to the business, it is important that the successor explores why that perception is held and what he or she can do to demonstrate improvement. The real value of this tool is to build self-awareness based on candid and objective feedback. It should not be used for promotion decisions or as a screening device for senior management.

Each individual successor should control their self-assessment process and the results of his or her feedback process should support the creation of his or her personal development plan.

Many successful family firms expand on this feedback process by employing 360-degree Evaluation for their executives as a basis for their annual performance review. The 360-degree Evaluation provides assessment from the employee's boss, sometimes senior management and also from co-workers and subordinates. This creates a broader picture of the employee's performance and creates a formal process to capture information to support additional training and personal development activities.

IDENTIFYING THE NEXT GENERATION OF MANAGERS AND LEADERS

Beyond the specific job performance criteria, there are other behaviors or characteristics that determine an individual's potential for senior management or leadership roles. These behaviors are related to management style and practices, which may be overlooked in discussions of the successor's performance because they are not quantifiable or always directly linked to a job task. There are Seven Characteristics (7-Cs) that strongly influence the decision over who eventually takes leadership roles. Figure 5.3 identifies these 7-Cs. They are conscience, credibility, coaching, capability, commitment, competence and communication.

Conscience is presented as the central behavior because this model assumes that most families would prefer a leader who they could trust and who demonstrates personal integrity and ethical behavior. The other six behaviors represent different measures of personal effectiveness. Three of these, commitment, competence and credibility, are expressed in relation to specific organization outcomes.

The remaining three, coaching, capability and communication, are personal behaviors that can be demonstrated in a variety of work and non-work settings. Family members, both successors and senior generation, can make these behaviors part of their discussions for personal development programs, mentoring and decisions about the next generation of leaders. Table 5.3 presents definitions of the activities that comprise the components of the 7-Cs.

It is unlikely that any successor candidate will possess all of these behaviors or characteristics. So it is the family and management's responsibility to prioritize their selection criteria based on the family's core values and the business situation. A family that places trusting relationships as its highest priority may choose a more trusted successor over a slightly more competent family member who lacks the family's complete trust. Identifying the family's selection criteria and making it part of the

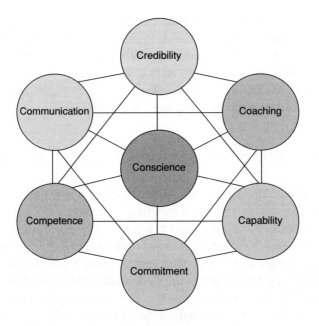

Figure 5.3   *7-Cs: behaviors contributing to successor performance*

family agreement helps the management team and successors to accept
and support the outcome of the selection process.

Larger families that clearly differentiate between family and business
roles may select two or more family members for leadership positions. For
example, a family member with demonstrated business skills (competence) and a proven performance record (credibility) would serve as CEO
of the business. Another family member with a reputation for ethical

Table 5.3   *Definitions of the behaviors contributing to successor performance*

Conscience:	Demonstrated ethical behavior in dealings with the family and the business
Credibility:	Respect of the family and business based on accomplishments, work performance and personal style
Coaching:	The ability to teach and develop other people's skills and talents
Capability:	The intellectual and emotional talents for future growth as a manager and leader
Commitment:	A personal decision to support the family's and the business' interests
Competence:	The technical ability or skills required to manage the business
Communication:	The ability to have meaningful relationships based on sharing information

behavior would serve as chairperson of the board. A third family member recognized for networking and building relationships would serve as chair of the family council. Some families will chose to rotate governance and family leadership roles based on terms. This model of shared leadership would optimize the family's talents, allow leaders to focus their efforts and expertise and create more opportunities for participation.

PLANNING FOR NEXT-GENERATION RELATIONSHIPS

One of the most important responsibilities of senior family and management in the succession process is creating structures that support positive relationships with and among the next generation. Families must be realistic about successor relationships and recognize that these relationships are shaped by a combination of genetic and environmental forces, including birth order, gender, family of origin, personality and individual and family experiences.[16] It is unrealistic for the family to expect that siblings or cousins who have had a conflicted relationship will suddenly work together for the good of the family and business. In fact, it is more likely that serious conflicts will erupt at the death of the parents, as the siblings attempt to create a new family structure without their parents. At this time, it is likely that old unhealed wounds and hurts resulting from competition, rivalry and parental favoritism will trigger serious sibling conflicts.[17]

Competitive tension is often healthy for a business. Siblings who are striving for the presidency, for example, will work hard to turn in excellent, individual job performances. Yet, if this effort becomes a rough-and-tumble battle – complete with efforts to derail other siblings or cousins – it will have a negative effect upon the company. Unfortunately, siblings' husbands and wives often unintentionally reinforce this sort of unhealthy competition.[18]

In successful family businesses, siblings, cousins and the senior generation work to make the effect of rivalry positive rather than negative. Their family agreements and business policies support this goal. They use such techniques as: rationalized salaries and promotions; assigning positions based on company requirements and individual career needs; and developing a code of conduct that will govern the next generation's behavior among them.

Rationalize Salaries and Promotions

Several approaches are available to the business based on Family Business Philosophy and on the business itself. One approach is that traditional business principles will apply. That is, salaries are based on market and performance criteria and one person will eventually be allowed to assume the presidency. This approach puts the business first. While competitive salary schedules encourage performance, they may also produce family conflicts.

A second approach puts the family first. Here, the opposite risk comes to the fore – that business performance is sacrificed for the sake of family harmony. All family members' incomes are equal. All difficult decisions are made by consensus. The 'president' may actually be a team of family members; their job is to see that consensus is reached rather than to make final decisions.

In any case, management should consider the benefits of openly publicizing compensation and perquisite levels among all family members. This minimizes the opportunity for spouses and in-laws to draw incorrect conclusions from lifestyles. It also says clearly that family members depend on one another for their mutual success, financial and otherwise.

Assign Positions Based on Business Needs

Until the moment that one is named president, family members should not be required to report to one another, if at all possible. Each should also have his or her own area or project within the company, from a special project to managing a full division. If they perform well and are rewarded for their efforts, they will feel that they are making valuable contributions to the business. This softens the sting of watching one sibling gain a higher title. Eventually, such separate career paths may pave the way for corporate spin-offs or new ventures led by individual sons and daughters.

Strengthen the Employment Provisions in the Family's Code of Conduct

This code is an agreement among family members to act in a manner conducive and supportive of healthy relationships and a healthy business. Often the code will need to be strengthened or expanded to create rules on how to work together and avoid serious rifts. Examples are: 'We will support each other with employees... We will not judge each other... We will assume that each has discretionary time to do with as he or she wants... We will respect each other... We will not take any assets out of the business except as salary and formal benefits.'

Work or employment issues that the family might want to consider for the code of conduct include the following topics:

- Keeping in-laws and spouses up to date on the business performance and plans.
- Publicly recognizing the various accomplishments of each family employee.
- Spending 'social' time with other family members employed in the business and ensuring open lines of communication with them.
- Maintaining family and work boundaries (not discussing work topics at social or family events).
- Publicly supporting each other, especially with employees, customers and suppliers.
- Behaving in an ethical and responsible manner related to company activities.
- Sharing publicity and recognition with each other.

SUMMARY

The family can provide a positive teaching ground for the next generation of family leaders and senior family mangers. Because businesses and families undertake similar activities from setting goals to sharing decisions, a synergy develops between the two systems and makes it possible to identify family activities that can serve as lessons for future business and family leadership.

There are two critical challenges for family businesses that want to prepare the next generation for leadership responsibilities. The first challenge is to create effective plans for the development of the next generation's capabilities; the second is to develop family agreements to ensure that the family will successfully address the issues of working together.

Table 5.4 summarizes the key ideas from this chapter, demonstrating the mutual contributions of developing career plans, Family Agreements and a code of conduct to successful family business careers.

The next chapter examines issues related to family business ownership. Developing plans to support capable and responsible owners is the third component of the Family Enterprise Continuity Plan.

Table 5.4   *Plans and actions supporting successful family business careers*

Family Activities

- Develop explicit family agreements for family participation in the business through family meetings, family values statement and expressed in the Family Enterprise Continuity Plan.
- Appreciate and adapt to the life cycle forces and life events that create change in the family and business.
- Encourage activities that teach family values, personal and business financial concepts, leadership, and business skills.
- Develop family programs for planning and decision-making that ensure Fair Process.
- Present a balanced picture of the family business' advantages and challenges.
- Protect family boundaries to ensure that family and social time are not invaded by the business.

Welcoming Family Members into the Business

- Communicate the invitation to work for the family business.
- Present the business as a possible career option.
- Make employment conditions clear and base them on the Family Business Philosophy.

Entering the Business

- Focus on providing an exposure to the business and its industry.
- Fill an existing position for which the family member is qualified, based on education and work experience.
- Assign the family member to work with a non-family mentor.
- Encourage training, education, and developmental experiences.
- Encourage exploration of the family and business history and an understanding of the business culture.

Managing Sibling and Cousin Relationships

- Design career paths with separate roles and opportunities for a meaningful contribution.
- Develop business policies on compensation and promotions that are supported by family values and the Family Business Philosophy.
- Update the family code of conduct, specifically addressing work and career issues.
- Encourage sibling or cousin meetings.

Selecting a Successor

- Share planning and decision-making responsibilities with the successor candidates.
- Recognize and accommodate individual and generational differences.
- Provide successor candidates with profit and loss responsibility.
- Develop a performance review and objective feedback system.
- Determine future leadership requirements as a part of the Business Strategy Plan.
- Involve the board of directors and key family members in making the selection.

---

6 Developing Effective Ownership

Developing effective ownership is not traditionally a part of a business' strategic planning, but it is a critical element of the Parallel Planning Process. The fundamental presumption of the PPP is the integration of family and business; therefore the family's goals as owners must support the business' strategy.

Ownership, in simple terms, addresses all of the family business dilemmas discussed in Chapter 1 (see Figure 1.1). Effective owners must ensure that the business has qualified leadership (careers), correctly allocates financial resources (capital), follows a plan (control), maintains the family's values (culture) and resolves disputes (conflict). To fail to consider the family's role and responsibility as owners ignores the fact that this business is family controlled.

Why is this so tough? First, unlike management, ownership has no standardized job description, required training or special qualifications. Through purchase, inheritance or gifting, family members become shareholders with all the rights and responsibilities of ownership, no matter what their training, experience or qualifications. Second, shareholders, in most cases, are shareholders for their lifetime. Third, shareholders have the right to elect the board of directors and therefore influence the selection of management, the direction of the company and even the company's continued existence. Fourth, and perhaps most significant to the future character of the family business, shareholders gift or sell stock to the next generation of owners, thereby shaping the future ownership group.

For all these reasons, a family concerned about creating a family business that is meaningful and valuable to future generations must plan for the effectiveness of the ownership group.

This chapter explores ownership as the last component of the Family Enterprise Continuity Plan. The starting point for discussing ownership is understanding family business Ownership Configurations and the influence of life cycle and ownership decisions on their development. This is important because different Ownership Configurations require different activities to support effective ownership. As the family business moves through the life cycle, the characteristics and requirements of the family owners change. Changes in ownership characteristics, such as number of shareholders, shareholders' business experience and percentage of the owners employed by the business create a need for ownership plans to ensure a committed and capable ownership group.

Families concerned about ownership continuity find that planning and developing four programs support this goal:

1. Ownership education programs provide knowledge about the business, an understanding of its culture and an overview of ownership roles and responsibilities.
2. Ownership Agreements clarify the family's understanding on ownership issues such as selling stock, voting, and dividends.
3. Estate plans address financial security, distribution of assets, and taxes.
4. Family and business governance structures support decision-making, conflict resolution and management accountability among the owners.

FAMILY BUSINESS OWNERSHIP CONFIGURATIONS

Business families potentially move through six possible Ownership Configurations:

- Entrepreneurship
- Owner-managed
- Family Partnership
- Sibling Partnership
- Cousins' Collaboration
- Family Syndicate (see Figure 2.3).[1]

It is important to realize that the six Ownership Configurations are not necessarily linear – not every family business goes through them or completes them.[2] In fact, the family firm may skip phases or circle back into a phase because of family ownership decisions or actions. An owner-manager may transfer majority ownership to his or her children but personally continue to control the firm's business direction. This business remains in the Family Partnership Phase until the parent's death.

Sometimes families will agree that the business should be owned by the family member who serves as CEO or only by the family members employed in the firm. In these cases the business would continually recycle itself in the Owner-managed Phase or the Sibling Partnership Phase.

Family ownership issues can also be mediated by family actions. Some families work hard to maintain the connection and identification of future generations with the business and its heritage. These families may never become disinterested owners even when they reach the Family Syndicate Phase.

FACTORS SHAPING OWNERSHIP CONFIGURATIONS

The interaction of life cycle forces and family ownership decisions determine the family business' Ownership Configuration. The different Ownership Configurations have unique ownership groups and characteristics.

Life Cycle and Ownership Configurations

The family's movement through the individual and family life cycles directly influences the family Ownership Configurations. Life cycle events such as birth, marriage, retirement and death create the potential for changes in the ownership group. Examining life cycle helps to identify its impact on the family business and demonstrates the need for the ownership education programs discussed earlier in this chapter.

The family needs to anticipate and plan for individual and family life cycle transitions because they create changes in personal goals, financial situations and investment objectives. Different life cycle stages are associated with behaviors that directly impact the family business system. Life cycle transitions often trigger events for changes in ownership. The founder's retirement or 65th birthday will often coincide with the transferring of stock to the next generation of family members.

Family Ownership Decisions and Ownership Configurations

It is important to consider the impact of family decisions on ownership transfer because it can have significant ramifications for the future of the family business. This can be demonstrated by analyzing the different Ownership Configurations that could develop in a fourth-generation family business when different ownership decisions are made. Figure 6.1 is a family genogram with the six Ownership Configurations displayed.[3] The example shown presents four generations of a business family and the Ownership Configuration that could result.

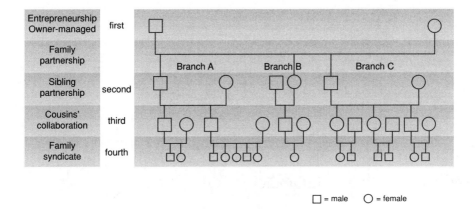

Figure 6.1 = male   ◯ = female

Figure 6.1 *Four generation genogram with possible ownership configurations*

Three ownership structure scenarios are presented to demonstrate how different family decisions on the transfer of ownership to the next generation will affect the business. The first scenario is equal distribution to all heirs, scenario two is distribution to males and scenario three is distribution only to family members employed by the firm.

Scenario One: Distribution of Ownership to all Family Members

This example demonstrates ownership that is based on a family decision of equal family ownership across each generation (see Figure 6.2). The founding couple divided their stock equally among their three children and this tradition has been followed by succeeding generations. By the fourth generation, this decision results in the single heir in Branch B controlling 33 percent of the company's stock. The remaining ownership is split among the other 13 members of the fourth generation based on the number of family members in their branch.

Scenario Two: Ownership Based on a Family Tradition Limiting Ownership to Male Family Members

This family decision creates an ownership structure that is based on a family agreement that allowed stock to be transferred only to male descendents of the founder (see Figure 6.3). Using this model of ownership transfer, the son

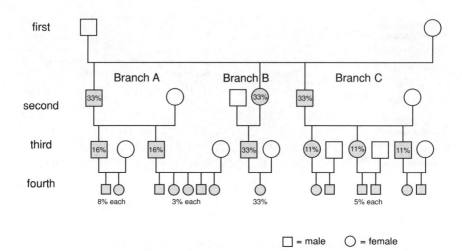

Note 1: Ownership percentages are rounded so they do not total 100%.
Note 2: Shading = ownership.

Figure 6.2   *Scenario one: ownership based on
distribution to all family members of each generation*

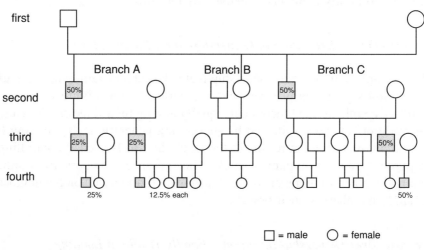

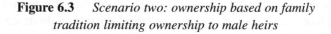

Note: Shading = ownership.

Figure 6.3   *Scenario two: ownership based on family
tradition limiting ownership to male heirs*

in Branch C will control 50 percent of the stock after four generations. His three cousins in Branch A will control the remaining 50 percent.

Scenario Three: Distribution Based on Employment in the Family Business

The final ownership structure demonstrates the effect of an Ownership Agreement that is designed to maintain control with family members who are employed by the firm (see Figure 6.4). The family's Ownership Agreement contains two stipulations. First, ownership is based on employment and the corporation redeems all shares at the employee's retirement or death. Second, each family employee is allocated shares annually based on their compensation using an ownership distribution formula. Under this plan senior family executives with long tenure own a larger share of the company's stock. This plan effectively redistributes the ownership to each new generation of family employees and prevents a concentration of ownership based on life events such as a family branch. It also allows family members to join the family business and earn ownership even if their parents were not involved with the family business. This is demonstrated in Branch C where two third-generation family members are significant owners even though their parent had no ownership in the business.

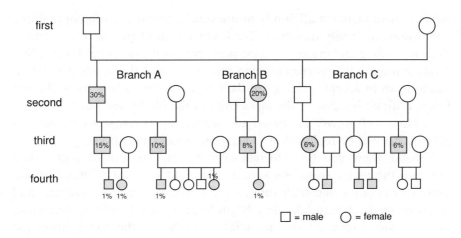

Note 1: Ownership percentages are rounded so they do not total 100%.
Note 2: Shaded symbols are family employees and owners. Some younger family members have not yet been allocated shares.

Figure 6.4   *Scenario three: ownership based on employment*

The three scenarios demonstrate that Ownership Configurations can vary dramatically, depending on the family's ownership decisions. There are no 'right or wrong' outcomes, but each decision does result in different ownership characteristics and varying levels of commitment to family business ownership. If a family makes no effort to plan the relationship between the family's Future Vision and its ownership structure, then an ownership pattern that undermines family continuity may result.

Family Ownership Forces

As the family matures and the ownership group changes, three ownership forces affect the characteristics of the ownership group. These three forces create changes in the characteristics of the ownership group resulting in the different ownership challenges that family businesses face. They include:

■ The participation of multiple generations of family members.
■ An expanded potential number of owners.
■ The separation of management and ownership roles.

Multiple Generations of Family Members

An important theme in all family businesses is the participation of multiple generations of family members. The involvement of two or more generations in owning and managing a business creates the potential for conflict. First, sharing power is required and this means that the senior generation has to learn to accept a change in their business and family roles. At best this is difficult because of the hierarchies of the family and business structure. How well power is shared and leadership is transferred creates a pattern that will be replayed in future generational transitions.

Second, there can be conflicts over personal or business priorities between the generations. As senior shareholders mature, they become more conservative and their tolerance for risk, personal motivations and financial goals change.[4] As they begin to plan for retirement, their goals become more focused on financial security. At the same time, the successor generation has most of its career ahead and is concerned more about business growth and creating future wealth. The two generations have age-appropriate risk/return criteria that may cause conflict over strategic choices and investment opportunities.

Expanded Ownership Group

As time passes, most families increase in size. A third- or fourth-generation business family can have a large and diverse group of shareholders. This larger shareholder group means a diffusion of ownership, often resulting in more shareholders with smaller ownership positions.

Separation of Management and Ownership Roles

As the ownership group expands it becomes increasingly unlikely that a large percentage of the owners will work for the business. The diversity of individual interests and the business' requirements for professional management result in many owners finding careers outside the family business. This separation of ownership and management roles fundamentally changes the firm's decision-making. By necessity, decision-making and management discussion have to become more formal as management – and ownership roles – separate.

There is also no longer a strong mutuality between career and ownership interests on strategy or reinvestment decisions. A 40-year-old family executive and shareholder sees an investment in the company as positive for his or her own career and ownership interests. However, his or her cousins who are not employed by the family business might not be so pleased to learn of a new strategy that cuts dividends for the next two years to fund a long-term growth opportunity.

Multiple generations, growing numbers of family owners and increased separation of management and ownership roles typically accompany the family's move through the life cycle. These forces shape the ownership issues and challenges facing the business and therefore the ownership programs that the business must eventually develop.

The characteristics of the family ownership group change in several key ways:

- The level of information-sharing changes.
- The percent of family members employed in the business changes.
- The family's level of business experience changes.
- Connections among family members change.
- The relationship between family members and the business' founder changes.
- The degree of wealth concentration changes.
- The degree of ownership concentration changes.

How to Establish a New Ownership Program

The Reardons share a challenge that many families face – how to create a capable ownership group.

The criticisms that the siblings are making sound as if they are expressing their frustrations over their uncertain ownership roles. They recognize that Bob's performance is strong but they feel a need for more influence on the family's relationship with the business. It is time for everyone to sit down and define what ownership in Reardon means and what it takes to balance the needs of the owners with the demands of the business.

Reardon family members have different definitions of what ownership in the company means. Here are some questions that they may want to discuss:

■ What are the rights and responsibilities of family business owners?

■ How does the family balance the capital demands of the business with the family's liquidity needs?

■ How do they strengthen the family's role on the board?

■ Is it time to identify a board with strong outside directors?

■ How do they improve the effectiveness and participation of the ownership group?

■ Who should decide on the CEO's compensation and review his performance?

For example, in early Ownership Configurations (Owner-managed, Family Partnership), all these issues are of low intensity because of the ownership characteristics. The relationships between management and ownership are strong and in many cases overlapping. Later, they are less directly connected. And as the ownership characteristics change the owners' need for ownership programs increases. The family must increasingly depend on proactive ownership programs to address issues such as the owners' 'lack of accurate information' and diffuse any conflict that might arise.

Table 6.1 reviews ownership characteristics and the changing need for ownership programs that a business family might consider. It also suggests the increasing need for ownership programs by each Ownership Configuration after the Owner-managed Phase.

Table 6.1 clearly demonstrates that each Ownership Configuration creates different challenges for the business family concerned about

Table 6.1   *Typical ownership issues, challenges and programs at different ownership configurations*

Ownership issues	OM	FP	SP	CC	FS*	Ownership challenge	Ownership programs
Level of information sharing						Lack of accurate information	Family networking/ governance
Split between ownership and management						Percent of family employed by business	Ownership agreements/ governance
Family's level of business experience						Complexity of family and business	Family education
Connection among extended family						Increased focus on marriage/ family/in-laws	Family social activities
Relationship with founder						Less connection to business values	Study business culture
Wealth concentration						Reduced shareholder commitment	Stock redemption plan
Ownership concentration						Diffusion of shareholders	Estate plans

Key: The need for ownership programs

Low	Medium	High

* Ownership Configuration

OM = Owner-managed Phase
FP = Family Partnership Phase
SP = Sibling Partnership Phase
CC = Cousins' Collaboration Phase
FS = Family Syndicate Phase

creating an effective ownership system. The three family ownership forces result in a diverse mix of people and problems that require well-crafted plans and programs. Four essential programs or plans follow:

1. Ownership education
2. Ownership Agreements
3. Estate plans
4. Overall governance design.

OWNERSHIP EDUCATION PROGRAMS

If shareholders are prepared for ownership roles and responsibilities, it is more likely that they will be willing and able to address the future challenges they will face. An owner, especially one who is not employed by the family firm, has two main challenges: understanding shareholder responsibilities and knowing the business.

No one doubts the importance and value of training and development activities to ensure qualified family managers and leaders. The previous chapter was devoted to exploring these issues. However, families typically do not pay similar attention to ownership education among members who are not as involved in the business. This is particularly unfortunate as the business grows because the shareholders' role becomes a more powerful factor in the firm's long-term success.

Fred Neubauer and Alden Lank, in their work on family business governance, suggest that as families move into the later stages of development an emphasis on 'enlightened ownership' is key.[5] Enlightened owners, they explain, are those who understand the firm's current position and have enough basic business knowledge to interpret that information. This book builds on their thinking, but also stresses governance and the organization's unique culture as additional topics for ownership education.

The value of ownership education increases as the ownership moves toward the Cousins' Collaboration or Family Syndicate Phases. Owners who take the time to participate in the training will not only gain insight into the nature of the business but will also find that it creates a relaxed, productive way to talk business with their parents and other senior family members. Senior family members also can use these sessions to develop an understanding of the next generation's expectations.[6]

Shareholder Responsibilities

Understanding the responsibilities of ownership – especially for those family members not employed in the business – is absolutely crucial to the PPP. Family owners concerned about improved family and business performance need to consider two broad responsibilities:

1. Understanding the ownership role.
2. Balancing individual interests with the shared interests of the other business and family stakeholders.

Understanding the Ownership Role

Shareholders concerned about the consequences of their actions need to understand their responsibilities as they make decisions or take actions regarding the family business. Being a capable and informed shareholder requires study and preparation. The following questions provide a brief overview of what it means to be a capable shareholder:

- Do I have the business information, knowledge and understanding to participate meaningfully in shareholder meetings and contribute to shareholder decision-making?
- Do I understand my family business' culture and how to contribute to it?
- What will be the long-term consequences of my decisions or actions?
- How will my decisions affect the family's Shared Future Vision?
- Am I willing to share my thinking and decisions openly with those affected by them?

Considering Other Stakeholders

Owners need to understand how their actions and demands will affect other stakeholders in the family business. Traditional business thinking saw the business run for the benefit of the shareholders with their interests placed above all others. That is changing. A concern for ethics and the realization that all interests are interrelated has led to a broader approach.[7] A stakeholder is anyone who is affected by the business' actions – not just shareholders. Typically stakeholders include employees, customers, owners, suppliers, partners, banks and the community at large.

Stakeholder thinking is a natural for family businesses since they are strongly influenced by values and long-term relationships. Stakeholder thinking can improve the quality and thoughtfulness of decisions since owners are required to consider a wider constituency. Knowing exactly who will be affected by everything a company does avoids problems and obstacles down the line. It might even lead to new business opportunities that owners had never considered.

The stakeholder decision-making process includes the following steps:

1. State the facts of the situation.
2. Identify the stakeholders affected by the decision.
3. Review the goals, desires or interests of each stakeholder.
4. Project future scenarios and consequences of possible decisions.

5. Examine the ethical and legal issues included in the decisions.
6. Balance steps 1–5 and make a decision and develop action steps and a follow-up plan.
7. Follow up to evaluate decisions and make adjustments.

The following *Family Experiences* on Malden Mills demonstrates stakeholder decision-making in action. It is a good example for owners not employed by the family business to consider, since they might not be aware of how a crisis or decisions about expansion, downsizing, overseas manufacturing or investment will affect the larger family business system.

FAMILY EXPERIENCES

Stakeholder Thinking in Action

In 1995 – two weeks before Christmas – a fire destroyed the Malden Mills Industries factory in Lawrence, Massachusetts. Malden Mills, with $400 million dollars in sales, was the area's largest employer with over 2,400 workers. In a region and industry plagued by chronic unemployment, the situation looked bleak for the employees and the adjacent communities.

Aaron Feuerstein, the 70-year-old business owner, needed only a few hours to organize an employee meeting to announce that not only was he rebuilding the plant, but also paying his employees while production was shut down. Many accused Feuerstein of 'grandstanding magnanimity' suggesting that he would have been better off pocketing the insurance money and retiring.

Feuerstein said he never thought about taking the insurance and retiring because he owed it to his employees, family and the community to rebuild. He is also a 'hard-nosed' businessperson who knows the value of highly productive employees in maintaining the superior quality that differentiates his products in the marketplace.

Note: Information from T. Teal, 'Not a Fool, Not a Saint', *Fortune*, **134** (Nov. 11, 1996) 201.

Business Knowledge

Developing a working knowledge of the business can be especially challenging when one's career is not in business. Ownership education must be designed to inspire basic business thinking and an understanding of the family business and how it operates. It must be conducted in a way that encourages learning and participation, particularly from the most inexperienced owners.

Understanding the Business' Strategy

As demonstrated throughout this book, the planning process is the company's recipe for future success. All companies have some model of planning, even if it is not formalized. It represents an implicit formula for creating a profit. Future owners, particularly those not employed by the family business, do not appreciate how planning can impact family and business outcomes. Discerning the planning model and understanding how decisions are made about the business and its strategy requires a review of the following topics (discussed fully in Chapters 7–9):

- Family and Business Vision
- Financial goals and family investment expectations
- Business strengths and weaknesses
- External opportunities and threats
- Industry and market trends
- Current situation and performance.

Organizational Culture

All organizations, and particularly families and family firms, have deeply ingrained cultures that dictate the way things are done.[8] The future owners owe it to themselves and the company to try to understand the culture of their family business – first to protect what is of value, and second to understand how to influence change.

Many next-generation owners, however, do not know the family business system and consequently fail to understand its unique culture. They eagerly propose new ideas, seeking to introduce changes that reflect their personal identity, training or experience. What these individuals must realize is that change in a family business is typically evolutionary, not revolutionary. This evolution should be a process of gradual movement based on agreed-upon core values. A new culture will result from new practices and behaviors built on the business' existing culture.

As the future owners observe and listen, they should keep in mind the following questions:

- How is the business different from others?
- What does the family add?
- What is unique about the history, values or experience?

When the inquiry is finished, future owners should be able to define the culture of the business in a few paragraphs.

To make sense of the business' culture, start by asking the following:

■ Who makes what decisions?
■ How much are the people and the company's history respected?
■ What does the organization celebrate (that is, innovations, loyalty, performance, risk taking, and so on)?
■ What stories are told around the organization about the founder? About the family?
■ What do the people who like to work at the business share in common?
■ How are power and authority handled in the family and business?
■ How does the organization structure hinder or support communication?
■ Is the formal or informal organization more powerful?

A family business that wants to work better has to create a friendly and structured environment for questions and discussion. Formal educational programs tend to work better than 'family talks' between generations because there is an opportunity for everyone in 'the classroom' to raise their hands and ask questions. On the other hand, unstructured 'talks' between family members tend to focus on what has gone right or wrong in the company, what is good or bad about the business, or who is successful or not in the business.

These topics do not necessarily evoke conflict in themselves, but they often deteriorate into debate on management styles or practices and on whose style or ideas is better – the senior or next generation's. These discussions do not teach anything. Most often, they simply end up rehashing old issues.

Understanding the culture of the family's business is perhaps the most important educational task. It is the business' reflection of the family's values and it creates more shareholder commitment than any other factor.

FAMILY EXPERIENCES

Developing Effective Ownership

Planning for ownership continuity is critical if the family and its descendants are to benefit from the economic value created by a successful family firm.

Family enterprises that last for generations must adapt not only to family and business challenges but also to the external environment. The Wendel family history began in 1704 when Jean-Martin Wendel acquired an iron forge in the French Lorraine region close to the German border.

Wendel's forges soon were a major supplier of iron bullets for the King's army and he rapidly gained prominence throughout France. His son Charles I further expanded the family business. He adapted a new production process using coal as a heat source, which increased production and reduced dependence on the area's forests. At Charles' death, his wife, Marguerite d'Hausen, took responsibility for managing the forges with the support of her two sons-in-law.

The French Revolution forced many in the Wendel family to leave France. Marguerite d'Hausen, despite her advanced age, stayed in France and continued to run the family forges until she was arrested in 1794. The forges were finally closed and sold as state properties.

During the Revolution, the Wendel coke cast iron process was temporarily lost. But Francois de Wendel, a great grandson of the founder, was able to reclaim the lost technology in England and restarted production in France after the Revolution.

The Industrial Revolution created significant opportunities and the company expanded. By 1825, the new Wendel enterprise employed over 3,000 people at their original location. Francois left ownership to his wife and with the help of their son, Charles II, and also a son-in-law, the family continued the dramatic growth of the company. The construction of railroads and iron ships allowed the company to prosper. By the 1860s, they employed over 10,000 people.

At Charles II's death in 1870, his mother created a company partnership to ensure that 100 percent ownership of the Wendel mines and forges would stay with her grandchildren. These articles of association stipulated that Francois de Wendel's descendants only could own shares. Active partners jointly received 10 percent of the company's profits but were personally liable for all of the company's debts.

The first shareholder group included nine men and women, all surviving grandchildren. A family agreement at that time stipulated that in-laws could not be owners but that they could be associated with the company through management.

Over the next 100 years, the Wendel family enterprise endured ongoing border disputes between France and Germany, economic booms and crashes and two World Wars.

The nationalization of the French steel industry in the late 1970s presented the family with an opportunity to liquidate its assets. The management team, led by Pierre Celier (in-law) and Henri de Wendel, proposed restructuring the non-steel holdings into a new family-controlled group. To insure the commitment of the 350 family shareholders, they asked for and received a unanimous vote of approval. The restructuring granted shareholders ownership in a family holding company restricted to descendants of Francois de Wendel; Marine-Wendel, a publicly traded company; and a newly created subsidiary, Compagnie Generale d'Industrie et de Participations (CGIP).

During the last 20 years, the Wendel family members have practiced what they describe as 'shareholder entrepreneurship' to significantly increase the value of these two publicly traded companies by diversifying into technology and manufacturing. There are currently more than 500 Wendel descendants as shareholders.

Note: Information from C. Blondel and L. Van der Heyden, 'The Wendel Family: Affectio Societatis, (Case A, 270 Years in Iron and Steel)' and 'The Wendel Family: Affectio Societatis, (Case B, CGIP, New Business Venture)'. Fontainebleau, France: INSEAD.

The Wendel family experience is a good example of maintaining effective ownership. This family has enjoyed a long business history despite chaos in the world around them. The family's ownership continuity is based on many of the concepts discussed in this chapter. In the late 1800s the family developed their first articles of association (Ownership Agreement) that stipulated ownership requirements and the responsibilities of management. The family's strong culture of 'shareholder entrepreneurship' helped the family to secure shareholder support for reformulating the family business after nationalization by the French government. This shareholder entrepreneurship and their sound governance structures have built a strong sense of Family Commitment that continues on today.

Governance Responsibilities

Governance is a fundamental responsibility of effective ownership. The PPP uses governance as a link between the family and business systems discussed in Chapter 10. In the family business context, governance takes on a double importance, requiring governance structures for both the business and family. As the family grows and ownership expands, there is an increased need for planning formal governance structures for both systems.

On the business side, senior managers and shareholders will recognize the need for a functioning board of directors when they feel that the business' size and complexity requires additional expertise. As the number of non-employed shareholders increases, the board must increasingly represent the interests of a growing group of owners.

Yet the next generation of owners have to educate themselves so that they can create an efficient governance structure for the board to follow. The well-governed family business is focused on the shared Family and Business Vision, not bogged down in debates about operations or family issues.

FAMILY OWNERSHIP AGREEMENTS

According to François de Visscher *et al.*, the Family Effect is an important competitive advantage of well-planned family ownership.[9] The Family Effect suggests that family shareholders provide patient capital if they understand the risk factors, have liquidity opportunities and are committed to the family business. Developing Ownership Agreements is a critical activity for stimulating the Family Effect.

Ownership Agreements serve three important purposes. First, they provide a framework for defining ownership relationships. Second, they create a framework for resolving disputes or conflicts over ownership issues. Third and equally important, they shape the ownership structure to support the family's vision of the business and itself. Just as it is important to develop employment and work-related family agreements before the next generation joins the firm, it is equally important to develop agreements on a wide range of ownership topics before shares are promised or transferred. These agreements should confirm who could own stock, how the stock can be transferred (sold, redeemed, and so on) and what benefits the stock creates (voting rights, board membership, dividends, and so on).

Essential Ingredients of a Liquidity Plan

A critical difference between ownership in a privately held company and a publicly traded company is the liquidity of the shareholders' investment. One of the most serious family business conflicts occurs when shareholders who want to sell are locked into an ownership position. This is particularly complex if one of the shareholders has an unexpected personal or business financial need and there is no way to get at the cash.

Transferability

A liquidity plan, often known as a buy–sell agreement, allows a family member to sell stock as a long-term strategy either to reduce their holdings or if they are discouraged with the investment. Whichever is the case, it is important for the family to have an efficient and easy way to administer a program to redeem, redistribute or transfer family stock.

A good ownership liquidity plan requires an internal market that establishes a formula for a sale price. The internal market can be created in several different ways, depending on the complexity of the family business and the number of shareholders. In a family business with a small number of owners, other shareholders are typically granted the right to buy the shares of any selling family member.

Clear Terms and Conditions

As a family business grows, there may be various branches of the family that want to maintain their branch's ownership position. Some families stipulate that shareholders within that branch have the first right to purchase stock that goes up for sale. If they waive that right, the stock is then available to any family member. These buy–sell agreements include limits on the amount of stock a shareholder can sell in any given period, as well as requirements for payment terms.

Companies also might structure their liquidity program around company buybacks – that is, when the company buys back shares when shareholders want out. This type of ongoing redemption program can be funded with the corporation's cash flow or by an employee stock owner-ship trust. These plans support the remaining shareholders' ownership position without additional investment. This type of plan is most workable in a mature family business with predictable cash flows and limited demands for additional working capital.

Terms of payment are also paramount in any liquidity plan. The company's owners might allow installment payments for stock if the purchaser cannot come up with all the cash at once. The family needs to examine this issue very carefully. Buy–sell agreements may also require purchasers or sellers to offer notice within a specific time period or set the line on a minimum or maximum number of shares that might be sold or purchased at a single point in time.

Valuation Formulas that Make Sense

The final element in any shareholder liquidity plan is an agreed-upon formula to determine a selling price. Families will develop a valuation formula (see Table 9.3) to represent the calculated value of the stock for buy–sell, buyback or other redemption activities. Using a valuation formula ensures that shareholders understand the price under which family stock is traded in the internal family market. It reduces the potential for disagreements on pricing between the seller and buyer.

Establish Shareholder Rights

Shareholders in family businesses have rights and responsibilities as in any partnership or corporation. Unfortunately, rights in privately held companies are more dependent on relationships and clear understandings than corporate charters, laws or government regulations. Shareholders in public companies have well-defined rights because stock markets, government agencies and courts set minimum standards and enforce regulations related to shareholder meetings, disclosure of financial information, boards of directors, voting rights and other structural issues.

In a privately controlled family business it is often impractical to depend on outside intervention for enforcing ownership rights. A family that manages its affairs based on strict interpretation of legal requirements or the threat of legal action loses its natural competitive advantage of trust. Many families find it useful to develop family Ownership Agreements that articulate the family's understandings about what it means to be a shareholder in the family.[10]

An Ownership Agreement should address the following issues:

- Who can own stock in the business?
- What is the dividend policy? Who determines if dividends are paid?
- How can stock be redeemed to provide liquidity for shareholders?
- Can family members transfer stock to each other?
- Can a former shareholder buy stock in the company at a later date?
- Does all stock have the same voting rights?
- How are members of the board of directors selected?
- What is the board's relationship to the shareholders?
- Can company stock be pledged for loans or other purposes?
- What financial information and business reports are issued to shareholders?

Financial Expectations

Businesses are created to generate economic value for the owners. Family shareholders, like all investors, are concerned about the financial returns on their investments. One of the challenges that investors in privately held businesses face is the lack of information about the prospects of their investment. Shareholders in public companies have the daily market pricing and professional analysts' reports to give them some indication of their investment's potential.

Family businesses need to begin this process of disclosure by discussing the business' financial policies and expectations. For example, a family business that reinvests 75 percent of its earnings into the company presents a very different investment from a company that pays 75 percent of its earnings in dividends. At least once a year, management and the board should review with the owners the business' goals and policies related to dividends, growth rate, leverage and operating risk, profitability and Economic Value Added. This regular disclosure and explanation can diffuse many family conflicts.

ESTATE PLANS

Creating estate plans is one of the toughest projects business families undertake. These plans are important because family businesses must balance the needs of the senior generation for financial security with the ability of the business to remain financially viable and competitive.[11]

Estate plans are also crucial to management succession. A study of 749 failed family businesses revealed that three of the five most frequently mentioned reasons for failure – as cited by the successor generation – were related to inadequate estate planning.[12]

Choice of Ownership Structure

One of the first decisions that a family should consider in estate planning is the type of ownership structure that best supports the Shared Future Vision. Choosing an ownership structure for the next generation is fundamental to working out an estate plan. This decision is influenced by the Family Business Philosophy (Family First, Business First or Family Enterprise), the family life cycle and the current Ownership Configuration. Often the first decision that is made in the transfer to the sibling group sets the future pattern for the family business. This first transfer is also the most controllable because it involves the founder and his or her children. Once the stock has been distributed to a sibling or cousin group, restructuring the ownership distribution is a significant family, legal and financial challenge.

There are many different ownership structures that a family can follow, but generally the pattern is one of the following:

■ Distribution to all heirs.
■ Distribution to the family members employed by the firm.

- Distribution to the family members employed in senior executive positions by the firm.
- Distribution of two classes of stock, voting to family members employed by the firm and non-voting to other family members.
- Distribution to a selected group of heirs, typically males.
- Distribution to the oldest heir (typically male).
- Redistribution at each generation transition to balance ownership across different branches of the family.

Retirement Funding

Glenn Ayres, an attorney and family business consultant, suggested that estate planning be driven by a family dialogue, using an equation that determines 'family need' and the 'business' ability to pay'.[13] This again demonstrates the importance of developing Ownership Agreements before attempting to finalize estate or other legal plans. If estate plans, and specifically ownership positions, are not clearly understood by the family, they often sustain long-term family conflicts that are not resolved before death.[14] A family that cannot discuss and agree on fundamental issues, such as future ownership, will have ongoing difficulties resolving other family business issues.

The starting point for discussing the estate plan is the current owners' needs. The first calculation includes the financial resources that the senior generation believes it 'needs' to ensure its lifestyle and economic security, as well as funds for philanthropy and assets to share with their heirs. This may include distributing some of the parents' assets to children who have decided not to participate in the family business.[15]

The second part of the equation explores the business' financial resources and its ability to meet the 'need' calculation of the senior generation. It is important to remember that, unless a business has accumulated significant liquid assets, the ability to fund the 'need' calculation is based on the business' future performance.

Thus, the next step is to determine the ability to pay by exploring the financial performance and capital needs of the business, the expectations of other creditors and the willingness of the successor generation to delay their financial rewards to fund the 'needs' payments.[16] The final plan should address retirement income, minimizing estate taxes, distribution of assets among the family, funding for taxes and business succession and philanthropy.

Distribution of Assets to the Family

The actual shift of assets from one generation to the next may take several years, which means that the next generation of owners should be identified well in advance of the senior generation's retirement date. This is another important advantage of clarifying the estate plan because most tools for efficiently completing the ownership transfer require a significant transition period. Taxes and other transaction expenses related to an ownership transfer can be minimized with early gifting, 'sales' of minority positions, compensation plans, consulting agreements, asset purchases, upgraded pensions, passive income from partnerships, or changes in corporate or legal structure.

Facilitating discussion of these uncertainties, of course, is what the Parallel Planning Process is supposed to do. It is meant to encourage honest exchanges and full disclosure of both family and business concerns. The only way to resolve the ownership challenge just outlined, for example, is for the senior generation to state openly the financial position of the business and the family. How well the family has attended to the family issues – such as Family Vision and Commitment and Family Agreements on compensation – will determine the business management's ability to reconcile business strategy choices with family plans. Chapter 9 discusses balancing the family's need with the business' strategy and the development of a reinvestment decision.

In some families, the estate planning process brings to the surface some unresolved family issues, such as who wants to accept the responsibilities of business ownership. In such cases, the family must then resolve these issues or uncertainties before the company can be sure that its business strategies are appropriate.

FAMILY BUSINESS GOVERNANCE

Effective governance is the fundamental responsibility of ownership. Family business governance requires parallel family and business thinking to support the development of planning, decision-making and problem-solving structures for both the family and business systems (see Figure 6.5). Most businesses have a board of directors (or supervisory boards) that oversee management actions, allocate capital and participate in the strategy process. Family councils are the family's 'board'. They provide a governance structure to support consensus decisions, coordinate family actions and provide leadership.

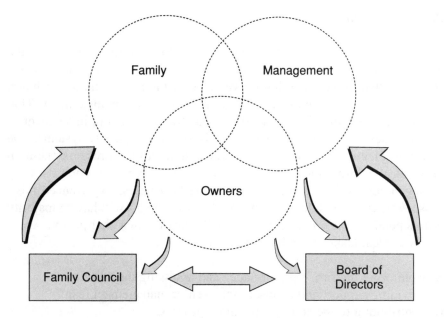

Figure 6.5   *Parallel family and business governance structures*

Sharing information and coordinated action between the family council and board of directors is often required because of the overlap in the family and business systems. These groups may simply offer counsel to each other, or, on difficult decisions, they may both be asked to participate in the decision-making process. Sharing decisions and plans related to Family Agreements, ownership transfers, management succession and business strategy ensures that the family and business policies and plans are complementary. The family council and board of directors are forums for that sharing.

Board of Directors

A family concerned about creating an effective business governance structure needs to consider decisions about the board's purpose, key tasks and structure.

Purposes and Tasks

In any company, the board of directors must do the following: protect the company's assets, ensure that capable management is in place and support strategies that create shareholder value. In a family business, the board also serves as a link between the family and senior management. That means the board may be involved in mediating ownership, investment or career issues created by the overlap of business and family systems. The board is elected by the shareholders and legally represents them in directing the corporation. The board of directors typically comprises top management, family members and, in the best cases, experienced businesspeople from outside the company. Ideally a board will have a majority of independent, outside directors and will elect its own chairperson.

The critical tasks of the board include:

- Monitoring the firm's performance and assessing the CEO.
- Providing support and counsel to the senior management team.
- Contributing to the strategic planning process.
- Providing mentoring to family employees on careers and family relationships.
- Acting as a link between the family shareholders and the management team.
- Representing the needs of non-family stakeholders in the decision-making process.

PLANNING TOOLS

For Your Business Library

Readers interested in more information on family business governance should read *The Family Business: Its Governance for Sustainability* by Fred Neubauer and Alden Lank (London: Macmillan – now Palgrave, 1998). Also, another good source is *Creating Effective Boards for Private Entrepreneurs* by John L. Ward (Marietta, GA: Family Business Publishers, 1991).

In addition to its formal governance roles, the board can also support the family's relationship with the business. The board can play an invaluable role in management succession decisions and provide objective counsel about which candidate may have the skills and talents needed to manage the business in the future. The board may also be structured as a training vehicle for future generation owners and directors. The future leaders may hold non-voting slots on the board if the company chooses to structure its board that way. An effective board with outside members also demonstrates to the next generation the family's commitment to professionalism in ownership and management – and new ideas.

Family Decisions on Creating Boards

Developing a functioning board, especially with outside directors, is a major task that must support the Shared Future Vision. Therefore the family should carefully discuss why they feel creating a board will add value to their family and business. This discussion will identify several issues that the family should consider:

- The board's role and decision-making authority.
- The composition of the board (the mix of management, family and outsiders).
- The selection process for members.
- A method for evaluating individual members' performance.
- How to compensate board members.

A board, when well conceived and given clear authority and responsibility, is an invaluable tool. The opposite is also true. A board comprising family members designed to counteract a strong CEO's authoritarian rule only creates another venue for conflict and negative feelings. The board's role should be clearly identified and discussed by shareholders and the senior management team.

There may be a reluctance to authorize a board of directors with outside members or even younger members of the family. For this reason, some families choose to begin their governance activities with a board of advisors who provide a new level of objectivity but without the formal or legal structure of a board.

Family Council

Family governance structures typically evolve from the informal family meetings. As the number of family members increases and the influence of the senior generation decreases, it becomes difficult to organize and conduct regular family meetings. The large number of family members may also reduce the effectiveness of the meeting process. At this time, the family develops a representative family council to formalize the planning and decision-making actions that are on the family meeting agenda.

Purposes and Tasks

Typically the transition to a family council represents a need for a more professional approach to addressing and resolving family issues. The family meeting often continues but on a less frequent schedule, typically annually or semi-annually, focusing on educational, social and informational activities. A multi-generational family or one with a large number of members may also benefit from the representational approach that opens up participation to more of the family. Younger family members, those who are not employed by the business or those not currently shareholders, may find that a representative family council is more open to hearing their ideas and addressing their concerns. The nomination or election of family council members also creates leadership opportunities for a more diverse group of family members.

The creation of a family council is a logical step to complement the business governance provided by the board of directors (see Figure 6.5). The family council's purposes can vary by family needs but typically addresses family planning, decision-making and resolving problems or conflicts. Specific projects often include: developing family education, revising Family and Ownership Agreements, resolving family conflicts and enforcing the family's code of conduct. Examples of ongoing family council tasks include the following list of responsibilities:

- Leading the development of family plans.
- Reviewing business strategy.
- Transmitting family values and the Family Vision.
- Offering a family forum for sharing ideas.
- Encouraging family participation and commitment.
- Supporting the family's ownership education programs.
- Developing family leaders from the next generation.
- Monitoring family and business interactions.
- Implementing family plans and programs.

Family Decisions on Creating a Family Council

Families that plan on using a family council should consider the responsibilities of the council in relation to the family and the model of representation.

If the family council evolves from a tradition of family meetings, then the family will have accepted the idea of shared planning and decision-making. Family members will have experienced the value of working together to create understandings about critical issues. The transition to a family council will be supported because the family appreciates the need for the change and feels that the entire family will still have influence on critical decisions. The family's concern over the council's decision-making authority can be addressed by providing a ratification procedure at the annual family meeting.

A more difficult issue is deciding how to select a representative group to serve on the council. Historically, family meetings may have been organized by the senior generation that played a leadership role in conducting family meetings. Some families may want to ensure representation from different branches of the family or seek a balance between family members employed inside and outside the business. Other families will try to maintain a balance based on generations of the family. Some very successful families try to avoid constituent council make-up and instead seek the best candidates regardless of family branch or generation.

STEWARDSHIP AS A FAMILY OWNERSHIP VALUE

Stewardship, as an overriding theme in the family values and vision statements, suggests that each generation will pass on a family business that is healthier and more valuable to the future generations. Stewards recognize that they are making decisions for their children's children and therefore consider the long-term interests not only of the owners, but also all the firm's stakeholders.

Families can encourage stewardship by reviewing important actions based on future outcomes and consequences. Discussing what stewardship values mean to the family during family and business planning sessions, at family council and family meetings and at board meetings creates awareness throughout the system.

SUMMARY

Ownership education programs and board or family council meetings can be therapeutic for families caught up in the everyday stresses of managing and governing a business. These processes provide a structure and an objective framework for communication on sensitive topics, which builds family trust. The parallel planning concepts developed in this book also encourage a type of communication that is more acceptable to business people because the output is a strategic plan while integrating the family's aspirations and values.

Early in the planning process, family managers, owners and the rest of the family may not be ready to share or hear constructive criticism. But even in conflict, a shared vision and focus is being created. Eventually, families will reach consensus faster based on the painful process of airing all their views. At that point, it is more likely that planning programs will reflect a Shared Future Vision, rather than focus on differences in short-term goals.

The participation of the owners in the Parallel Planning Process is critical to developing business plans that will be supported with the necessary family reinvestment. It is important to develop agreements on a wide range of ownership and governance topics before ownership is transferred. These family procedures become the basis for effectively directing the actions of the family and its relationship with the business. The worst circumstance for any family business is a conflicted family or shareholder group.

Educated and well-informed owners are important to the planning process when management needs to make investments that require patient capital. The owners need a sound understanding of business and finance concepts, an appreciation of the responsibilities of management, boards and shareholders and an appreciation of the family business' culture. These areas of knowledge are important to becoming active and effective shareholders.

The following is a review of the basic ingredients of the Family Enterprise Continuity Plan addressed in Chapters 3–6.

Securing Family Commitment

- Discussing core values.
- Identifying a Family Business Philosophy.
- Crafting a Family Vision.
- Drafting a Statement of Family Commitment.

Encouraging Family Participation

- Addressing family conflict.
- Creating family fairness.

- Planning and conducting family meetings.
- Preparing participation agreements.

Preparing the Next Generation of Family Managers and Leaders

- Understanding the business' future needs.
- Exploring the family business as a career possibility.
- Launching a family business career.
- Planning a meaningful career.
- Addressing next-generation relationships.

Developing Effective Ownership

- Understanding life cycle influences on ownership.
- Developing ownership education programs.
- Preparing Ownership Agreements.
- Crafting estate plans.
- Designing governance structures.

The Family Enterprise Continuity Plan has described the family's support of a Shared Future Vision (see Appendix E). Chapters 7–9 develop the business side of the Parallel Planning Process. This process begins in Chapter 7 with an assessment of the firm's Strategic Potential. Chapter 8 reviews possible strategies and Chapter 9 concludes with the selection of a strategy and the family's reinvestment decision.

Part III

Planning for the Business

7 Assessing the Firm's Strategic Potential

Strategic planning for any organization is about assessing the firm's capabilities and matching those capabilities with the external environment. The Parallel Planning Process helps business families to integrate this strategic thinking with their Shared Future Vision. Understanding the company's current situation and recognizing the commitments required of the family is the essence of the PPP.

Traditional family business thinking often encourages planning based on past business experience. This practice, built on the assumption that change is incremental, worked well until the last decade. The current business environment finds all organizations encountering turbulence, threats and unimaginable opportunities. This dynamic environment reduces the value of planning based on the past. Nothing can replace management's business experience, but as the business grows in size and scope, a more structured approach, based on formalized planning, improves the consistency and quality of the plans and decisions.

The Business Strategy Plan, proposed in this book as a part of the PPP, is a systematic approach to exploring three key questions:

1. Where to compete?
2. How to compete?
3. What is the required investment?

The challenge that family businesses face is deciding on a strategy that positively addresses these three questions. The next three chapters present a process for identifying options and making decisions regarding the Business Strategy Plan. This chapter begins with an assessment of the firm's internal capabilities and the external environment. This information is used to create a matrix that identifies the firm's future potential. This information is also used in Chapters 8 and 9 to identify where and how to compete. Chapter 8 will explore 27 possible business strategies and Chapter 9 focuses on making the final strategy and reinvestment decisions.

Together, these three chapters are designed to provide an overview of business strategy activities that support the PPP. Business models and tools are included to support the development of business strategies and decision-making. When the business planning activities are completed, management and the board or shareholders should be in a position to finalize a business strategy and a reinvestment decision.

The authors have purposely provided only an overview of strategic planning techniques because the focus of this book is family business planning not business strategy. There are several excellent books written on business strategy if the reader needs a more in-depth discussion of the strategy process or of any of the specific topics discussed in this book.

DEFINING THE FIRM'S STRATEGIC POTENTIAL

This book proposes the development of a decision-making matrix to help to organize business planning factors into a structure that supports effective planning. The business planning model proposed in this book is based on a two-dimensional matrix using the strength of the firm's internal capabilities and the attractiveness of its external environment. Figure 7.1 displays this matrix and the relationship between these two variables. The result, as is described in this book, is the firm's Strategic Potential.

The two variables are central to all aspects of the business planning process. The firm's internal capabilities are the resources that management uses to develop the Business Strategy Plan. These capabilities include the firm's financial, marketing and organization resources. The firm's external environment includes the market, the industry and the general environment. The external environment describes everything that goes on outside the firm including customers, competition, government actions and new technology. An attractive external environment allows the business to implement its plans and creates new business opportunities.

Throughout the next three chapters the Strategic Potential concept is used for assessing the firm's current position and its future potential, identifying the firm's priorities, evaluating possible business strategies and finalizing the investment decisions. Strategic Potential is important to family firms because it ultimately determines the business strategy and investment options.

In Figure 7.1, a firm in the three upper-left-hand boxes (labeled A) is a strong business in an attractive environment. This firm has excellent profit potential, which creates more resources and new capabilities. On the other hand, an assessment that reveals either a business weakness or an unattrac-

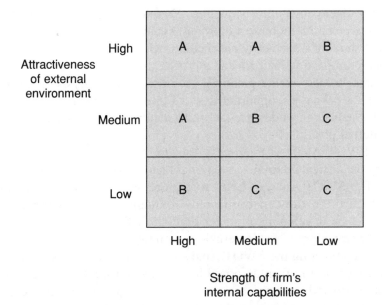

Figure 7.1   *Strategic potential matrix*

tive market indicates that management will need to identify new business strategies (middle boxes labeled B). These businesses are moderately successful but have greater potential if management can develop a strategy to help the firm to exploit its current market or identify a new market.

The businesses in boxes labeled C are weak businesses in unattractive environments. These firms face the most serious threats because they lack a positive market situation and the strengths to exploit a new opportunity.

Identifying and discussing the firm's Strategic Potential is a valuable activity for the family and management because it builds a shared awareness of the firm's situation. As discussed in Chapter 8, determining the firm's Strategic Potential naturally leads to thinking about what type of strategy the firm needs to pursue. A strong firm in a growing market is probably not going to abandon its position. Most people would understand that a weak firm in a declining market needs to make some changes.

THE SWOT ANALYSIS

The logical place to begin exploring the firm's future potential is by analyzing the firm's current position. It is critical to develop agreement among the management team about the firm's current status as a starting point for discussing future strategies. Developing an accurate picture of the firm's potential requires a thorough evaluation of both its internal and external situations. One efficient method, which offers both an analysis of the factors impacting the firm and a process for engaging management and other stakeholders in the planning process, is the analysis of the firm's strengths, weaknesses, opportunities and threats (SWOT). The goal of the SWOT Analysis is to develop an understanding of the business' internal and external position.

The SWOT Analysis is an easy tool to use that provides a summary view of the critical internal and external factors that are of strategic importance. The SWOT Analysis helps to capture data in order to qualitatively plot the firm on the capabilities/environment framework discussed in Figure 7.1 by developing an understanding of the firm's strengths (capabilities) and opportunities (external environment).

When completing the SWOT Analysis, it is useful to consider as many perspectives on the firm as possible. The candid thinking of employees and other trusted stakeholders who have a unique perspective can help management to recognize their own blind spots. One technique for securing SWOT data is to ask key employees, managers, family members, directors, and possibly even outside stakeholders (customers, suppliers) to list two or three strengths, weaknesses, opportunities and threats that they believe are important to the firm. The exercise not only provides new information but is a simple way to stimulate the organization's thinking about change and future business strategy. Additionally, asking people's opinion builds their commitment to the firm and its ultimate plans. The information collected can be used as input to the management team charged with developing strategic plans.

The information from the SWOT Analysis enables management to locate the firm on a Strategic Potential Matrix (see Figure 7.1). This 'plotting' of the firm's position forms the basis for discussions of the firm's possible business strategies (Chapter 8) and the family's reinvestment decision (Chapter 9).

THE INTERNAL ANALYSIS

The internal assessment explores the firm's capabilities (strengths and weaknesses) related to assets, resources, technologies and skills. These factors are important because they directly influence the choice of strategy. Generally, management would specifically examine the firm's strategic capabilities in finance, marketing and organization. These three broad functions should be evaluated to assess their potential contribution to the strategic plans that management may propose. The firm's strengths should be the focus of this analysis because what the firm does better than competitors or in a unique way is the basis for creating a new strategy. For example, a firm with a sophisticated distribution system may want to identify related or new products for a diversification strategy in order to capitalize on its distribution skills.

Table 7.1 identifies generic marketing, organization and finance capabilities that management should consider in its internal assessment of the firm. This generic list is included to suggest possible factors that may represent strengths and weaknesses of a family firm. Firms should identify factors important to their situation and industry for analysis. The family's impact as a strength or weakness should also be addressed. Family factors for analyses are identified at the bottom of Table 7.1. Often the information that the SWOT Analysis identifies as strengths or weaknesses is well known to the management team and the family, but not addressed. One of the benefits of using the SWOT process is that it provides management and the family with a format to constructively discuss difficult issues and new ideas.

The SWOT Analysis is a starting point to generate ideas and discussion. Management should do additional in-depth thinking about the internal factors that shape the firm's finance, market and organizational strengths. It is valuable to use a SWOT Analysis to determine the firm's current position and then to explore how the firm's strengths can contribute to a new business strategy.

The next three sections of this chapter discuss the firm's capabilities by analyzing the finance, marketing and organization position of the firm. After completing this internal analysis on strengths and weaknesses, management is prepared to assess the strength of the firm's capabilities – high, medium or low – based on the competition they face. It is valuable to attempt to gain a management consensus on where the firm's internal analysis places the firm on the vertical axis of the Strategic Potential Matrix.

ASSESSING THE FIRM'S FINANCIAL STRENGTH

The discussion of the firm's internal situation begins by examining financial performance and financial structure. The firm's financial strength tells a lot about the effectiveness of the current plans and is a critical factor in assessing its Strategic Potential. A firm with growing profits and a positive cash flow or additional debt capacity has a greater range of strategic options. It can invest in new facilities, fund new promotional activities or

Table 7.1 *Examples of internal factors for analysis*

Marketing Capabilities	Organizational Capabilities	Financial Capabilities
Customer reputation	Information technology	Financial controls
Trademarks or copyrights	Planning systems	Cash flow
Customer reputation	Employee development	Leverage
Market share	Physical facilities/capabilities	Credit capacity
Promotion strategies	Employee relations	Balance sheet
Competitive market position	Management team	Budget and control system
Distribution channels	Research & development	Annual financial reports
Sales force	Manufacturing technology	Banking relationships
Product mix	Performance evaluations	Cost/control systems
Pricing strategies	Organizational structures	Capital expenditure budget
Market research	Quality control	Performance measures
Customer data base	Employee morale	Inventory control system
Customer support systems	Union relationships	External audit or review
Brands and trade names	Policies and procedures	Asset utilization
	Technology competencies	Access to capital
Family relationships with customers	Family values	Family investment policies
Family marketing power	Family employees	Family payouts
Family public image	Family management	
	Family agreements	

make an acquisition. This section will explain the assessment of the business' financial strength and the adequacy of its current investment levels. This analysis will indicate whether the business is adequately funded for its future or underfunded and risking future decay.

The financial analysis is divided into two parts:

- A set of assessments to analyze the business' performance.
- A set of assessments to determine whether the business is adequately investing for its future.

The assessments of current and future financial position are quite distinct. Overall, the barometers of current weakness include declining profitability, declining productivity, inefficient use of cash and declining competitive strengths. Barometers that indicate a company is compromising its future include a declining investment level or reduced sustainable growth rate.

A business that is already decaying looks unhealthy right now; by contrast, a business that is compromising its future by a lack of investment may not show signs of decline until much later. In fact, the latter may often look quite healthy. Sales may be growing and so may profit. The analyses are thus intended to uncover signs of trouble that indicate future decay – signs that develop when too much of the cash flow or profits are being taken out of the business for Family Payouts. Family Payouts in the form of dividends, bonuses, stock redemption, and so on, reduce the funds available for reinvestment in the business. This lack of investment is often hidden beneath an apparently promising trend.

FAMILY EXPERIENCES

Assessing the Future Opportunities

The Barcelona-based Puig Corporation is a vivid example of how assessing the firm's capabilities supports planning for continued family business growth and profitability. 'Take a leap forward, turn Puig into a major multinational player' was the challenge of the advisory board to the four-member team composed of three third generation family members and one non-family executive.

This board challenge called on the successors in the third generation to take time and assess the business' capabilities and the firm's markets and competition to develop a thorough understanding of the challenges they faced. This strategic review explored the company's brands, marketing position and future opportunities. The new strategic plan identified a mission, strategy and structure that met both the business' and the family's needs. The new strategy plan became the foundation for the transition of leadership to the third generation and their blueprint for future strategic success.

As a part of their internal assessment the successors confirmed the value of their team culture by developing a new organization structure to support the business strategy they were developing. The new management structure, termed the 'Team at the Top', creates an executive team of three cousins and one senior non-family manager who serve as the firm's executive leadership.

The new strategy, developed completely by the third generation of successors, expands their international marketing based on targeting selected segments and exploits the company's manufacturing and marketing strengths.

The third generation's seven years of strategic thinking and planning reflects the Puig belief that, 'Each generation develops the business in its own entrepreneurial way.'

Note: Information from M. Wagen and J. Schwass, 'Corporacion Puig', *Family Business Network Newsletter,* **22** (1998, December) 5.

Analyzing Business Performance

The barometers of business performance that a family business requires in order to make strategic decisions are usually difficult to find in standard accounting or management information systems. Uncovering these measures requires a variety of calculations ranging from figuring the Economic Value Added (EVA) of the business, to utilizing the Balanced Scorecard, to determining the firm's capital expenditure investment. Neither the EVA, which calculates the firm's profitability while also considering the cost of capital, nor the capital expenditure investment, which quantifies how much the firm is investing for future growth, is typically included in a firm's quarterly or annual financial statements. Further, the Balanced Scorecard (see *Planning Tools*) offers some critical non-financial measure of business performance.

Once the resulting measures have been tracked over time, important trends can be identified and interpreted. The process is not complex and the insights gained will provide a solid groundwork for later planning.

PLANNING TOOLS

The Balanced Scorecard

Accurate and timely information is critical to assessing the internal capabilities of the firm. Monitoring and evaluating the firm's current performance is an important first step in the internal analysis. One way many families find to focus attention on critical performance variables is the Balanced Scorecard. The concept behind the Balanced Scorecard is that each organization needs to identify important performance measures that support its strategic objectives.

This model suggests that a firm should assess its performance from four different perspectives: financial, customer, internal and innovation and learning. One of the reasons that the Balanced Scorecard method is very appropriate for family businesses is because it focuses on key performance indicators to avoid overloading people with information. Thus, the Balanced Scorecard prevents an overemphasis on analysis, rather than action. Focusing on key information can be very important to family members who are not actively involved in the business and may not have the time or the interest to fully analyze the firm's current financial position and operating performance.

Note: Information from R.S. Kaplan and D.P. Norton, 'Using the Balanced Scorecard as a Strategic Management System', *Harvard Business Review*, **74**(1) (January–February 1996) 75–85.

It is worthwhile to share the insights gained from the business analysis with the family and key managers. Everyone then learns to interpret the performance of the business in the same way. They will all know, for example, that two years ago the company invested in a new sales office in Europe and that the majority of the current sales growth is from the international market. Everyone also begins to use a common language and agree that measures such as EVA or the Balanced Scorecard are the criteria for reviewing business performance and making investment decisions.

Everyone, including the family, will watch critical business issues surface, recognizing, for example, that profitability is falling or that reinvestment rates are declining. This focuses the attention of managers and the family on the business itself – on actionable information – and puts the emphasis on objectivity and rational analysis. It is more likely then that personal conflicts and personal agendas regarding bonuses or dividends will be discussed in the context of their impact on the business' long-term financial health.

Analyzing Profitability

Most senior family executives describe their business as 'profitable', 'increasingly profitable', or 'about breaking even'. They rely on three financial measures, net income, sales growth and the ability to fund growth, as important indicators of financial health.[1] Many are not aware of other more

REARDON FAMILY CHALLENGE

Assessing Strategic Potential

Bob and his management team have done an excellent job of identifying fast-growing markets. Their decision to pursue the Internet components market, however, creates significant challenges because of rapidly changing technology, new competition and the industry's explosive growth rate. The high growth rate attracts competition that can threaten Reardon's continued growth and profitability.

The resources and capabilities that the company needs in the future will change dramatically if they are to maintain their competitive position or exploit new opportunities. Additionally while Bob and the team have a clear idea of this position, it is important that they develop some systematic way to share that information with the full management team and the family shareholders.

They need to assess their firm's Strategic Potential as a basis for making strategy and investment decisions. Some questions to ask include:

- What are the firm's internal capabilities?

- What impact can the external environment have on the firm?

- What opportunities exist?

- What threats do technology and competition create for the firm?

meaningful measures of business performance beyond profitability. As a result, they do not know just how efficient their companies are compared to other businesses or investments. They are also unaware of negative financial or operating trends that may be revealed by analyzing beyond profitability and sales growth.

Most business executives use some variation of net income in assessing and planning financial performance. Unfortunately, this measure only indicates the profit a business was able to generate rather than measuring how efficiently the business uses investments to make a profit. Return on Investment (ROI) measures provide a much more accurate picture of the value of a business for family and strategic planning, but the most accurate measure for overall business performance is EVA.

EVA, better than other measures, discusses the economic return to family owners. EVA is ideal for family firms because too often they do not consider the true cost of invested capital in calculating financial returns. What EVA measures is a relationship between the profit generated by a business and its cost of capital. The underlying principle of EVA is that a company is really not creating value for its shareholders, no matter how good its accounting earnings look, unless it is returning value above its cost of capital. EVA is determined by taking the annual operating profit after tax before interest expense, minus a calculated charge for the cost of capital (see Table 7.2). The importance of that charge is that it allocates a cost for the owner's equity that is invested in the business as well as the cost of debt.

Using traditional accounting standards, there is no cost allocation for the equity invested in the business. In effect, companies pay nothing on what may be the family's largest asset. From an accounting standpoint, it is simply free money. The calculated charge should represent a return to family shareholders that they could earn if their owner's equity was in a portfolio of tradable securities with the same risk as their family business. This return would probably be in the range of 15–25 percent per year. This

Table 7.2 *Calculating economic value added*

Operating profit (no interest but after taxes) $	*minus* **Cost of capital $**	**= EVA $**
1,000,000 operating profit	3,000,000 total capital	
– 400,000 taxes	× 15.33% weighted average cost*	
600,000	– 460,000	= 140,000

* Note on cost of capital:	Bank debt	1,000,000 @ 6% (after tax)	
15.33%	Equity	2,000,000 @ 20%	
	Total capital invested 3,000,000		

percentage represents the opportunity cost of the equity capital invested in the business. It also challenges management to plan for economic value, not just sales growth or profits.

The calculation completed in Table 7.2 demonstrates the difference between EVA and accounting profits for assessing business performance. In the example shown, there is a significant difference between the accounting operating profit of $600,000 and the real economic value created for the shareholders of $140,000. Tracked over time, EVA shows what is happening to the earning power of the business. Whether the ratio is actually increasing or decreasing, however, is not as important as why it is changing. EVA might slump simply because of changes within the particular industry or market. In such situations, management and ownership may want to consider a new strategy to reduce their long-term investment in this industry.

A positive EVA trend is a good indication of a well-managed company. A company's improving EVA usually results from one or more successful business strategies.

EVA can be a very important tool for providing accountability to a large family business with diverse shareholders or non-family management. Multi-generation family businesses often face the issue of maintaining the family's investment and ownership commitment. EVA is an excellent tool for increasing accountability and ensuring value creation for these shareholders. The objective nature of the EVA calculation provides a good tool for discussing management's performance and the benefits of investing in the family business. Planning a compensation plan for family and non-family executives that is based on creating economic value for shareholders will meet the needs of both management and shareholders. The simplicity of the EVA calculation makes it a useful tool that all members of the family business can understand and support.

Analyzing Cash Flow

The business' ability to generate positive cash flow is critical for supporting the company's growth strategies and meeting the family's needs for retirement funding, dividends or stock buybacks (Family Payouts). The analysis of the firm's cash flow will reveal much more than would statistics about the current growth rate and level of profitability. An analysis of cash flow – the uses and sources of cash – clearly identifies the cash available for business expenditure and family use.

Understanding the business' cash flow is critical to developing workable family and strategic plans. It may be necessary for management to support family members who do not have a strong business background in developing an understanding of the differences between cash flow and profits. Analyzing cash flow helps to develop future financial projections and it also assesses operating performance. Many business problems are revealed in an analysis of cash flow. In simple terms, cash flow reveals the sources of money in a business – whether bank borrowing or sales increases – as well as its ultimate use.

Management or their accountants can determine cash flow by comparing this year's balance sheet to last year's and asking a few questions. Did inventories increase or decrease? Have receivables gone up or down? Are payables and debt higher or lower? Such comparisons reveal whether managers are using cash to build a better business or simply to fund the status quo. For example, if analysis reveals that receivables rose along with sales and that inventory held steady, this would indicate that cash is financing increasing sales to new customers. That is a good use of cash. But if it reveals that sales declined while inventory rose, management is not controlling its purchases or production. It indicates that cash is tied up in assets that are not being used efficiently.

During the planning process it is important to assess cash flow at three levels. First, what is cash being used to finance? Has cash been used to finance programs with future benefits (such as new equipment or research projects) or merely to reduce debt (a conservative measure that often has no business purpose except providing a stronger balance sheet)? Second, how efficiently is cash being used? Are receivables and inventories rising proportionally to real sales growth or because of a lack of managerial discipline? Signs of the latter include allowing customers to delay payment or allowing manufacturing lines to produce more inventory than sales would warrant. Third, what are the cash requirements of the strategic opportunities management is considering? An important management action is to decide how to fund strategic initiatives. Cash flow may be sufficient if the new strategy can generate enough cash from operations. If not, debt or additional capital investments may be required. This understanding is, obviously, very relevant to family owners.

Analyzing Investment Levels

The internal analysis of the firm's financial position may reveal weaknesses in the company's profitability or investment of cash flow. If weaknesses exist, sales and profits are probably already on the decline. Developing immediate plans to eliminate them is essential. A thorough analysis must go one step further, however, because other kinds of financial threats, which are often hidden, can seriously damage the company's future fiscal health. These threats can be present even though sales and profit look robust. Ironically, these weaknesses may be created by management's desire to improve profitability through cutting investment. Such firms work to reduce debt. They reduce capital expenditures for new equipment or facilities. They do not develop programs to expand the company's markets. While limiting investment may increase current net income and increase cash for Family Payouts, it will lead, almost inevitably, to a loss of market share and, ultimately, future economic value for the owners.

Alternatively, weaknesses may result because of the family's desire to improve their standard of living. If profit and cash flow are good, for example, they may use that capital for bonuses, dividends, or hefty salary increases. The result is the same as above: without reinvestment in the business itself, profit is likely to slump in the years ahead. The assumption, of course, is that money spent on the business will help to secure a brighter future and that money invested outside the business will erode its prospects. There are three areas that indicate if the business is investing adequately for future growth: capital expenditures, innovation projects and strategic expenditures. Analyzing funding in these three areas provides a measure of the management's commitment to the future and the security of the family's investment.

Capital Expenditure Budget

A useful indicator of commitment to the future is the size of the company's capital expenditure budget or its annual investment for future growth. In a growing business, this budget should be greater than the cash savings that result from depreciation expense (the amount written off for tax purposes each year). Guidelines for capital expenditures vary based on:

1. The type of business (manufacturing, high tech, distribution, or service).
2. The industry life cycle.
3. The intensity of competition.

It is also possible to use leasing or other financial arrangements to acquire assets without directly investing capital. Most growing businesses should have a capital budget 1.5–2 times more than annual depreciation to allow the business simply to maintain its current level of fixed assets, let alone improve that level.

Innovation Projects

Still another way to discern the rate of reinvestment in the business is to count the number of innovative projects underway. These include any new projects that have as their goal increasing the sales growth rate, improving profitability, or strengthening the competitive position of the business. These projects might involve developing an extended product line, testing a new distribution channel, using a substitute material in production or adding salespeople in a new market. Such experiments do not have to be risky or expensive. What is important is that they allow the company to explore new ways of doing business.

Multiple projects of this type should be underway at all times. They are the best available indicators that the future prospects of the business are bright. Management and family owners are encouraged to attempt to quantify and monitor these investments.

Strategic Expenditures

Trends in strategic expenditures – money spent on market research, research and development, employee training and new (not replaced) fixed assets – are an excellent indicator of commitment to future business growth. These trends can be calculated by translating each category on the income statement and balance sheet into a percent of sales. Market research expenditures, for example, may be 1.3 percent of sales. Managers should plot these expenses for several years running and note the resulting trends. If the business is not spending aggressively on new opportunities, these ratios (market research to sales, research and development to sales, training and development to sales and new equipment to sales) will decline. If the business is investing in the future, the ratios will hold steady or rise.

ASSESSING THE FIRM'S MARKETING SUCCESS

The most important measure of the firm's marketing capabilities is understanding the firm's position and performance in the marketplace, knowing the firm's market share and what is causing market share to fluctuate. In other words, it is what causes customers to buy more or less of a company's product or service versus the competition and is therefore essential strategic information. Customer preferences are strongly influenced by a number of variables, ranging from the price and quality of a particular product to special company promotions, such as new product campaigns. The variables that attract the most customers can be collectively described as a company's relative competitive strengths. This section begins with a discussion of market share, one of the most crucial measures of business strength, and some possible ways to measure it.

Market Share

Many managers are satisfied if sales and profits are growing because they feel that these are adequate measures of business health. Yet those interested in a more insightful analysis will want to study what creates strong sales and profit. They will track those indicators as closely as they do the bottom line. In this regard, increasing market share is one of the most important factors in creating a high level of future profitability.

If a company's market share is not only sizable but also increasing, management may expect higher profits in the future, as it indicates that customers are increasingly satisfied with the company's products or service. In contrast, if sales are not growing as fast as the market or as fast as competitors' sales, then the company is probably in trouble and its market share is declining. Unless customers are increasingly pleased with the company's products and willing to buy more and more of them, the company will eventually lose market share and, thus, will suffer a decline in profitability.

Competitors' Growth

Management can monitor the growth of major competitors. While they will not know the actual results achieved by other companies, observable signs such as the number of employees, store traffic (count cars in the parking lot), raw materials purchased (talk to suppliers), or recent renovations are good clues. The company growing the fastest is probably gaining the most market share.

Participation in Fast-growing Segments

Still another approach is to identify the fastest growing segments of the market and to try to ascertain whether the company is competitive in these new markets. A few questions asked of colleagues or suppliers would provide clues to markets that will be good for the long haul. A company should be growing at least as fast as anyone else in these segments, since they hold the most potential. Monitoring such trends will help an adaptable company to increase its market share, especially since many of its competitors will never expand into new growth segments; they are more likely to continue selling only to that segment of the market that they have traditionally served.

Growth of Customers and Suppliers

Finally, managers who want to measure their market share can look at the growth of their major customers and suppliers. If their suppliers or customers are growing faster than the family business, then it is likely that some competitors are also getting increasingly more of the business.

Relative Competitive Advantage

There are several marketing variables that can contribute to a firm's relative competitive strength. A well-conceived marketing strategy based on an analysis of the industry and competition and an assessment of customer needs is the foundation for building a relative competitive advantage in the marketplace. The following list identifies several generic factors that may comprise a competitive advantage. How well the firm performs, relative to the competition, on each of the following factors can help to predict future changes in market share and eventually changes in profitability:

■ *Service:* Providing customers with support appropriate for the type of product they are buying.

■ *Quality:* Reputation, offering customers a higher perceived quality based on differences in product design or characteristics.

■ *Product characteristics:* Design, durability or fashion.

■ *Technical specifications:* Offering a customer products to meet their specific needs; for example, medical products or computer technologies.

■ *Brand:* Offering the customer recognized quality based on a well-known brand name.

■ *Product or service reliability:* Designing product performance to meet customers' expectations for reliability.

■ *Geographic coverage:* Offering the customer convenience for purchasing a product.

■ *Promotional effectiveness:* Communicating with the customer in a way that captures their attention and stimulates purchasing decisions.

■ *Distribution structure:* Using channels to supply the product in an efficient, timely way to customers.

Another important factor in maintaining competitive advantage is the development of new products and services. The rate of new product introduction, as measured by the percentage of sales drawn from new items over the last three years, is a very meaningful barometer. Once this percentage has been determined, it should be compared to the estimated percentage of the company's competitors. If the company's percentage is larger than that of its competitors, it will likely gain market share in the years ahead. If the converse is true, the company is likely to lose share instead.

ASSESSING THE FIRM'S ORGANIZATIONAL RESOURCES

The firm's organizational competency is the final factor in the assessment of the firm's internal capabilities. Every business needs to create an organization that optimizes its ability to generate, formulate and execute new strategies and to implement effectively current strategies. Great ideas implemented by an ineffective organization will not create sustainable success.

Assessing organizational capability requires the management team to explore a wide range of variables. The McKinsey 7-S Framework is a valuable tool for analyzing organizational capabilities and their fit in support of the firm's overall strategy.[2] The 7-S Framework (see Figure 7.2) demonstrates the interdependence of the seven organizational variables and need for internal consistency among the variables for the firm's long-term performance.

It is essential to consider the systemic relationship of these elements when assessing capabilities. A weakness in any organizational element, or elements, will affect the overall effectiveness and performance of the firm. For example, a traditional retail organization with strong experience in operating stores would have a difficult time expanding into an Internet strategy. Without new systems and new skills, based on Internet marketing, the firm will be seriously challenged by the demands of an Internet strategy. The framework can be used as a planning checklist when assessing the relationship between the firm's organizational capabilities and current or planned strategies.

Examining the 7-S model from a social and technical systems perspective shows that three elements (strategy, structure and systems) are more technical or task based; the other four elements (style, staff, skills and

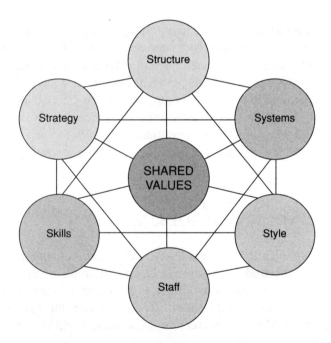

Figure 7.2   *The McKinsey 7-S framework*

Source: R.T. Pascale and A.G. Athos, *The Art of Japanese Management* (New York, Warner Books, 1981) p. 125. Copyright 1981 by Warner Books. Reprinted by permission.

shared values) are oriented to the social or human dimension. Most managers find it more natural to focus on the tangible or task-driven activities of developing a strategy, designing operating systems and creating an organizational structure. The technical elements often receive more attention because they represent the 'hard' tasks of management – what managers feel is their 'real' work.

However, the 'soft' tasks are of equal importance and often represent weaknesses as the business' strategy is implemented. New strategies can be developed in a few weeks but creating a capable organization and supportive culture to implement those strategies requires time and an organizational commitment. Table 7.3 defines the 7-S organizational variables, creating a good checklist for examining the firm's organizational capabilities.

After management has developed an understanding of the business' internal capabilities, it can plot the perceived strength of the firm's internal capabilities on the Strategic Potential Matrix (see Figure 7.1). The firm's management needs to discuss fully and develop consensus whether the firm's internal strengths are high, medium or low. Reaching this shared understanding on the firm's capabilities creates the foundation for identifying the appropriate future business strategy.

Table 7.3   *Definitions of the 7-S organizational variable*

- *Strategy:* The game plan used by the company to allocate resources, meet customer needs and achieve its competitive goals.

- *Structure:* The framework for organizing the company, describing reporting relationships, decision-making and how the various functions or profit centers relate to each other.

- *Systems:* The different procedures, often based on technology, for transferring information, monitoring employee performance, allocating capital, reporting results, compensating employees and generally ensuring that things get done within the firm.

- *Style:* The way the company conducts its business, particularly how its senior management interacts with both internal and external stakeholders.

- *Staff:* People who work in the organization.

- *Skills:* The unique capabilities required of key people within the firm. These skills often form the basis for core competencies, which give the firm an advantage over its competitors.

- *Shared values:* Represent the culture of the organization, defining what is important to the organization and its beliefs about how work gets done. Shared values are at the center of the diagram because an understanding of how we do things in this firm influences all of the other interactions.

Source: R.T. Pascale and A.G. Athos, *The Art of Japanese Management* (New York: Warner Books, 1981). Copyright 1981 by Warner Books. Reprinted by permission.

At that point management can proceed to the second component of the SWOT Analysis, opportunities and threats in the external environment. There is obviously an overlap in the assessment because marketing, organization and finance factors are interrelated to the external environment. A change in market share, discussed in the review of the relative competitive position, is often related to market or competitive changes, both external factors.

THE EXTERNAL ANALYSIS

Founding entrepreneurs typically depend on personal effort to exploit opportunities and overcome threats. As a result, they come to believe that the fate of their company lies completely within their own control. As the business grows and their direct control diminishes, formally analyzing the external environmental forces affecting the firm's future needs to become a part of the firm's planning practices. Unlike internal factors that managers can directly influence, the external environment must be addressed by identification, anticipation and planning.

The external environment is divided into two elements that influence the firm and its strategy – the firm's industry and market and the larger general environment that surrounds the industry and market. Figure 7.3 illustrates the relationship of the industry and market, general environment and business and family systems. The external environment represents everything that occurs outside of the firm. For example, changes in government regulations, the introduction of a new technology or changes in customer values are all in the external environment. Forces and trends in the external environment are an important consideration in developing strategies and in making investment decisions.

A significant trend or force can positively or negatively affect the results of a strategy decision regardless of the firm's capabilities or management's implementation. For example, a new technology such as the Internet can support the growth rate of a retail marketing organization if it uses this technology to reach and service its customers. Likewise, if it ignores the new technology, it creates opportunities for competitors to apply it successfully to gain a competitive advantage and increase their market share.

The goal of the external analysis should be to identify trends or forces that affect the environment in which the firm competes. In his article, 'The Future Has Already Happened', Peter Drucker suggests:

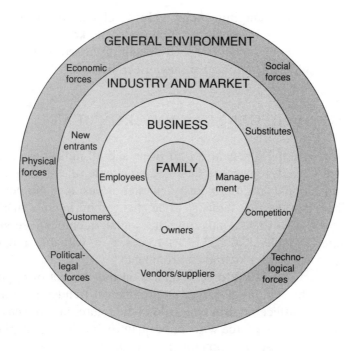

Figure 7.3   *The external environment and the family business*

It is possible – and fruitful – to identify major events that have already happened, irrevocably and that will have predictable effects in the next decade or two. It is possible, in other words, to identify and prepare for the future that has already happened.[3]

No one can predict the future, yet, based on Drucker's thinking, there are known trends and external forces that will affect family businesses in the future. This suggests that successful managers will be those who ask questions about the external environment and, based on the answers, develop their plans accordingly. Examples of questions that the external analysis should stimulate include the following:

- What strategic action will major competitors take?
- Will foreign trade barriers be relaxed or tightened during the next 10 years?
- What new technologies will change the business' marketing or manufacturing processes?
- Will inflation return to double-digit rates during the next 10 years?

■ What effect will changing social values related to spending and consumption have on the business' products or markets?

■ What social or demographic trends are being discussed in the media or industry or trade publications that may affect markets?

ANALYZING THE GENERAL ENVIRONMENT

General environmental forces affect all firms and all industries. They are often difficult to analyze because there are no simple rules for identifying what will impact on a specific industry, market or business. No one could have predicted that the first industry to be changed by Internet marketing would be book retailing. Analyzing the social, technical, economic, political-legal and physical (STEPP) forces is a valuable model for thinking about the firm's external environment.

The discussion of STEPP forces expands on the concept of opportunities and threats by looking at larger environmental trends or forces that may not currently affect the firm but could in the future. In some cases, the specific implications of a force will not be quantifiable during the planning process and may simply be something to monitor as strategic plans are reviewed. Possible factors in the general environment that may affect the firm's strategy are displayed in Table 7.4. A thorough STEPP Analysis should attempt to identify the forces, trends or events that are relevant to the specific business and industry being explored.

The process for using the STEPP Analysis is very similar to the larger SWOT Analysis. There is one exception – an attempt should be made to identify both in-house and external experts (suppliers, consultants, vendors and professionals) that can support the firm's efforts in scanning the environment to identify treads or forces that influence opportunities and threats. The trends identified in the general environment represent important topics that should be considered in the planning process. It is essential that the management team and family ownership understand the impact that the general environment may have on the future of the family's business. A family business in an industry that is being made obsolete because of technology changes needs to understand the consequences on their plans for family ownership and continuity. Additionally, time should be allowed as part of strategic plan reviews to monitor these forces on an ongoing basis.

These external forces provide a good framework for asking questions about the general environment. It is obvious from the type of information represented in the STEPP Analysis that business managers need to review these factors if they are to develop strategic plans that are relevant and

Table 7.4 *Examples of STEPP trends or forces for analysis*

Social	Technical	Economic	Political-legal	Physical
Changing values	Global communications	New economic cycles	Increased workplace regulation	Natural disasters
Changing gender roles	Expanded application of digital electronics	Fluctuating currency values	Expanded environmental regulations	Climate changes
Increasingly democratic organizations	Genetic engineering	Micro markets and specialization	Increased demands for social benefits	Pandemic disease
Influence of baby boom generation	Increased business applications for the Internet	Inflation rate	Increasing government regulation	Industrial or nuclear accidents
Aging population	Internet convergence of communications and entertainment	Interest rates	Regional government relationships	Residual effects of pollution
Immigration		Regional trading alliances		Substitutes for petroleum and chemicals
Ethical constraints	Unlimited computing power	Global mergers and acquisitions	Regional conflicts	Space technology
Pluralistic values		Volatile global financial markets	Changes in tax rates	Ocean mining
Ethnicity	Access to communications	Market economies	Changes in estate taxes	
		Free trade and new trade barriers	Emerging market economies	

effective over the long term. As Drucker's comments suggested earlier, simply exploring the significance of events that have already occurred on the business' future is a good starting point.

The strength of the forces and their relationship to the organization should also be considered because not all the forces in the external environment are important to an individual firm's planning process. Families concerned about continuity of their family business must be sensitive to the pressures and changes these forces may create on their organizations. The dynamic environment of the 21st century makes it difficult to make formal predictions, but identifying forces and monitoring trends that may affect the firm is a valuable activity to improve the ability to determine the firm's Strategic Potential.

ANALYZING THE MARKET AND INDUSTRY

In addition to considering the global forces of the general environment, management must be aware of the trends occurring in the firm's specific market and industry. What is happening with the firm's customers and competition strongly influences the attractiveness of the market and industry to current and potential competitors. The market's attractiveness, as measured by the potential for increased sales and long-term profits, is a key factor in determining where to compete.

Generally, a market is attractive if it is growing, profitable and offering an opportunity to perform activities that are different from those of other competitors. It is important to identify those distinctive competitive activities because, when all firms in an industry compete in the same way, eventually there is a competitive convergence.[4] When this convergence occurs, competitive advantage is replaced by a contest for operating efficiency and overly intense competition results. Many other factors may contribute to a market segment's underlying attractiveness.

Two analyses are invaluable to determining a firm's overall market and industry attractiveness: industry dynamics and competitive advantages. Table 7.5 identifies several factors that are likely to influence a market's attractiveness within its particular industry.

Industry Dynamics

Understanding the dynamics of the industry is important to understanding how intensely participants compete. According to Michael Porter, five

Table 7.5   *Factors affecting market attractiveness*

- Actual and potential market size
- Growth rate
- Life cycle stage
- Buyer profitability
- Cyclical and/or seasonal fluctuation
- Buyer sophistication
- Loyalty of buyers to suppliers
- Fragmentation or consolidation of the industry
- Industry pricing and cost structure
- Industry production or marketing capacity
- Trends in competition, customer behavior or the general environment

forces influence the nature of competition: customer power, intensity of competition, substitute products, potential new entrants and supplier power.[5] An analysis of these industry forces will prompt an understanding of the industry structure and the possible opportunities or threats in a firm's competitive position.

The structure of the industry in which the firm competes directly influences the industry's attractiveness. Industries are more or less attractive depending on the trends in the five forces mentioned above. The essence of strategy is to understand the trends driving these five forces in one's industry and develop plans that will help the company to exploit opportunities, avoid threats and create a sustainable competitive position.[6]

A business can use the Five Forces Model to identify forces that may affect its strategy. For example, if a major competitor is acquiring other firms in an industry, the probability of increased competitive rivalry should be acknowledged in the firm's business planning. If the acquirer is well managed and has financial resources, it is likely that a firm will experience pressures on profit margins and a reduced market share. These realities should be a part of the strategy and investment considerations.

Another benefit created by thinking about the industry is a better understanding of how much of the company's profitability (or lack thereof) is due to industry pressures that are beyond management's immediate control, as well as what forces are actually shaping the future of the industry. The more favorable these industry circumstances and trends, the more bullish a company can be in its choice of strategies and its reinvestment decisions. The more unfavorable the conditions, the more conservative it would be in the future. It is important for family owners to be able to differentiate between industry factors and internal actions that influence profitability when they make their investment commitment (discussed in Chapter 9).

In addition, recognizing that much of a company's profitability is related to external or industry factors has special value in a family business. Very frequently, changes in the firm's profitability are attributed purely to 'good' or 'bad' management. This can cause tension in a family, especially between members of different generations. Sharing the simple realization that other important factors may be at work in any given situation can significantly ease such tension.

Competitor Analysis

Identification and review of specific competitors is always a planning consideration because their actions directly affect the effectiveness and success of the future plans. Management should identify the company's top two to three competitors in each market or industry segment in which they compete. They can do this by ranking each market player (including their own company) by using the Competitor Analysis Worksheet (Appendix F).

PLANNING TOOLS

Analyzing Your Competitors

The Competitor Analysis Worksheet (Appendix F) provides a detailed description of your market and an analysis of major competitors. Competitors' actions are always of interest because competitors' weaknesses create potential opportunities and their strengths need to be addressed in the final selection of business strategy. Monitoring the competition's strategic and tactical actions is an important tool for understanding the competitive pressures this firm is experiencing. It also provides a measure of the effectiveness of a firm's activities. If the competition is frequently reacting to or copying your new marketing tactics, it is a good indicator that your actions are positively influencing customers.

The analysis should reveal some competitors who compete similarly with the company in similar segments, as well as some that compete differently and/or emphasize different segments. Competitors who are similar to the company are its key competitors; in other words, they are the company's strategic group. The firm is most vulnerable to competitive attacks from those within the same strategic group.

Developing a comprehensive competitor profile provides management with an understanding of their key competitors' approach to the market. A few possible factors to explore include the following:

■ *Market position:* How is the firm or their brands perceived by customers?

■ *Marketing strategy:* Do they compete based on differentiation (unique product or services), cost (lower prices and cost structure) or focus on a specific market?

■ *Marketing tactics:* How do they compete (brand names, low price, distribution channels, innovative products, heavy promotion)?

■ *Current performance:* How are their sales and profits? What do suppliers think of their strategy? Are other competitors copying their tactics?

■ *Mission or goals:* What does their advertising or sales force communicate about future intentions and commitments? Does their market position present a direct challenge to other competitors?

■ *Weaknesses:* What internal weaknesses can be exploited?

DETERMINING THE FIRM'S STRATEGIC POTENTIAL

This chapter introduced the concept of a firm's Strategic Potential for developing business strategies. The internal and external assessment should provide management with a realistic picture of the business and its future prospects. Management's experience and judgment should enable them to use assessment data to identify the firm's position on the Strategic Potential Matrix. The qualitative nature of the analysis and the grid used do not require exact answers. In fact a management team that cannot decide and therefore positions the firm in two very different boxes on the Strategic Potential Matrix will eventually clarify their thinking as the process continues. Plotting the firm's Strategic Potential on Figure 7.1 creates the starting point for linking the firm's current situation and its final strategy and reinvestment decision.

SUMMARY

The internal and external assessment helps management to develop a shared understanding of the firm's Strategic Potential. The important outcome for this first phase of the planning process is agreement on the firm's Strategic Potential because this is the starting point for identifying possible business strategies. If the management team, board or shareholder group are strongly divided on their interpretation of the firm's Strategic Potential then they need to stop and reconsider their situation. This may mean asking a consultant to facilitate a planning session or using a strategy consultant to assess the firm and share their findings. A rough consensus is necessary because it is very difficult to complete a new plan if there is not a shared starting point. Family shareholders, also, need to have a consensus view of the firm's Strategic Potential. If they do, they have more confidence in assessing management's strategy proposals to the board of directors.

The next chapter narrows the choice of possible strategies using the Strategic Potential concept. After the firm's Strategic Priority is discussed, seven strategy groups are proposed that lead to 27 possible business strategies. A decision template will be proposed for considering the critical factors that contribute to success with each of the 27 different strategies.

Chapter 9 will then address how the overlap of the family's commitment, the firm's internal capabilities and the attractiveness of its external environment are the three critical influences on the final choice of strategy. A decision-making matrix is offered that relates the Family's Reinvestment with Family Commitment and the firm's Strategic Potential. This decision matrix will guide the owners and management team in formulating strategies that are realistic both from a business and a Family Commitment perspective.

8 Exploring Possible Business Strategies

By this point in the planning process, management should have gained many insights into their company regarding the business' current situation and possible new business opportunities. The internal and external assessments should have provided management with a solid understanding of the firm's Strategic Potential – based on the firm's internal capabilities and the nature of the external environment. The next challenge facing management is to identify possible strategy alternatives based on the firm's Strategic Potential. These strategy alternatives provide the input for the final decision on a business strategy and the family's reinvestment discussed in Chapter 9.

In Chapter 7 management plotted their assessment of the firm's Strategic Potential on a matrix, as in Figure 7.1. This action graphically represents management's understanding of the firm's capabilities and its external environment. The strategy exploration process presented in Figure 8.1 uses the assessment of Strategic Potential as a starting point for thinking about and making strategic decisions.

The three steps identified in Figure 8.1 narrow the alternatives available and link the firm's Strategic Potential to its final choice of strategy. First, based on the firm's Strategic Potential, a corresponding strategic priority is discussed (see Figure 8.2). The strategic priority clarifies the organization's thinking about the broad strategy actions required. Second, using the strategic priority, a related strategic direction can be selected. This decision narrows management's option by focusing on a group of basic business strategies in the strategic direction group selected. Third, management reviews the strategies in the strategic direction group and recommends possible strategies to the board and owners for a final strategy and investment decision. Management makes its recommendation based on an evaluation of the possible strategies using the template offered in Table 8.1 and after considering the specific family business advantages the firm possesses. Each of these three steps is reviewed and discussed below.

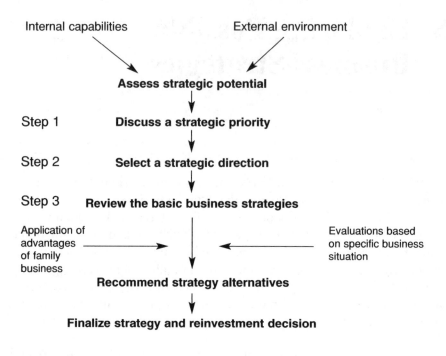

Figure 8.1 *The strategic decision process*

DISCUSSING THE FIRM'S STRATEGIC PRIORITY

Before discussing specific strategy alternatives there needs to be a shared awareness of the limits that the firm's Strategic Potential places on strategy development. Identifying a strategic priority supports this thinking. The purpose of discussing strategic priority is to ensure that the organization's strategic thinking makes sense based on the firm's situation. This can be a difficult process because different generations of the family often have very different assessments of the firm's current position and its future potential.

There are three possible strategic priorities: renew, reformulate and regenerate. In simple terms they represent capitalizing on the existing strategy (renew), improving the strategy (reformulate) or dramatically changing the strategy (regenerate). A strong firm in an attractive market executes a renewal strategy to fully exploit its potential. A moderately strong firm in a moderately attractive market suggests a reformulation strategy to move it into stronger business and competitive positions. A weak firm in an unattractive market demands a regeneration strategy or it will eventually be driven out of business. Figure 8.2 plots the three strategic priorities using the Strategic Potential Matrix presented in Figure 7.1.

The discussion of the firm's strategic priority challenges the organization's thinking on what action the firm needs to take to improve or strengthen its position. A discussion of the strategic priority should leave no doubts about the reality of the firm's situation or which of these three actions the firm needs to take. Consider the case of two electronics manufacturers. One is the eighth largest competitor in a mature market, the other is the second largest competitor in a high growth market. These two firms could be similar in size, financial structure, and organizational skills but they face very different challenges. The following questions demonstrate the differences in discussions for the three strategic priorities:

1. *Renew:* How can the business leverage existing capabilities to maximize opportunities in existing markets? What are the risks and potential returns of high growth? What level of investment is required?

2. *Reformulate:* How does the business strengthen internal capabilities and/or identify new market opportunities? Does the business have a long-term future? Should the firm begin harvesting assets while the business is still relatively strong?

3. *Regenerate:* How does the business with weak capabilities and an unattractive market improve its own position? What are the alternatives to

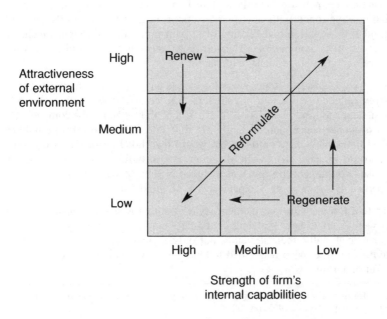

Figure 8.2 *Identifying the firm's strategic priority*

selling the business or its assets? What level of investment is required to significantly reposition the firm?

Renewing the Business' Strategy

All business organizations need to constantly strengthen their business strategy by making improvements, identifying new opportunities or expanding already successful efforts. The ability to improve on a strategy that is working is the sign of a company that understands the importance of exploiting environmental changes and market opportunities.

In 1927, J. Willard Marriott and his wife Alice invested $500 of their savings into a nine-stool soft drink stand called the Shoppe. The soft drinks sold well during the hot summer months, but the business needed a boost during the winter. So the Marriotts added tacos and tamales to their menu. Later, Marriott noticed his customers buying snacks to take on airplanes. This new opportunity became another chance to expand, and Marriott branched out into in-flight catering in 1937. In the 1940s, Marriott opened five new restaurants; in 1955, he entered the hospital food service market; and in 1957, he opened the first motel in Arlington, Va.

The founder's son, Bill Marriott Jr., became president in 1964 and he began to grow the business rapidly through acquisitions, creating new ventures and international expansion. He followed his father's growth strategy of leveraging existing experience with new market opportunities. In the 1980s, Marriott expanded through internal funding of growth rather than through franchising like most of his competitors. Marriott built hotels and then sold them, while preserving the rights to manage the facility.

In the early 1990s, this strategy was threatened due to changes in tax law, which sharply reduced real estate tax shelters. The company was left with a $3.4 billion debt and limited potential for expansion. To regenerate the company, Bill Marriott conceived a plan to divide Marriott Corp. into two separate publicly traded companies, one company that would own hotel properties and another that would manage them. The decision was initially controversial, mainly because two thirds of the debt was assigned to Host Marriott, which owned the properties. However, both companies went on to post strong earnings.

Despite differences in management styles, the two Marriotts' business strategies were similar. New strategies continually emerged after periods of slow or no growth. Finally, their strategies not only logically extended past business activities but they also responded to changing environmental forces and new market opportunities.

Note: Information from P. Kepos (ed.), *International Directory of Company Histories*, 3 (Detroit: St. James Press, 1995) pp.102–3.

SELECTING THE STRATEGIC DIRECTION

After reaching agreement on a strategic priority, the management team needs to begin its exploration of possible strategies. The next step is to identify the strategic directions that are possible based on the firm's strategic priority.

The strategic direction is a grouping of business strategies that are appropriate in terms of the firm's Strategic Potential (see Figure 8.3). Each strategic direction represents a group of related basic business strategies. The seven groups contain the 27 basic business strategies proposed in this book. This step begins the process of considering possible strategies that will support the family's and management's Shared Future Vision.

It is important to note that all firms may choose innovation as a strategic direction. Innovation strategies are 'out of the box', such as creating a whole new market or developing a strategic alliance with a competitor. Innovation strategies may not always be within the limits of the firm's Strategic Potential, but risk-taking managers pursue them anyway.

Figure 8.3 also shows a reduced exit area and expanded harvest and redeploy and guerrilla areas. This reflects the reality of family firms where

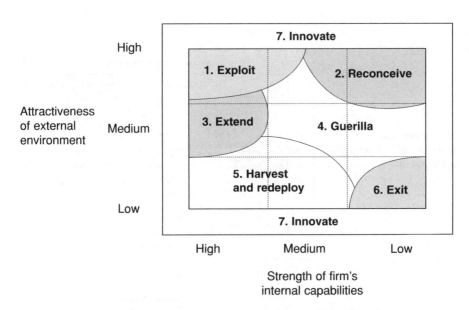

Figure 8.3   *How strategic potential influences strategic direction*

Adapted from: J.L. Ward, *Keeping the Family Business Healthy* (San Francisco: Jossey-Bass, 1987). Copyright 1997 by the Business Owner Resources. Used by permission.

the family is often reluctant to sell the business despite failing to invest or take strategic action to strengthen the firm's position. Often during the transition of management and ownership it is necessary to use harvest and redeploy or guerrilla strategies as a basis for the firm's business strategy.

SEVEN POSSIBLE STRATEGIC DIRECTIONS AND THE BASIC BUSINESS STRATEGIES

The selection of a strategic direction enables management to focus their evaluation on a smaller group of related basic business strategies rather than the entire set of 27. Figure 8.4 positions the 27 basic business strategies on a strategy map based on Strategic Potential. The location of the various business strategies on the map suggests which one might be most appropriate, given management's assessment of the industry and the firm.

For instance, if the industry and market attractiveness is relatively high (say, 8 on a scale of 1–10) and the company's capabilities are also relatively high (say, another 8), then an exploit strategic direction is the logical choice. The exploit strategic direction contains five possible basic business strategies to consider including expansion of the product offering, aggres-

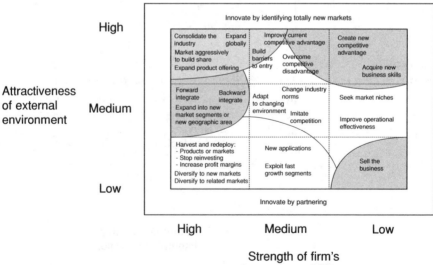

Figure 8.4   *Map of possible basic business strategies*

sively building market share, consolidating the industry, building barriers to entry or expanding globally.

Closely related is the extend strategic direction that includes expanding into new markets, forward integration or aggressive marketing to build share. In all there are several alternatives that are similarly appropriate.

A review of the 27 basic business strategies is followed by a discussion of a decision-making template that considers the critical variables that influence their success.

Strategic Direction Number One: Exploit Strengths in Existing Markets

The first and most aggressive strategic direction is intended for those who can fully exploit the strengths of their company in their existing attractive markets. In this situation, managers will have determined that their business has relative competitive strength and competes in an attractive industry. They will want to capitalize on those advantages, aggressively invest more money in the company, capture market share and continue to grow. The options are:

1. *Market more aggressively to build share.* Increase promotion. Reduce prices to stimulate sales. Intensify marketing efforts with new advertising or an expanded sales force. Do whatever it takes to gain more market share and thus dominate the market.

2. *Build barriers to entry.* Discourage small and potential competitors from realizing profitable opportunities in the market. Such barriers may include threats of lawsuits over patent infringements, long-term contracts with suppliers and customers, changes in product specifications that increase capital requirements for new entrants or the establishment of a strong brand identity. Do not pursue high prices or other policies that will offend customers or distributors. That only invites new competitors to enter the field.

3. *Expand the product offering.* Broaden coverage of niches so that competitors can see no unfilled opportunities that could ultimately lead to a strong foothold in the market. Offer a broad line of models and services in order to take full advantage of business strengths.

4. *Consolidate the industry.* Acquire competitors to strengthen market position and increase operating efficiencies. Successful acquisitions

may leverage brands, core competencies or technology resulting in increased profitability.

5. *Expand globally*. International expansion can take many forms and is available to all size firms because of improved communication and transportation. Many smaller firms are finding international marketing of their products as a natural market extension. Global expansion can take many forms including licensing and export agreements, foreign manufacturing, joint ventures and subsidiaries operating as a new corporate entity. The advantage of international expansion is the ability to leverage the distribution of existing products into new markets.

Strategic Direction Number Two: Reconceive Core Strategies

In the second circumstance, reconceiving a new strategy is required because the business appears fairly weak. The industry, however, seems in excellent health. Managers must then come up with some new ideas to significantly improve the company. They must compete in a new way, thereby gaining new strength. The options are:

6. *Create new competitive advantage*. Find a new way to make, distribute or promote the product or service. For example, if everyone else is selling through retail stores, consider using the Internet to build an electronic commerce market. If strong competitors are making standard products, consider specialty products or services. The weak competitive condition of the business requires innovative ideas to take advantage of attractive industry and market circumstances.

7. *Improve competitive advantage*. Take the firm's strengths and enhance them. If customers perceive the business as a quality supplier, invest money in strengthening those perceptions; if the firm has the advantage of being the lower-cost supplier, strengthen that aspect.

8. *Overcome competitive disadvantage*. If, for some reason, customers do not prefer the company's product or service, identify the chief relative disadvantages – a weak sales force, an inferior product, a high price – and work to rectify it.

9. *Acquire new business skills*. Purchase a firm that is strong where the company is weak – one that has more plant capacity, perhaps or a larger, more effective sales organization. Or recruit and hire people with the specialized skills necessary to strengthen the business. For example,

an international opportunity is ripe enough to justify the investment in staff with global marketing competencies. When it is probably too late for the company to build up the needed skills, acquiring them is the better alternative.

Strategic Direction Number Three: Extend Current Approaches

In the third category of strategic direction, the business appears fairly strong, but the market and industry are mediocre. Managers must extend what they are already doing. This will probably entail either marketing current products in new markets or selling new products to current customers. The options are:

10. *Expand into new market segments or new geographic area.* Take the excellent strengths of the business and pursue new types of customers based on usage, new product applications, or channels, or look for new customer demographics. Geographic expansion requires moving from a local to a regional or regional to national operation. This is a logical progression for a well-managed company with strong management and control systems.

11. *Forward integrate.* Expand by moving downstream in the product flow, enter customers' businesses by acquiring some of them – or go into competition with them. Note, however, that this is among the riskiest of all strategic directions, as it puts the company into new markets that managers may not understand. The advantages include improving economies, full control of the product and opportunities for innovation. This strategy also runs the risk of offending and losing current customers who might resent doing business with a supplier who is also a competitor. This strategy requires tremendous business strength.

12. *Backward integrate.* Add increased profitability to the current business by improving access to raw materials or products at an earlier stage of the value chain – such as making what the company used to buy. Assemble what was assembled for it, paint what was painted, package what was packaged and so on. Like forward integration, backward integration can be accomplished through acquisition of another company or through internal development. But it is typically a less risky path than forward integration.

Strategic Direction Number Four: Guerrilla Tactics

In the fourth case, both the business and its environment are only mediocre. Hence, managers should adopt a guerilla strategy. This situation requires flexible efforts in the marketplace and a consideration of the long-term vision of the firm. The business is successful but currently offers limited potential for growth or creating shareholder value. It might seek a fresh market niche or reposition itself in a new way against a market leader. The options are:

13. *Change industry norms.* Pursue strategies that keep competitors off-balance by rewriting the rules of the game. This might be a matter of altering the industry's seasonal pattern of promotional expenditures, selling through a new channel, offering new credit terms or providing a new package of related services, such as training or support programs.

14. *Adapt to the changing environment.* Here, industry and environmental analysis will have revealed several concerns – perhaps a shortage of skilled labor, rising insurance costs or stiffer governmental regulations. Responding to these threats and opportunities with new programs or a task force analysis will provide the core of the company's strategic direction. The business competes based on flexibility and response time rather than spending money on expensive innovations or pursuing aggressive strategies.

15. *Seek market niches.* The company's weakness will not allow it to effectively compete in the larger market. Managers should identify a few market niches (such as local deliveries, private label production, a particular customer group and so on) that the company can target. These will not be big enough for larger, stronger competitors or they may be too demanding for them. As a result, the business will perform in a relatively sheltered environment, which may help managers to gain sufficient strength to broaden the strategy later on.

16. *Improve operating effectiveness.* In situations where neither the market nor the business promises exciting new directions, correcting internal weaknesses often becomes the core of future strategy. Such weaknesses, revealed through the planning process, might include offering a higher level of service or customizing products.

17. *Imitate the competition.* When a company's market and business strength do not justify speculative investment and competitors are obviously pursuing superior ideas, the best strategy may simply be to mimic their products, use similar packaging, provide the same kinds of services or replicate their pricing and promotion methods.

Strategic Direction Number Five: Harvest and Redeploy Assets

In the fifth category, the business is strong, but the external environment looks very weak. This can occur when a firm stays in a mature industry too long. Such an assessment should prompt managers to harvest the company and redeploy financial resources, that is, they should extract funds from the company in order to spend them elsewhere on new opportunities. The options are:

18. *Exploit fast growth market segments.* Even mature markets, such as manufacturing or retailing, boast pockets of high growth ranging from new distribution channels to electronic commerce. A strong company can identify these segments and decide to enter them aggressively.

19. *Harvest: products or markets.* Eliminate mature products and/or marginal customers. Perhaps planning reveals a need to maximize the return from the current business in order to redeploy funds into new, more attractive markets or business opportunities. Companies may harvest some income by selectively raising prices to discourage less-profitable customers. Companies might also choose to discontinue less-profitable mature products.

20. *Harvest: stop reinvesting.* Stop reinvesting in the company's current competitive strengths. Planning may reveal that the business is stronger than the future of the market warrants. If the company is a high-quality operation, it might consider becoming only average in its product or service quality. If it is a low-cost supplier, it should cease to emphasize that advantage and allow the cost of the operation to slowly rise. It could then funnel the freed cash into new market opportunities.

21. *Harvest: increase profit margins.* Harvest cash from a deteriorating market situation by raising prices or cutting expenses on all products and services. Again, the purpose is to funnel the cash into fresh businesses.

22. *Diversify into related markets.* This strategy applies a company's current strengths to new but related markets. For example, a bicycle manufacturer might begin making stationary exercise equipment, perhaps utilizing the same brand identity or distribution system. A seafood distributor might add a line of sushi products. Market weaknesses require that the business identifies new opportunities where it can effectively use its strength.

23. *Focus on new applications.* Another approach when the business is facing a weak Strategic Potential is to find new uses for old products that do not demand much adaptation. For example, a firm that sells industrial thermostats can refocus that product toward a high-end market in home greenhouses or saunas.

24. *Diversify into new businesses.* Although the business itself is fairly strong, related market opportunities may be unattractive. So, funds may be better spent on new types of businesses. An industrial products manufacturer might move into manufacturing consumer products, or a restaurant might develop a line of frozen foods.

Strategic Direction Number Six: Divest and Exit

The sixth category – the very weak business in a very weak environment – usually includes only one option. Owners must sell the business, divesting themselves promptly before the value of the company erodes even further. They must sell the company for as much cash as possible and then seek out new opportunities. This situation can result from not developing new management talent or from failing to invest in the business. The result is that needed business strengths are simply not present. The options are:

25. *Sell the family business.* A business without good market opportunities and without the strength to capitalize on new ventures is obviously trapped. It can only erode the family's and the company's capital. As a result, the only logical strategy is to prevent further erosion by investing capital in other financial assets, such as equities, bonds or real estate.

Strategic Direction Number Seven: Innovate Outside Industry and Current Business Strengths

The seventh option is open to any firm in any position that is willing to innovate by identifying a totally new market or new business relationships. This category of action is shown as a box around the grid in Figure 8.4, because any firm willing to take risks on a new venture can access it. This entrepreneurial action requires reinvesting in an opportunity that may be unrelated to the firm's current experience. The innovation strategy typically utilizes new technology or new partnerships. The options are:

26. *Innovate: identify totally new opportunities.* Most family businesses were created by an entrepreneur who identified a market opportunity and created a product or service. Sometimes businesses in any of the previously discussed six categories may have the opportunity to grow based on changing markets or new technology. This type of innovative strategy can use technology to help a small or weaker company increase its market share.

27. *Innovate: create a new partnership, joint venture or strategic alliance.* This partnering action can include licensing, franchising, joint marketing agreements, overseas manufacturing, importing or export relationships. This type of alliance can include working with suppliers, competitors, buying groups, customers or any other organization that can create and support value creation.

EVALUATING THE BASIC BUSINESS STRATEGIES

The concept of a strategic direction is an important step for narrowing the strategy decision. Unfortunately, as was discussed in the previous section, a strategic direction may still contain several possible basic business strategies. It is now time to focus the decision on the most appropriate and workable basic business strategies to submit to the board or shareholders for a final strategy and reinvestment decision.

The decision template presented in Table 8.1 can help management to explore the requirements and business implications of different strategies. It summarizes the critical family and strategy success factors for the 27 basic business strategies suggested in this book. Thus it can serve as a discussion checklist to evaluate the various alternatives in relation to the business and family circumstances. The table suggests that strategy decisions are influenced by assessments of the industry, the business strengths, available capital, confidence in management, and Family Commitment. A strategy that meets all the business and family criteria discussed in Table 8.1 has a higher probability of being successfully implemented.

As Family Commitment often evolves or some family members are ambiguous about their commitment, strategic decisions must sometimes be made without full family support. Table 8.1 identifies which strategies can be implemented when Family Commitment is low or uncertain and also those that require a high Family Commitment. It clearly illustrates the impact of family assumptions on the final choice of strategy.

After management has evaluated the possible business strategies against the five-point template in Table 8.1, it is time to consider the unique strengths of the family business and how these strengths can be leveraged to create additional competitive advantage for the firm. For example, if a family business chooses to extend its current market by forward integration, it could create additional competitive advantage based on the family's long-term investment orientation. A family with a five-year investment horizon may be able to exploit a niche market that a large publicly held company could not enter because of short-term investment goals.

UNIQUE ADVANTAGES OF FAMILY BUSINESSES

Whatever the choice of strategy, it may be possible to use the advantages of family firms to create additional competitive advantage. Well-crafted strategies artfully capitalize on every possible strength or advantage. Although it is impossible to list all the unique advantages that any one family company might possess, there are some strengths that successful family businesses often possess by the very nature of the fact that they are a family business. The following section summarizes some typical family business strengths.

Long-term Investment Horizon

Family businesses are in business for the long haul. They do not have to answer to outside shareholders and Wall Street. Instead, if the family is committed they may focus their vision 5–20 years out. They can afford patience. They are freer than public companies are to experiment with distant, future markets and to wait for the eventual payoff.

Flexible Organization

The management and staff of large corporations often waste valuable business time on political warfare and they pay a double price for this behavior. Companies lose productivity while these battles are underway, and management often finds it difficult to respond to change because it is engaged in a turf war instead of developing new products or services. The family business that develops its plans based on a Shared Future Vision can usually react more quickly to changing circumstances. It can add a

Table 8.1 *Evaluation of basic business strategies*

	Industry attractiveness	Business strength	Capital available	Confidence in management	Family commitment
Exploit Strengths					
1. Market aggressively to build share	+	+	$$	+	H/L
2. Build barriers to entry	+	+	$$	0	H/L
3. Expand the product offering	+	+	$$	0	H/L
4. Consolidate the industry	+	+	$$$	+	H
5. Expand globally	+	+	$$$	+	H
Reconceive Core Strategy					
6. Create new competitive advantage	+	–	$	+	H/L
7. Improve competitive advantage	+	0	$	+	H/L
8. Overcome competitive disadvantage	+	+	$	+	H
9. Acquire new business skills	+	+/0/–	$	+	H
Extend Current Approaches					
10. Expand into new market segments	0	+	$	+	H
11. Forward integrate	0	+	$	0	H/L
12. Backward integrate	0	+	$	0	H/L
Guerrilla Tactics					
13. Change industry norms	0	0	N$	0/+	H/L
14. Adapt to the changing environment	0	0	N$	0/+	H/L
15. Seek market niches	0	0/–	$	–	H/L
16. Improve operating effectiveness	0	0	N$	0	H/L
17. Imitate competition	0	0	N$	0/–	H/L

cont'd

Table 8.1 *(cont'd)*

	Industry attractiveness	Business strength	Capital available	Confidence in management	Family commitment
Harvest and Redeploy Assets					
18. Exploit fast growth segments	–	+	$	+	H/L
19. Harvest: products or markets	–	–	N$	0/+	H/L
20. Harvest: stop reinvestment	–	+	N$	0	L
21. Harvest: increase profit margins	–	+	N$	0/+	L
22. Diversify into related markets	–	+	$$	+	H
23. New applications	–	0	$	0	L
24. Diversify into new markets	–	0	$$	+	H
Exit					
25. Sell the business	–	–	N$	0/–	L
Innovate					
26. Innovate: identify totally new market	–/0/+	–/0/+	$ or $$	+	H
27. Innovate: partnering	–/0/+	–/0/+	$ or $$	+	H

Key:

+ = Strong; 0 = Neutral; – = Weak

$$$ = Large amount of long-term capital investment needed and available

$$ = Internal cash flow needed for working capital and available

$ = Small amount of cash flow needed and available

N$ = Does not require reinvestment of funds

L = Low or uncertain Family Commitment to the vision

H = High commitment to the vision

Adapted from: J.L. Ward, *Keeping the Family Business Healthy* (San Francisco: Jossey-Bass, 1987). Copyright 1997 by the Business Owner Resources. Reprinted by permission.

new manufacturing line, design a new marketing program or develop a new business unit. It can do this because a few people make these decisions, not a slow moving corporate bureaucracy.

Strong Commitment to Quality

Larger companies often must seek a standard of excellence through a costly and time-consuming set of personnel and management controls. But family companies have a natural pride in their products or services. It is their name on the door. They are inherently motivated not to tarnish it with poor workmanship or service. Family firms often respond more quickly than larger, widely held companies to customer complaints. Family companies take such complaints personally since they come from neighbors. For customers large and small, a family business can provide that 'personal touch' so important in today's frequently impersonal business world.

Positioning in Niche Markets

Niche or specialty markets often provide greater opportunities than larger, mass markets because fewer players mean more profit. The company that first makes a name for itself in such a market usually can create a barrier to other competitors. The family business is eminently suited to take advantage of such market opportunities.

Greater Investment in People

One of the oldest clichés about business is also among the truest: good people are a company's most important asset. As a result, big and small businesses alike invest time and money in improving their personnel. They offer training programs, weekend seminars, time off for professional or industry associations, even funding for further formal education. Family companies can gain high return from such an investment because their employees tend to develop long-term loyalties and become 'part of the family'. A family company that develops, promotes and rewards based on performance benefits from their relationship with the people whose growth they have encouraged.

Tradition of Innovation

Family firms can install that specialty manufacturing procedure that turns out products at low volume but also at high quality. They can find a slow growth market to dominate profitably while others are looking elsewhere. The profit premiums inherent in this course of action exist only for those willing to innovate.

Strong Organizational Culture

Family businesses typically exude a camaraderie that extends to non-family members working in the business. They usually live in the same community, often working at one location for years. They form strong bonds with the company, as well as with the family. In such a closely-knit environment, people know the standards and know what is expected of them. Those standards – the corporate culture – are reinforced in a thousand ways, from wall photographs and company folklore to special awards. Such clear standards make it easier to establish business direction and get everyone pulling together in that direction, thus increasing a company's chances of success.

POTENTIAL DISADVANTAGES OF FAMILY FIRMS

Family businesses do, typically, have particular weaknesses. Good strategy rests on minimizing weakness as well as exploiting strength. Smaller businesses with less diversity and limited financial resources can be vulnerable to technological advances and market changes. These same characteristics also often discourage investments in speculative markets or new technologies. They make those directions riskier for a small company than for a larger, more financially stable concern. The following list summarizes the potential disadvantages of family firms.

Investment Decisions May Be Too Personal

Shareholders and senior managers often personalize their investment in the company and fail to recognize the true financial or opportunity costs when making investment or divestiture decisions.

Family Relationships May Be Too Close

The overlap of the family and business systems creates opportunities for unresolved conflicts or disharmony in personal life to spill over into the business.

Culture Is Rigid or Closed

A strong culture tends to resist outside influences and to trust its own employees, which may limit their exposure to outside ideas, new technology or recognition of new market opportunities.

Product Lines Are Too Narrow

Their long-term success in one product or a focused market reduces their exposure to new opportunities enjoyed by companies that have multiple products or multiple-market exposure.

Organization Transitions Are Difficult

In periods of ownership transition, there is competition between the family and the business for capital, as well as a period of uncertainty as management transitions are completed.

Business families can often beat these problems by using the Parallel Planning Process to develop programs or activities that address the issue. For example, a family that knows that ownership transitions are difficult for them may find it helpful to hire a family business consultant to facilitate family meetings or coach the family. Families that see their weaknesses on this list should not ignore them. Most of these weaknesses are related to topics that are discussed as the family develops a Family Enterprise Continuity Plan. Knowing their weak spots will help the family to neutralize them by emphasizing strengths.

RECOMMENDING POSSIBLE STRATEGIES

The final step is management's recommendation of one or more basic business strategies to the board, owners and family. If management has done their job, they have considered the fit between the basic business strategies identified in this chapter and the unique situation of their family firm.

The act of choosing a business strategy is, and forever will be, more art than science. To be truly effective, business strategies must be creative, in that they must challenge patterns of the past by using improved strategies and tactics to exploit new opportunities. But the strategic decision process (see Figure 8.1) will, hopefully, make the thinking about and choice of strategy more explicit and more productive.

REARDON FAMILY CHALLENGE

Exploring Business Strategies

One of the challenges that any business in a high-growth market faces is which of many opportunities to pursue. Reardon's participation in the Internet component market could be pursued through many different types of strategic action. Reardon's Strategic Potential indicates that one of the four basic business strategies in the exploit group would best support their future vision. Management's challenge is to evaluate (1) a consolidation strategy based on acquiring others, (2) an aggressive marketing strategy to build market share, (3) expanding their product line or (4) global expansion.

Their management team needs to ask:

■ What strategy is most appropriate based on the capital available?

■ Is the management team capable of executing these strategies?

■ Does the family's commitment support any of these strategies?

■ Which strategy best leverages their distinctive competency in technology?

SUMMARY

The Business Strategy Plan cannot answer every future contingency or event that the firm will face. What it can do is address the most likely events and establish a process that guides the firm's planned actions and its reaction to unplanned events. A well-crafted plan will provide a framework for decision-making and problem solving that is based on a Shared Future Vision. When a new opportunity or challenge is identified, the plan provides the roadmap to steer the firm to this point; but now management will need to reconsider its future actions based on the current situation.

At this point in the planning process, management has done enough to make informed recommendations about one or more possible business strategies. They have considered existing markets and identified new opportunities that show promise. They have screened a variety of business strategies and focused their attentions. They have decided how their company strengths can best penetrate the markets identified, and they have assessed whether any weaknesses in the company or threats in the external environment will stand in the way of implementing those plans.

When the business inquiries are complete, management will need to work with the owners and board of directors to make a final strategy decision and the family's investment commitment. The goal of Chapter 9 is to help the family, board and management to decide on a business strategy and the related investment requirement. The owners or board of directors can then make informed decisions regarding continued investment or harvesting.

9 The Final Strategy and Reinvestment Decision

The logical conclusion to the Parallel Planning Process is securing agreement among the family (or shareholders), management and board of directors on business strategy and a reinvestment decision. The PPP is structured so that the family and management team can work together to create an overlap between Family Commitment, the external environment and the business' internal capabilities.

The interaction of these three most fundamental planning factors creates the business strategy overlap (see Figure 9.1). This area of overlap represents the strategy options that meet the objectives of the family, leverage the strengths of the firm and address the realities of the environ-

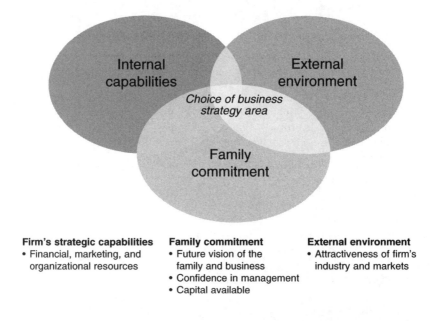

Firm's strategic capabilities
• Financial, marketing, and organizational resources

Family commitment
• Future vision of the family and business
• Confidence in management
• Capital available

External environment
• Attractiveness of firm's industry and markets

Figure 9.1　*The overlap area for identifying family business strategies*

ment. A firm with a large overlap has many strategic options. A firm with a small or no overlap may have no options other than selling or downsizing the business.

The final choice of strategy from the above options dictates the level of reinvestment that family ownership must make in the business. In practical terms the actual decision evolves as the two systems work together to identify actions that support their Shared Future Vision. This should occur throughout the planning process because of family and management linkages created by the Shared Future Vision, as well as through the board of directors' efforts to integrate and enhance the family and business plans. The board's role is discussed in Chapter 10.

REARDON FAMILY CHALLENGE

Finalizing Strategy and Investment Decisions

In the past, the Reardon Family has not paid much attention to the family concerns regarding business strategy or investment decisions. This was one source of conflict because the shareholders did not feel they had any input on the decisions that were affecting their financial future. The Parallel Planning Process allowed Bob and his family to appreciate the interrelationship between family and business decisions and consider strategies that support the needs of both systems.

The final challenge that exists for the Reardon family is to analyze the possible alternative strategies that exist for the firm and the required level of family reinvestment. Reardon Technology has an advantage because their Strategic Potential indicates that any of the exploit strategies could support their future vision for the company. But what are the family shareholders willing to commit in terms of financial investment? Bob's challenge, as CEO, is to evaluate each of the exploit strategies to assess their impact on the family.

The strategy and investment package that Bob proposes to his family must meet both the Strategic Potential of the business and the investment and personal goals of the family. Traditionally, Reardon's CEO would have made these decisions based on the business' needs only. After completing the Parallel Planning Process, he now recognizes the importance of family and shareholder support.

Questions to ask include:

- What is the family's commitment to the business?

- What is the balance between Family Payouts and business reinvestment?

- Does the Family Vision support continued investment in the business?

IDENTIFYING THE BUSINESS' STRATEGY

The business strategy decision process began by assessing the firm and its environment, proceeded to identifying the firm's Strategic Potential and concluded with an exploration of possible strategy options available to the firm. After exploring all possible alternatives, management proposes one or more possible business strategies to the board and to the owners for a final strategy and investment decision.

However the process evolves, the final choice of a business strategy for the family business will reflect, either formally or intuitively, the family's and management's ability to create an overlap between the Family's Commitment and the firm's Strategic Potential. Understanding and managing this overlap creates a powerful tool for deciding on the final family business strategy. Descriptions of the elements that contribute to the final decision are listed below.

■ *Family Commitment*
  – The family's support for the future vision of the family and business.
  – The family's confidence in management.
  – Capital available to fund business strategies as well as family needs.

■ *Internal Capabilities*
  – The firm's financial, marketing and organization strengths.

■ *External Environment*
  – The attractiveness of the firm's industry and markets.

It is important to remember that the strategic variables identified in Figure 9.1 are not intended as prescriptions for successful family business strategies. Rather, they provide a decision-making framework designed to help families and management teams think about the factors that will influence their success. During the family and business planning process, each family needs to test and modify this framework based on their unique situation.

The value of this template is that it creates a structure to support systematic thinking, planning and decision-making. Some family businesses may choose to identify their own planning variables or modify the five presented in Figure 9.1 to meet their family's unique situation.

The concept of Family Commitment has been developed throughout this book as a foundation for the family's support of the business. Until this point in the decision process, Family Commitment has represented the family's intentions of support for the business. The Family's Reinvestment

Decision requires an enactment of that commitment based on funding of the business' new strategy. Demonstrated Family Commitment is the basis for the investment decisions discussed in this chapter. This enacted Family Commitment requires the exploration of three questions identified in Figure 9.1:

1. Is the family committed to the Shared Future Vision?
2. Is the family confident that management can run the company well?
3. How much money are the owners willing or able to reinvest in the company?

The answers to these three questions will influence the choice of strategy as much as the firm's Strategic Potential.

ASSESSING THE FAMILY INVESTMENT DECISION

A critical decision that all family businesses face is determining the rate of reinvestment or disinvestment in the family business. Typically the discussion is framed as balancing the business' demands for capital with the family's demands for payouts (dividends, bonuses, stock redemptions, and so on). As discussed throughout this book, life cycle forces at work on the family and business create the potential for conflicts between reinvesting and disinvesting financial assets in the firm.

Many successful families are unaware of the damaging effects of a failure to plan adequately for the financial requirements of the family and business. Often, family businesses are not aware that funding a stock buyback or retirement plan takes funds that are also needed to grow the business. Most assume that all is well if profits are strong and sales are rising. They think that they can easily afford high levels of personal spending. And yet, successful businesses absolutely require a minimum level of reinvestment if they are to continue to grow and maintain their relative market strength.

This chapter begins by helping the family business to analyze its current priorities for reinvestment and disinvestment. The rate at which the family is currently reinvesting or disinvesting provides powerful evidence of the strength of the family's commitment to the business. This analysis also helps to measure and monitor whether the business is doing what the family intends.

Sustainable Growth Rate

One way to understand the rate of reinvestment or disinvestment is to calculate the firm's Sustainable Growth Rate (SGR) – the capacity for funding growth internally from retained earnings. The issue of how much a business can grow versus how fast a family wants it to grow can spark heated debate among family members. Business growth can be funded in three ways: internally through retained earnings, externally through additional debt or new equity or operationally through improved efficiency in using assets. Undertaking the following kind of analysis, which reveals how rapidly a company can grow internally – without selling more stock, taking on proportionately more debt or changing its operations – is one way to add some objectivity to the issue. It puts in perspective discussions about management's estimates of growth potential, shareholders' tolerance for risk and the family's expectations for Family Payouts (that is, bonuses, dividends or stock redemptions).

Without a reasonable level of profit, a family firm cannot fund Family Payouts nor can it finance future growth strategies. It is useful to consider the effect of these various financial demands on the business during the planning process. The family must realize that business growth depends on invested capital, which provides funding for inventory and accounts receivable, new staff and other assets that will support additional sales.

A simple method for estimating SGR is dividing the annual addition to retained earnings (net income after tax and owners' bonuses or dividends) by the amount of equity the owners have in the business. This calculation estimates the sales growth that continued earnings would fund. This calculation assumes that an increase in sales will require a proportional increase in assets. There are more sophisticated formulas that calculate the implications of the firm's financial actions on SGR, but this model is used here to demonstrate the concept.

Table 9.1 demonstrates the effect on the business' growth potential if profits are used for Family Payouts. This firm is paying $100,000 in retirement consulting expense and $150,000 in dividends. The firm creates an additional $90,000 of retained earnings resulting in a SGR of 9 percent. This firm can grow sales by 9 percent a year with no changes in operating efficiency or additional capital or debt.

Table 9.2 presents the same firm, but the firm is retaining all its profits to support additional sales growth. This firm retains $360,000 of earnings resulting in a significantly higher SGR of 36 percent. In both of these examples, the firms are healthy and their owners' equity is increasing.

Table 9.1 *Calculating sustainable growth rate with bonus and dividend payments*

Estimated sustainable growth rate	=	Retained earnings	=	$90,000	=	9%
		Beginning owners' equity		$1,000,000		

Net income after tax $	Dividends $	Retained earnings* $
500,000 Operating profit – 100,000 Consulting expense 400,000 Pre-tax income – 160,000 Taxes (40%)	150,000	
240,000	– 150,000	= 90,000

* Assumes no change in proportion of assets (inventory, receivables) or in operating efficiency

Table 9.1 and 9.2 calculations are intended to show the effect of family financial decisions on planning for growth, not to suggest what that decision should be. A critical issue in the strategy decision process is: do the family's investment actions support the Shared Future Vision, the business' capabilities and market attractiveness? The family in the second example, Table 9.2, has the potential to double its size in approximately

Table 9.2 *Calculating sustainable growth rate without family payments*

Estimated sustainable growth rate	=	Retained earnings	=	$360,000	=	36%
		Beginning owners' equity		$1,000,000		

Net income after tax $	Dividends $	Retained earnings* $
600,000 Operating profit 600,000 Pre-tax income – 240,000 Taxes (40%)		
360,000	Nil	= 360,000

* Assumes no change in proportion of assets (inventory, receivables) or in operating efficiency

two years, whereas the family that is taking payouts will require eight years to double the size of its business. A firm that has strong capabilities and good market opportunities would ideally want a business plan to optimize its growth potential; whereas a firm with moderate strengths and a less attractive market may opt for more family payouts as a form of harvesting.

Some family businesses will find that the strategic plans they are considering cannot be supported by internally generated funds. They may discover that due to Family Payouts, their annual retained earnings do not allow much growth at all, perhaps 5 percent or less. These businesses will need to improve their operating efficiency (reduce inventory or speed up collection of receivables) or increase their debt load to finance new projects designed to create sales growth. Others will find that their business can support additional growth beyond their current plans. In fact, annual sales growth could reach as much as 30 percent in many profitable businesses, without any changes in operations or increasing the proportion of debt.

One of the reasons that many companies go public is to sell stock in order to raise funds for growth. That option is not open to family businesses that wish to keep their stock privately held. As a result, businesses that want to continue to grow may have to take on a certain level of debt. The important consideration is to understand the implications of funding a growth strategy or a retirement program with debt. The use of debt as a form of capital is discussed later in this chapter.

Families that do not make the commitment to reinvest and instead spend the company's profit in other ways run the risk of unintentionally harvesting the business. They set in motion forces that silently depreciate the business, often in ways that will not show up at the bottom line for years. At that point, it may be too late to reinvest. Analyzing Family Payouts compared to business reinvestment will determine if the family is reinvesting sufficiently in the business to support its future growth and profitability.

Analyzing Family Payouts Versus Business Reinvestment

Another way to study the business' rate of reinvestment is to analyze the balance of the family's investment in the business with its Family Payouts for bonuses, dividends and ownership redemptions. The discussion begins by presenting several ways to calculate the rate of reinvestment. This can be done by examining:

- Ownership returns versus business reinvestment.
- The family business annuity.
- The capital expenditure budget.
- Strategic innovation.
- Strategic expenditures.

Family Payouts

One way to calculate whether the family is absorbing too much cash at the expense of the business is to calculate Family Payouts. This includes bonuses (retirement plans and other family perquisites), dividends and stock buybacks as a percentage of the total sum available for future business opportunities. That total sum available is typically measured by net income before taxes. To calculate the percentage, simply divide Family Payouts by the net income before taxes. Family Payouts should rarely exceed 33 to 50 percent of operating income for mid-sized companies with more than 50 employees. This analysis assumes that the business is profitable.

A family or board reinvestment goal might be that this percentage should decline even as new family members enter the business or family members begin to retire. Such a decline indicates that net income is increasing relative to monies paid to the family. That, in turn, frees up more cash to invest in the business. An increasing ownership payout percentage signals the converse; that is, more and more money is flowing out of the business for family uses. Over a long period of time, this outflow is an ominous sign if the family wishes to pass on a strong company to future generations.

The Family Business Annuity

Another way to determine whether the family is taking out 'too much' is to calculate the family business annuity. This calculation clearly reveals how dependent the family is on the business for its current standard of living. Table 9.3 is an example of the family business annuity calculation.

To make this calculation, first note the approximate worth of the business on the open market; that is, what it would bring tomorrow if it were sold after tax. Let us say $4 million is the rough estimate. That number, then, is the 'endowment'. Now consider what return the family could earn on that same $4 million if it were safely invested in stocks or bonds. Assume the return to be 7 percent, which means that the earning power of the business asset is potentially 7 percent times $4 million, or about

Table 9.3   *Calculating family business annuity*

		$
Endowment	Estimated cash sale value of business	4 million
Annuity	Risk-free return on endowment if invested elsewhere (7%)	280,000
Family payouts	Cost of all family salaries, perquisites and bonuses, retirement	350,000
Replacement cost of salaries	Less market value of family held jobs	(150,000)
Return on ownership	Family payouts less replacement cost	200,000
(Family payout) or reinvestment	Return to ownership less 'annuity'	80,000

$280,000 per year. That amount is the perpetual annuity. Any more than that annuity sum flowing out to the family (in the form of dividends, bonuses, retirement costs, salaries and perquisites in excess of market compensation for family management) means that the business is being devalued. Any less than that annuity sum (given that the rest is invested back in the business) means that the family is building the value of the business and, consequently, the benefits available to future family generations. This family is reinvesting $80,000 per year in additional capital.

The fictitious sale is a good device to test this particular calculation. In the real world, however, a sale is unlikely to occur if the family's draw is greater than the annuity value of the business. Under such circumstances, the family really cannot afford to sell. Accustomed to spending more than the business is truly worth, they are trapped in a negative spiral of consuming business capital. This makes it increasingly difficult to increase the profitability of the business or to build a stronger business for the future.

Families that wish to avoid this trap might consider making an Ownership Agreement to take out no more than, for example, 5 to 10 percent of the market value of the business annually for all Family Payouts of compensation, retirement, perquisites and dividends. This keeps investment in the family in proper relationship to investment in the business.

ANALYZING THE BUSINESS' MARKET VALUE

A review of changes in the company's market value over the past five years is another valuable way to discuss the family's investment in the business. When the company's market value is steadily increasing, the shareholders can be fairly confident that the company's strategy is working. Many family businesses are more profitable than their publicly held company competition and this supports a decision for continued investment.

If the company's value is not increasing, it indicates a need for an additional review of the strategy and a discussion of the business' long-term prospects. A family that is supporting a business with a declining market value needs to rethink its strategy or consider selling the business. For this reason, valuation calculations should be completed on the business annually and included on the agenda for family or annual shareholders' meetings.

There are many generally accepted valuation methods that will provide a guide for the family's discussion of the business' value (see Table 9.4). Different valuation techniques will provide different estimated values because they emphasize different information in their calculation. A calculation using book value emphasizes historical results, whereas an earnings multiple model is more sensitive to recent earnings performance. If the family were planning a high-growth strategy and a possible public offering, a discounted cash flow method would provide a more accurate valuation of future earnings. The rule in selecting a valuation method is to consider the planned use of the valuation information. If the valuation is for planning discussions, the overall trend is more important than the size of the valuation. If the valuation is for a buy–sell agreement or for estate tax purposes, the family's long-term goals and legal or tax requirements are a consideration.

There are benefits to deciding on a valuation method, developed with a professional advisors' support, to use for business, ownership and estate planning purposes. An agreed upon valuation method reduces the chance of family disagreements from unplanned transitions (death or termination) and establishes a basis for planning estate taxes. The methods discussed here were selected because they are simple to calculate and, more importantly, easy to communicate to the family. They are appropriate for beginning business planning discussions.[1]

Table 9.4 *Business valuation techniques*

Balance sheet valuation techniques: The simplest valuation that a family business can use for meaningful discussion is the adjusted book value. The adjusted book value calculation begins with the book value from the firm's latest balance sheet and adjusts it for discrepancies between the assets' book value and the true market value. Assets such as land or buildings and equipment may be recorded on the books significantly below market value because of depreciation or other accounting requirements. Increasing the valuation because of assumptions about these undervalued assets becomes a part of the adjustment to the book value.

Income statement valuation techniques: A more objective valuation technique is a formula based on the firm's earnings. This calculation uses the firm's earnings before interest and taxes (EBIT) multiplied by an earnings multiple. The earnings multiple is similar to the price earnings multiple assigned to publicly traded stocks. The earnings multiple used is a subjective decision with private companies but should reflect the industry and market attractiveness and the firm's relative internal capabilities.

A guideline for beginning a family's discussion of an appropriate multiple is as follows:

8+ times earnings: Attractive market and industry; strong internal capabilities;
5–7 times earnings: Moderately attractive industry; moderate internal capabilities;
1–4 times earnings: Unattractive market and industry; weak internal capabilities.

It is important to reiterate that the family and management need to select an earnings multiple that they feel offers a reasonable valuation of the business based on their experience and long-term goals.

FAMILY INVESTMENT CONSIDERATIONS

Resolving the questions of how aggressively to reinvest in the future is one of the most fundamental, and difficult, tasks for those involved in a family business. If a family misjudges its business' potential, it can lead to family discord – especially between conservative and risk-taking members of the family. Proactively approaching investment questions in a professional and objective manner focuses the shareholders on the future vision and possible strategies, instead of on differences in personal philosophies. This process will also begin to reveal the ownership's true financial commitment to the continued investment in the business.

The family's commitment to the business is a major theme of the Family Enterprise Continuity Plan discussed in the early parts of this book. The family's commitment also has an economic dimension. Family Commitment in economic terms is measured by the family's reinvestment or disinvestment rate – decisions including the uses of earnings and cash flow, whether to add new capital and how to use debt. The idea is that a committed family will support the future success of the business by reinvesting and foregoing current financial rewards.

The Family Business Reinvestment Matrix

The allocation of financial capital is the final step in the family business planning process. As the business grows and generates profits or requires additional capital, the decision to reinvest earnings or distribute them to the shareholders becomes the definitive strategy decision. Business families have six possible reinvestment scenarios based on different levels of family investment commitment and business Strategic Potential: sell, harvest, hold, reformulate, renew, and regenerate. Each of the six scenarios represents an increasingly higher level of capital reinvestment than the preceding alternative.

The Family Business Reinvestment Matrix presented in Figure 9.2 is one means of considering the allocation of business capital in relationship to the family's commitment. According to this matrix, two key concepts of this book influence family business reinvestment decisions: Family Commitment and Strategic Potential. The firm's Strategic Potential is important because it defines the business' reinvestment requirements.

The reinvestment requirements and business tactics for each of these six scenarios are very different. Clearly, each requires a different level of Family Commitment and consequential level of reinvestment. In reality, all businesses need to reinvest and to continually improve their plans and

| | | Family commitment | |
		High	Low
Strategic potential	High (A)	Renew ++	Harvest – –
	Medium (B)	Reformulate +	Hold –
	Low (C)	Regenerate +++	Sell – – –

+ indicates the level of required investment (low +, medium ++, and high +++)
– indicates the level of capital returned to owners (low –, medium – –, and high – – –)

Figure 9.2   *The family business reinvestment matrix*

execution. Family Commitment is obviously important because it supplies the Shared Future Vision that is enacted through the allocation of capital to the business. A mismatch between the family willingness to invest and the business' financial needs creates a difficult situation often loaded with family conflict. A high potential business, with an uncommitted family will lack the financial resources to fully exploit its potential. At the other extreme, a challenged business with a committed family can reposition itself by using the family's reinvestment to strengthen its capabilities.

Figure 9.2, like all the planning or decision templates presented in this book, is a tool designed to facilitate the family's thinking about investment in a more objective and structured manner. Instead of an unstructured discussion of personal views and feelings about investment, the family can use management's assessment of the firm's Strategic Potential, and their recommended strategies, as input for the Family Business Reinvestment Matrix. If there is an agreement on the business' potential and the strategy's financial requirements, the family or shareholder group's only issue is to determine their level of investment commitment.

Reinvestment Scenarios

The Family Business Reinvestment Matrix creates six boxes based on different combinations of Strategic Potential and Family Commitment. Each box is named to indicate an investment scenario. Additionally, there is a symbol representing the capital allocated for either reinvestment or disinvestment.

Table 9.5 illustrates the reinvestment of operating profits – before taxes and owners' dividends or draws in excess of marketplace compensation. For example, a regeneration investment scenario expects to require almost all the firm's available operating cash flow; a hold scenario requires less than half of operating cash flow for business needs and allows more than half to be paid out to the family owners.

Needless to say, the percentages are merely illustrative propositions. They are not empirically proven – that would be a valuable research project. The propositions in this table are also greatly affected by the investment requirements (fixed and working capital requirements) of the industry and by whether the business is increasing or decreasing its use of debt. For example, if debt to equity ratios are declining, then the investment scenario will require an even higher percentage of operating cash flow; if the debt to equity ratio is increasing then debt is funding some of the business' needs and operating cash flow can carry less of the load.

Table 9.5   *Rates of reinvestment for different investment scenarios*

Reinvestment scenario	Rate of reinvestment of operating profit (%)
Regenerate +++	80–100
Renew ++	60–80
Reformulate +	40–60
Hold –	20–40
Harvest – –	0–20
Sell – – –	0

+ indicates the level of required investment (low +, medium ++, and high +++)
– indicates the level of capital returned to owners (low –, medium – –, and high – – –)

Renew and Harvest

In Figure 9.2, the Family Business Reinvestment Matrix, the upper row contains businesses with high Strategic Potential and either high or low Family Commitment. Businesses with high Family Commitment can optimize their growth potential and will therefore require high levels of capital investment (renew). At the same time, they are well managed and profitable so they have the ability to make payouts to families with a low commitment (harvest).

The strong competitive position provides more committed and less committed families with flexibility in determining an investment strategy. Based on Table 9.5, the more committed owners may choose to reinvest 60–80 percent of their operating profits in a high potential strategy such as an industry consolidation. Less committed owners may remove up to 80 percent in the form of Family Payouts. Some capital is retained because most businesses require a minimum reinvestment to maintain their competitive position.

Reformulate and Hold

The middle row of the Family Business Reinvestment Matrix represents businesses that are successful but either compete in moderately unattractive markets or lack some internal capabilities. These are often mature organizations in mature markets, so they are profitable. The high commitment family will want to reinvest to reformulate the business strategy. These reformulation strategies are typically less capital intensive than a renew or regenerate strategy and involve using assets differently or repositioning the firm in its market. According to Table 9.5, owners pursuing reformulation strategies will reinvest 40–60 percent of their operating profits. The low commitment family will pursue a hold position with Family Payouts of 60–80 percent to transfer wealth. The risk of a hold position is that under-reinvestment can lead to loss of capabilities and a reduced market share.

Regenerate and Sell

The lower row of the matrix in Figure 9.2 typically contains businesses in unattractive markets that lack internal capabilities. These firms have the least options and face the most serious competitive threats. High commitment families interested in regenerating their family business face significant challenges because of the lack of resources and capital for reinvestment. These businesses are not highly profitable and usually require investment of 80–100 percent of the scant operating profits. They may also require an additional infusion of capital or debt to improve their competitive position. Low commitment families see selling the business or its assets as their only alternative. If the family sells the business, the business' value is returned to the shareholders.

Overall, the idea of this matrix is to demonstrate the different reinvestment scenarios that result from the interaction of Family Commitment and strategy. Family shareholders and managers need to consider these factors and understand the following implications for family business planning:

- Family businesses that require reformulation need a high Family Commitment or reformulation will never happen.

- Family members who express uncertainty or low commitment to the business should be offered a chance to redeem their shares.

- If the family does not have a strong commitment to the business, a strategy should be developed to sell or harvest the business.

- There is an inherent conflict between low commitment owners and a capable management team in high potential businesses. Low commitment owners are not interested in high levels of reinvestment and, consequently, their actions limit the business' potential. Family or non-family managers who are not allowed to pursue business opportunities that support their career goals will become frustrated. This frustration results in business disputes, family conflicts and eventually the loss of management talent. The loss of talented management reduces the firm's capabilities and affects its competitive position and financial performance.

- Business families can become dependent on the family business annuity (family payments for bonuses and dividends, and so on) and resist reinvesting for the business' future. This result in failing to adequately reinvest in the business means that the future generations inherit a weak business ready to fail.

Increasing Family Commitment

Certain investment decisions can boost the level of Family Commitment, but so can two key concepts introduced earlier in this book: articulating values and developing the Family Enterprise Continuity Plan.

On the investment side, one way to increase Family Commitment is to redeem the ownership of those with low commitment – pruning the family tree. Buying out some family shareholders is an expensive use of precious financial resources. But many families find that the resulting increase in Family Commitment unleashes more proactive business strategies and better eventual financial performance.

If capital is really scarce and 'pruning' is really important, some families choose to sell part of their business to finance the redemption of shares. An important source of funding for this type of financing is the private equity investor. The private equity funds are often backed by large family investors who become 'temporary owners' to fund family buyouts or regeneration strategies.

A less dramatic but possibly valuable way to increase Family Commitment is to have a somewhat diversified portfolio of businesses. With several businesses instead of just one, different family members may perceive less risk and, therefore, be willing to be more committed to their investment. In addition, a modest diversification strategy allows for the future possibility to sell one unit or spin off one unit to redeem some owners and to increase Family Commitment.

Finally, Family Commitment can be raised by pursuing a strategy of controlled growth, which means that the direction of the strategy is clear but the owners and management are more patient in realizing it. Controlled growth can permit slightly less financial resources to be used for the strategy, hopefully in exchange for more Family Commitment and long-term reinvestment persistence. Of course, there is a gamble in a controlled growth strategy – that the increased Family Commitment will not be enough to help the business to realize its potential.

OTHER FACTORS AFFECTING THE REINVESTMENT DECISION

The Parallel Planning Process hopes to make the strategic planning efforts for an emotionally complex family business more objective and constructive. But there are two very common phenomena in business families that deserve special attention because they importantly affect the reinvestment decision.

For example, the analyses of this book have assumed that the business' current business strategy has not been inconsistent with its Strategic Potential as assessed in Chapter 7. In real practice this is rarely true; the business' current strategy is either more or less ambitious than its actual Strategic Potential. The gap most commonly results from a lack of certainty about Family Commitment. Further, the family business often has to change its financial structure or business strategies to secure and fund the senior generation's retirement and the succession process.

Gaps Between Current Business Strategy and Strategic Potential

The possible gap between current strategy and Strategic Potential is illustrated in Figure 9.3. For Firm A, its Strategic Potential (X) is approximately equal to the appropriateness of its current business strategy (O). No adjustments to the thinking about the Family Business Reinvestment Matrix (see Figure 9.2) are needed.

Firm B is pursuing a current strategy less aggressive than its Strategic Potential would suggest. This scenario appears to be a common experience of family firms because of family considerations.

The Impact of Family Considerations

One of the early family business research studies by John Ward, of twenty family firms from different industries and different locations, showed that family business leaders often pursued strategies that were less than their

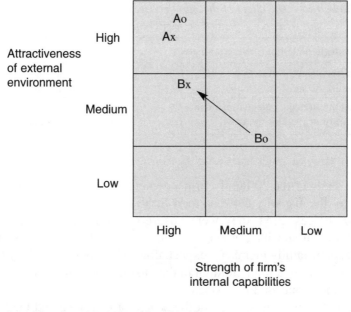

Ao and Bo = Current strategies of firms A and B
Ax and Bx = Strategic potential of firms A and B

Figure 9.3   *Analysis of current strategy versus strategic potential*

Strategic Potential.[2] The study first asked owner-managers to determine the relative strength of their company and, next, to explore the attractiveness of their markets. They were then requested to select their actual strategy from a list similar to the 27 alternatives identified in Table 8.1 in Chapter 8. Much to their surprise, the vast majority of the business owners discovered that they were 'undershooting' their Strategic Potential. They were pursuing strategies less ambitious than their own assessments would justify. Many were simply fine-tuning past strategies. Meanwhile, in their assessments of the actual potential of their situations, they suggested that they could use much more aggressive tactics, such as expanding product lines or building market share.

Based on this research, the most typical family business situation is that exemplified by Firm B in Figure 9.3 – current strategy (O) is less than the Strategic Potential (X). In this case, the family can strengthen its strategy to better optimize its Strategic Potential by increasing its reinvestment, or it can maintain its strategic reinvestment rate but not optimize its Strategic Potential. (An adaptation to Table 9.5 appears as Table 9.6.)

Table 9.6   *The effect of the gap between current business strategy and strategic potential on family business reinvestment*

If strategic potential > current strategy	Investment requirement
Strengthen current strategy to capitalize on strategic potential	Increases rate of reinvestment required
Given the strategic potential maintain current strategy below potential	Reduces rate of reinvestment required

In the study of the 20 family firms, owners offered the following explanations for the disparity between their Strategic Potential and their current strategic choices. First, they were unsure of the kinds of influence that their families might have upon their businesses. They did not know, for example, their family members' expectations of the business. They had not planned how to treat their children in the business or how to provide financially for those outside the business.

Second, they were unsure about the degree of their own and the family's commitment to the company's future. They were unsure because they had not discussed some key issues, ranging from the amount of money available to fund new projects to the interest or talent of the next generation of owners.

As a result of these uncertainties in the Family Commitment – all related to their families – the owner-managers usually selected more cautious, conservative business strategies than their Strategic Potential suggests. They chose this route despite their confidence in their respective companies. The unacknowledged influence of the family had overridden the business considerations. Such a study illustrates that family considerations shape business judgment, whether their power to do so is formally recognized or not. Under such circumstances, the most advisable course is to admit their influence and then turn that to the best possible advantage for the company. Otherwise, owner-managers are likely to misunderstand the real forces at work, which may, in turn, lead to poor decisions and frustration.

This research also reinforces the value of the PPP and its special attention to integrating the family's expectations and the business' opportunities.

REINVESTMENT ISSUES

In the study just cited, the owners' explanations for their conservative course revealed an inability to answer two fundamental questions:

1. Does family uncertainty about the ability to satisfy family needs lead it to conserve available funds?
2. Does the family have sufficient confidence in management's ability to develop and execute successful Business Strategy Plans?

These fundamental family-based issues will strongly shape the final selection of strategy by the family. Uncertainty about either of these issues will increase the shareholders' conservatism and make them less willing to reinvest in their companies. Families that have undertaken the family planning process outlined in this book will have already explored these questions. Their work on Family Commitment and a Family Enterprise Continuity Plan will answer the first question, and the next generation's career progress combined with the management team's performance throughout the planning process will help to supply the answer to the second.

Meeting the family's financial needs is obviously an important consideration in discussing business strategy and reinvestment plans. As explained in Chapter 6, timely estate planning can ensure that there are sufficient funds for family needs, estate taxes and retirement funds for the senior generation. But there is often another critical dimension beyond the actual financial considerations – the senior generation's need for control.

Balancing Control, Liquidity and Capital Needs

Reinvestment decisions force the family to plan formally how to balance the family's needs for payouts or liquidity with the business' demand for capital. But the issue is often complicated by the desire of the senior generation to maintain control of the business. Figure 9.4 examines the conflicts inherent in balancing the conflicting family business goals of maintaining control, increasing liquidity and securing business capital. This figure clearly demonstrates the conflicting goals of providing family liquidity and creating sufficient business capital to support business growth which have been substantially addressed in this book. A business family must, however, also recognize that making a generational transfer of ownership of a growing business requires new financial assumptions about debt, control and compensation. So far, all the analyses have not considered the issues created by the senior generation's transfer of voting control to the junior generation.

Through their early years, entrepreneurs and owner-managers typically reinvested all of the funds generated by the business in anticipation of future returns. As a result, the business consumed all available capital. The

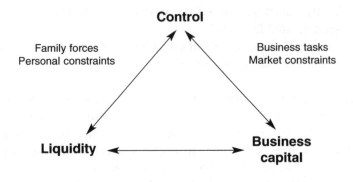

Figure 9.4   *Balancing control, liquidity and capital needs*

Source: F. de Vissher, C. Aronoff and J. Ward, *Financing Transitions: Managing Capital and Liquidity in the Family Business* (Marietta, GA: Business Owners Resources, 1995).

founding generation greatly sacrificed their personal financial security. The prospect of a future payoff made the sacrifice more acceptable. Unfortunately, as the family business grows and more family members become owners, there are increasing demands on the business' financial assets. Eventually, the highest priority for a family is to address the security and liquidity needs of the senior generation in order to support the transition of ownership to the next generation. Unfortunately, without careful planning, that need for liquidity to support ownership transitions may result in insufficient capital for business growth.

Senior Generation Liquidity Needs

The next generation of owners usually must meet the financial obligations or financial commitments to the retiring or senior family members. Typically, the senior generation wishes to accumulate a safe, liquid nest egg that would guarantee them and their spouses a secure, comfortable life. That generation wants to make the assumption that they will live a long life and that they will never be financially dependent on their children.

Second, the retiring senior generation seeks to ensure a very comfortable and generous standard of living through the retirement years. Very often, however, there is rarely a fully funded retirement plan or other investments to provide for such a secure retirement. Consequently, retirees either continue to draw their salary or arrange to receive a consulting fee from the business. They justify this expense by reasoning that they were underpaid in the past and so deserve continued compensation now.

Third, retiring family shareholders with some children in the business and some not in the business seek to distribute their assets fairly for all their children. They want to make sure that no one feels less valued or cheated, and they seek to leave everyone a reasonable financial legacy.

Fourth, estate and inheritance taxes in a private company can be a substantial cost in many countries such as France, Germany, Japan and the United States. If not carefully planned, they can cost up to half of the value of the business.

Business' Future Capital Needs

High levels of reinvestment, therefore, very commonly threaten the real and perceived financial needs of the senior generation in the business. To protect their needs, the senior generation often seeks to retain control of the business to be sure that business strategy reinvestment ambitions do not compete for or compromise their need for personal security. Much conflict between the generations is created in the strategic planning process. To avoid that conflict, strategic planning is actually discouraged. Neither succession planning nor strategic planning is valued by the senior generation as they focus almost exclusively on retaining control. Unfortunately, however, that choice will deprive the business of the planning it needs.

It seems like a vicious circle. Indeed, satisfying the financial demands of both the family and business is one of the greatest challenges to family business survival. Creating a business so strong that it can readily support the needs of both family and business is, of course, one solution. But most families will have to make certain choices in an effort to minimize the constraints that stem from competing capital demands. In order to complete the transfer of control and also to realize the Strategic Potential of the business, they will probably choose one or a combination of the following solutions to create more capital:

■ The family will structure ownership of the business and its real estate or other tangible assets so that they can be split in order to support ownership transitions and retirement planning. This allows the business and its related profit stream to be sold or gifted to the next generation of family members, while the other assets and their associated rents are

used to support the senior generation or transferred to the next generation of family members not involved with the business.

■ The business may take on more debt. Increasing the amount of debt can
serve one of two purposes. The business can go into debt in order to
finance new strategic developments, or the debt may be used to buy out
the previous generation of shareholders to help them to finance their
estate plans and personal retirement needs. Debt used to retire the
ownership of parent generations and pass control to successors within
the family can be accurately described as a leveraged buyout between
the generations.

■ The business may divest itself of one part of the business. In effect, the
successors choose to shrink the business for a while in order to fund the
buyout of the senior generation and thereby defer addressing the full
Strategic Potential for the business.

Discussing the senior generation's needs for liquidity and control demonstrates the inevitable interdependence between family business succession planning and strategic planning. Because the issues of succession
planning – especially the senior generation's capacity to let go of control
of the business – are so complex, they are beyond the scope of this book.
However, it is important to point out in this discussion on strategic planning how some family emotional uncertainties do powerfully affect the
strategic planning process. While the Parallel Planning Process does not
attempt to resolve all of these emotional issues, it does help to put them
into focus and it does attempt to point out their effects on the final choice
of strategy and reinvestment decision.

PLANNING TOOLS

Making Your Own Business Strategy Plan

Appendix G: A sample Business Strategy Plan is an example of how the
Reardon family might finalize their business and investment strategy. This plan
is not full of facts or numbers but, rather, it explains their firm's values, vision,
Strategic Potential, the business strategy and the tactics they will pursue.

SUMMARY

The future strength of the family business depends on continued financial reinvestment in it. Profitable growth is a result of developing strengths and minimizing weaknesses. It is achieved when a firm is developing the right customer strategies and allocating financial resources to markets that provide the best return. An important task for family shareholders is to analyze how the company is building its long-term profits, whether it is through marketing momentum, creating new customers, or cutting long-term reinvestment. Investment typically includes capital expenditures for new equipment or facilities, research and development, training and development and marketing (for such activities as new products, increased sales forces, or customer research).

The longer family members want the business to live and the more prosperity they want to enjoy in the years ahead, the higher their rate of reinvestment must be. Yet, as we discussed earlier, the converse is often the reality. The longer business owners live, the lower their reinvestment rates are likely to be. Instead they typically choose to take out money to satisfy their own needs, as well as those of their families and other stakeholders. Unfortunately, many families, especially those with profitable businesses, are unaware that they are making the family comfortable at the expense of the business.

Business families need to be alert to early warning signs, including the following:

- Declining profitability.
- Inefficient use of cash.
- Cash flow problems.
- Decline in business capabilities or increase in weaknesses.
- Declining number of strategic experiments.
- Declining reinvestment in marketing, equipment, research and training.
- Declining valuation of the company.
- Declining Economic Value Added.

All the above are the early warning signs, telling a family that it may need to reconsider its financial and business plans. For some families, these warning signs may indicate that it is time to harvest or divest itself of the business. Perhaps a family has concluded that the future of the business is bleak or even hopeless for reasons beyond its control. If that is the case and the family still wants to find a long-term prosperous role for itself in business, the family should harvest or sell the business and seek out other ventures in which to invest. However, if the family concludes that the business has a satisfactory future, reinvesting and Strategic Planning will help to take it where it wants to go. Divesting clearly compromises the future vitality of the family business.

None of these issues can be decided easily. They require a certain amount of study, forethought and planning in the formal sense of the word. The PPP provides a methodology by which the family and management can together decide whether to reinvest in or disinvest from the company.

The final chapter of this book explores the role that the business' board of directors can play to support and enhance the PPP. Ensuring effective governance, as discussed in Chapter 6, is a fundamental responsibility of family ownership.

Part IV

Integrating Family and Business Plans

10 The Role of the Board in Family Business Planning

The choice of strategy is one of the most profound decisions for any business. For a family business, as discussed throughout this book, the decision is even more complex and more significant. For the welfare of the business represents not only most of their financial resources and security, but also their reputation and values as a family. Hence the special need to integrate the family's interests and the business' interests in the strategic planning process. Without the family's commitment to the business, the business' strategies will never reach fruition.

The Parallel Planning Process integrates and balances the family's and the business' interests. It promotes a continuous, interdependent dialogue between business management and family ownership around the issues of family and business continuity.

But the most committed and progressive of business families augment this planning dialogue with the benefits of a third perspective: a board of directors, including several independent, outside directors. An effective board integrates and enhances the PPP in two fundamental ways. The board strives to ensure that the communications and content of management's views and the family's views are well heard and understood by the other. In addition, the strong outside directors bring unique and well-experienced questions and comments to the process. (For more on the make-up and workings of effective boards, see the work by Neubauer and Lank[1] and Ward.[2])

This chapter will both briefly summarize the family business strategic planning process developed throughout this book, but also illustrate how an effective board can strengthen that process. The board helps the owning family and management to affirm their commitment to business continuity. It also helps the family to feel solid with its Family Enterprise Continuity Plan. And, the board can bring great value to management's development of the Business Strategy Plan.

AFFIRMING FAMILY AND STRATEGIC COMMITMENT

Many families draw on their boards as they develop and articulate their core values and Family Business Philosophy. Identifying family values by asking only the family often lacks insight into the ways in which the family is most distinct in its beliefs and principles. Independent directors can see the family's history and behaviors through fresh and objective eyes. They can challenge the family to draft a values statement and a commitment statement that has more richness and particulars. When it does, those statements are more compelling and more gratifying for the owning family. Their commitment to the business and what it represents is more meaningful and stronger.

The board also can play a helpful role as management explores its long-term goals and its management philosophy. The board can challenge management to be more focused in their view of the business and to be more realistic and precise in their long-term goals. As important as any role for independent directors is to ask challenging, thought-provoking questions of management. When they do, good management teams appreciate the sharpening of their own thinking.

Finally, integrating the board into these early phases of the PPP can provide an excellent forum for family ownership representatives and management leadership to confirm a Shared Future Vision. Having each party supported in their understanding of the other's views helps to assure a full hearing and confident commitment. And, when each party acknowledges their support of the Shared Future Vision in the audience of the board, everyone's commitment is firmer.

SUPPORTING THE FAMILY ENTERPRISE
CONTINUITY PLAN

Families with independent directors who genuinely care about the family's growth and welfare are most fortunate. Probably no resource can objectively support a family's needs more than an effective board.

As the family discusses family participation the board helps in many, very important ways. The directors can serve as a valuable sounding board for family thinking as it develops its Family Agreements. Many families use independent directors to help check their thinking as they discuss Family Agreements. They write a draft agreement and ask the board for input before finalizing their agreements. Doing so helps to assure that the business perspective is well considered, without the possible concern that management's views on the matters may be biased by their interests.

Chapter 4 also tells of the role of family meetings and Fair Process in the family planning process. One special contribution that boards with independent directors provide is a role model for the objective decision-making process. The openness and vulnerability that this requires is a great endorsement of Fair Process. It is also encourages the family to formalize their governance structures to complement the board.

To help take advantage of the board's enhancement of the feeling of Fair Process, families can invite the independent directors to come to family meetings and become personally known to the family members. Familiarity between the independent directors and the family owners can also be promoted by sharing meeting agendas and minutes. Another simple technique is scheduling some family and board meetings for the same day. The family or shareholders meet in the morning, followed by a lunch with the board, and then the board meets in the afternoon. The shared lunch creates an opportunity for family and board interaction within the context of family and business governance activities.

As the family prepares the next generation for management and leadership, the board can play many helpful roles. Directors can be mentors for the next generation as they progress in their careers. Directors can help to provide networks of contacts for outside work and life experience. The board can offer an objective perspective on family compensation policies and decisions. And, perhaps most valuably, the board can provide independent and respected feedback to family members on their job performance and personal development.

The board is also an important player in the management succession process. One of the board's generic functions is to work with the CEO to ensure that a qualified successor is being developed. An independent board that is actively involved in the succession process can make succession decisions that are difficult or impossible for family members to make. A board that is known and respected by the family makes these decisions easier to accept and can reduce unhealthy rivalry in the family.

Addressing the future ownership and estate plans of a family, as discussed in Chapter 6, is often the most difficult of family decisions. A trusted board serves as a catalyst and source of encouragement for the family to face these decisions. The board also offers a powerful symbolic contribution; the mere existence of a board with independent directors demonstrates a commitment to professionalism. Independent directors also exemplify the family's commitment to practicing stewardship. When a family goes through the effort to build an independent, outside board and voluntarily shares accountability with it, care for the interests of others and for the future of the business is reinforced to all.

CONTRIBUTING TO THE BUSINESS STRATEGY PLAN

Family business managements with strong boards have a special advantage. Experienced outside directors provide creativity and a fresh perspective to the strategic thinking and formulation processes. Their independent view can be particularly helpful during management or ownership transitions. Family-owned businesses know that the resulting decisions can be made with long-term performance in mind. The board can also provide stability and continuity in times of family or management turbulence.

As management does its SWOT Analysis, as described in Chapter 7, a good board adds distinct value. Wise management will share the preliminary results of their internal capabilities assessment with the board. It is a well-accepted principle of strategic planning that management teams have a tremendous temptation to overappreciate the company's strengths and underappreciate its weaknesses. This phenomenon comes up in both the capability analysis and in competitive analysis.

The board also strengthens management's efforts to scan the external environment as it works to determine the business' Strategic Potential. Directors with diversity and breadth of experience bring new understanding of changes in the general environment. They also may have personal experience in how external trends may influence the business.

In addition, the outside view from independent directors also stretches management's thinking on the definition of the industry and of the relevant competition. All the analysis in this book presumes that the industry boundaries are clear to all. That is less and less true in these days of converging industries and rapid changes in technology. The independent directors have the best view of whether management has the most accurate sense for the parameters of industry and market analysis. An experienced board can ask tough questions to challenge management's assumptions and help them to look at the business in new ways.

Chapter 8 is a relatively descriptive identification of available strategic options. But the chapter also emphasizes how management can augment the fairly mechanical choice of strategy provided by customizing strategy to creatively exploit special family business competitive advantages and avoid particular family business disadvantages. Here the board can again be helpful.

A well-run board meeting with a diverse group of experienced independent directors is a very creative forum. The variety of thinking and the brainstorming environment in the boardroom easily stimulates new insights for final strategic choice and formulation. The final choice of strategy and the owning family's reinvestment decision close the book in

Chapter 9. The board again can help. An independent board is the most logical group to assist in the development and monitoring of the sophisticated financial and reinvestment analysis tools outlined in the chapter. As emphasized, these analytical tools require wise subjectivity to apply. Directors aid by assisting the family to feel confident in their attitudes about risk and in their interpretation of the reinvestment rate calculations.

In specific, the board is the most knowledgeable group to explore the appropriate debt to equity ratio for a particular business and a particular family. In addition, the board has the best vantage to decide what business valuation approach is most appropriate for the family's purposes.

This chapter closes with the critical recognition that the insecurities of 'letting go' by the senior generation can disrupt all the rational analyses generated by the PPP. Here again, an independent board can make a special contribution. Often the only people who can help the senior generation to face the ambivalence and pains of succession are trusted board members.

SUMMARY

This closing chapter attempts to summarize the book and to illustrate how an effective independent board of directors can add special value to the PPP. The board adds a third dimension to the integrated dialogue between the business' management and the family owners.

As business families become older and larger and include more family members in ownership, the PPP becomes more critical to strategic planning. There is more and more reason to work conscientiously and explicitly to recognize the distinct perspectives of ownership and management and to integrate those perspectives. That is the purpose of this book.

The PPP provides a comprehensive framework to guide both management and the family in their study of their interests and their commitment for continuity of the family business. Such a framework helps both better understand their roles and to appreciate the functions of each other. As the complexity of the overall business environment compounds the special challenges to family ownership and harmony grows, effective planning becomes more and more important.

The results of planning for a family business are not, of course, predetermined. For most, this book presumes that planning – especially the PPP – will sharpen the choice of strategy and strengthen the family's commitment to it. If so, the increased ownership reinvestment into the business will enhance the chances for success of the strategy and the long-term continuity of the family's business.

For some families, the PPP will lead to a different, but perhaps equally appropriate, result. Some families will learn more conclusively and comfortably that family business continuity is not the best goal for them. The lack of Family Commitment or the lack of business potential may preclude continuity.

For others, the PPP will help them to realize that potential exists and that commitment is for some family members, but not all. They may choose to strengthen commitment by providing ownership redemption opportunities for those less interested. Coming to that conclusion pro-actively and gracefully strengthens the chances for both business success and family harmony.

The board of directors, properly designed and led, enhances the strategic planning process. It affirms the family's and management's philosophies, goals, values and commitments. It reinforces and strengthens the family's agreements and plans. It provides creativity and objective perspective to management's strategic thinking.

Most importantly, the board represents and enhances the two most important attitudes of successful business owning families: stewardship and Fair Process. If ownership acts as stewards and if the family feels that processes are fair, the full potential and benefit of family and business planning are realized. Families that respect both stewardship and Fair Process will find the PPP an invaluable tool and worthwhile adventure.

Appendices

APPENDIX A: A FAMILY BUSINESS ASSESSMENT

Use this checklist as a guide to review important family business topics from the many different perspectives of family business stakeholders. Using it as a systems assessment will help you to identify family and business planning themes that are relevant to your family business situation. The value of doing this exercise is that it will build awareness of some of the opportunities available to your family to improve business performance and strengthen family relationships.

Business Situation

1. Do we have an ongoing planning process to address the 'strategic issues' facing the business (that is, changing markets, new products, new technologies, new marketing channels, new opportunities)?
2. Are decision-making and management actions influenced by the planning process?
3. Do we actively spend time 'getting close to customers and suppliers' to learn what is important and changing in our industry and market?
4. Are we marketing more aggressively than our competition?
5. Are we entrepreneurial in our management approach; that is, are we encouraging innovation and new ideas and taking risks and happily making some small mistakes?
6. Are we reinvesting capital in growing the business rather than harvesting?
7. Is the business profitable and growing enough to support the family in the future?
8. Are we outperforming the industry on key performance measures (for example, sales growth rate, market share, sales per employee, EVA)?
9. Are we efficiently managing the business' resources (cash, accounts receivable, inventory, labor costs) at industry standards or better?
10. Do we have consistent policies and expectations for all employees?
11. Do we set challenging yet attainable objectives for our employees?
12. Do we evaluate people based on measurable results and their contribution to the business?
13. Do people think we listen to our employees, ask their opinions and actively consider their suggestions?
14. Do we articulate a vision and goals for the business and hold our family and ourselves accountable?

The Role of the Senior Generation of Shareholders and Managers

1. Are we committed to family management and ownership succession? Is it a goal that influences behavior?
2. Do we have personal financial security after retiring from full-time employment with the business?

3. Have we identified a successor and shared the decision with key stakeholders? Have we announced a date for the transition in leadership?
4. Do we have a new challenge or interests that will keep us satisfied so we do not have to go back to the business?
5. Are we willing to accept the loss of personal control in delegating decisions and authority to the next generation?
6. Are we still willing to share new business risks to support the next generation's plans?
7. Do we share financial information and business goals with the family members?
8. Do we know the EVA performance for the family business?
9. Are our Business Vision and Family Vision aligned and mutually supportive?
10. Do we have an active board of directors? Are there any outside board members?

Family Participation

1. Does the family know the Family Agreements regarding employment and careers in the family business? What are the qualifications for an entry level position?
2. Do we offer qualified family members an existing job to begin their careers?
3. Are our most business-competent children in the most responsible positions?
4. Do we pay family members what their job is worth on the open market?
5. Do we have procedures to formally and objectively review and reward family member performance?
6. How do we balance control (governance) between management and owners?
7. Do we keep all family members fully informed of financial and estate decisions and arrangements?
8. Do we have Ownership Agreements covering liquidity and stock sales?
9. Do we have a family council or a regular schedule for family meetings?

Successor(s) and Next-generation Development

1. Are the possible successors personally motivated about working for the family business?
2. Is the successor group encouraged to get outside business experience to learn new ideas and develop self-confidence that is based on successful performance?
3. Do we have a clear personal and career development program for members of the successor group?
4. Is our successor group being taught and mentored by someone other than other family members?
5. Do the candidates for senior management have an opportunity to manage a profit center and participate in the long-range planning process?

6. Is our next generation continuing to be educated through university, industry or other personal development opportunities?
7. Are we purposefully teaching the next generation about our history, core values, vision, relationships, structure and planning?
8. Does the next generation have outside-of-the business opportunities for leadership and participation (for example, philanthropy, family, community)?
9. Does our next generation have a Shared Future Vision that supports their commitment to the family business – one that sustains them when things get tough?
10. Does our next generation have an opportunity to be with peers from other family businesses to share interests and concerns?

The Role of the Family

1. Does the family perceive the next generation and specifically the successor(s) as enthused, stimulated and challenged by the business?
2. Does the family value careers equally – in or out of the family business?
3. Do family members experience 'the family' as overly controlling or demanding?
4. Do family members believe that participation in the family business is a responsibility?
5. Does the family believe that owning a business together is valuable to the family?
6. Does the family actively teach in-laws and younger family members about the business – especially if they do not work for the business?
7. Does the family work to protect family and social time from intrusion by the business?
8. Does the family teach business values related to saving, consuming, sacrifice and investment to its young members?
9. Does the family have the means for and experience in resolving conflict?
10. Does the family review and update Family Agreements regarding employment, ownership and participation for family members?
11. Does the family have a successor to 'Mom' (that is, whoever has fulfilled the role of 'Chief Emotional Officer')?
12. Does the family have a clear understanding of the relationship between the family and the business (that is, a Family Business Philosophy)?
13. Does the family practice 'Fair Process' in decision-making and planning?

APPENDIX B: FAMILY BUSINESS COMMUNICATION QUESTIONNAIRE

Part I: Family Business Issues

All families have issues or conflicts that affect the quality of their family and business relationships. Families sometimes avoid addressing these topics because of the discomfort associated with discussing issues that may lead to hurt feelings or direct conflict. Unfortunately, not dealing with conflict reinforces avoidance behaviors and allows small issues to accumulate until they grow into large problems.

The following family and business issues inventory will help to identify topics that may require additional discussion and exploration by your family. The individual responses may vary significantly because of different perceptions held by family members. This is good because it helps the family to review differences on a proactive rather than reactive basis.

This exercise is designed to stimulate thinking and help the family to decide if additional work on the family's communication processes is required. Many families will use outside help to facilitate discussion of challenging issues or as a basis for team building activities.

For each topic below, check the box that best reflects YOUR assessment of your family's discussion of the topic.

Discussion topics	Needs discussion			Well discussed	
	1	2	3	4	5
Career expectations					
Money					
Difficult family relationships					
Family 'secrets'					
Love/feelings for each other					
Handling conflict					
Past actions or injuries					
Management practices					
Balancing career and personal lives					
Fairness					
Family rivalries					
Differing communication styles					
Quality of communication					

Appendices

	Needs discussion			Well discussed	
	1	2	3	4	5
Personal behavior/conduct					
Business policies					
Family leadership					
Business leadership					
Wealth					
Stewardship (care of family assets)					
Risk taking					
Family responsibilities:					
– To parents					
– To siblings					
– To extended family					
– To in-laws					
Decision-making					
Inheritance					
Other: _____					

Review together your family's individual responses to the previous activity and identify the topics or issues that are difficult for your family to discuss. Write these topics in the box below and during your next family meeting or discussion, explore the most serious topics in depth. Work continually to improve family communications and sharing about these difficult issues.

Most difficult topics	Reason for difficulty

Part II: Addressing Ongoing Family Stress or Conflict

Many families experience a pattern of ongoing conflict and stress caused by individual or family behaviors. There is no formula for the proper amount of tension in a specific family system, but frequent conflict because of unhealthy or inappropriate individual or group behaviors can create unnecessary tension within the family. Review the following checklist of behaviors to determine if there is an existing problem that may require additional action, such as intervention by an outside family business consultant or professional.

Individual or family behavior	✓
Constant arguments	
Referral to old disputes or hurts	
Deliberately hurtful actions	
Unwillingness to discuss business activities	
Personal criticism or attacks	
Unexplained decline in work performance	
Chemical abuse by a family member	
Family or business 'secrets'	
Stress from work or family demands	
Exclusion of family members from social events	
Intense sibling or other family rivalry	
Marital problems	

Part III: Family Communication Patterns

How you communicate is often as important as the message you communicate. Examining your family members' communication styles may be an important step to improving your effectiveness in understanding and working with the family. This exercise is designed to help family members assess individual communication styles and receive feedback from each other. The goals of this exercise are, first, to consider how your communication style affects your effectiveness and, second, to identify steps for improvement.

Communication style assessment

Communication skills	Needs work			Very good	
	1	2	3	4	5
Listens without judging					
Expresses personal needs					
Willing to consider new information					
Treats others with respect					
Encourages others to share ideas					
Discusses sensitive issues					
Takes ownership for ideas (I feel…)					
Creates family trust					
Considers others' feelings					
Handles conflict well					
Supports other family members					
Does not take control of discussions					

Part IV: Improve Individual and Family Communication

After each family member has completed his or her individual assessment, discuss the group's reactions to each individual's responses. The discussion should focus on your observations about each family member's communication style and its effect on you and the family. The group should identify in the grid below at least one constructive action for each family member that will contribute to improving the family's overall communication effectiveness.

Communication goals

Family member	Planned actions

APPENDIX C: EXPLORING FAMILY BUSINESS PHILOSOPHY QUESTIONNAIRE

The Family Business Philosophy Questionnaire is composed of two sets of questions: Part A: Business Issues and Part B: Family Issues. Each family member should complete and score the questionnaire based on his or her individual responses. There are no right or wrong answers. The most important outcome of this exercise is to encourage family members to share their beliefs about the family and the business and how these should relate to each other.

A. Business Issues

1 Are you generous with shareholders in providing them with liquidity and dividends?	1	2	3	4	5	Or do you favor retention of capital in the business?
2 If a shareholder wants to redeem, does the share valuation formula provide a high price?	1	2	3	4	5	Or do you seek to keep shares at a low value?
3 Does your business focus on current profitability?	1	2	3	4	5	Or more on long-term growth?
4 Do you prefer a few diverse businesses?	1	2	3	4	5	Or one focused business?
5 Is your business mostly domestic?	1	2	3	4	5	Or are you more global?
6 Does your business prefer public privacy?	1	2	3	4	5	Or see visible public relations as important?
7 Do you prefer the decision-making speed of a private company?	1	2	3	4	5	Or the discipline and accountability of public ownership?
8 Do you do business with relatives who are suppliers or vendors or advisors?	1	2	3	4	5	Or prefer a strict no conflicts of interest policy?
9 Does your company regard loyalty highly?	1	2	3	4	5	Or, more so, celebrate achievement and merit?
10 Do you offer non-family executives a sense of career security?	1	2	3	4	5	Or reward them with stock options?
11 Are your decisions based heavily on family values?	1	2	3	4	5	Or, more so, on maximizing share price value?

12 Are you more respectful of tradition?	1	2	3	4	5	Or a promoter of change?
13 Is wealth preservation a key objective of owners?	1	2	3	4	5	Or is entrepreneurship more the focus?
14 Do you look for independent directors who are supportive in nature?	1	2	3	4	5	Or those who are more dispassionately critical of decisions and policies?

SCORE FROM PART A:_____

B. Family Issues

1 Do you welcome family employment regardless of experience or educational qualifications?	1	2	3	4	5	Or have very selective family employment requirements before joining the business?
2 Is dissent accepted among family members so that people may express different views to management?	1	2	3	4	5	Or does the family attempt to be of one voice in communications to managers in the business?
3 Do individual family branches pass on ownership?	1	2	3	4	5	Or are there efforts so family future generations will have more equal ownership (per capital) regardless of size of different branches?
4 In decision-making, is there respect for elders?	1	2	3	4	5	Or more aggressive 'take charge' leadership?
5 Are non-employed owners involved in business decision-making?	1	2	3	4	5	Or quite 'hands off'?
6 Do family members feel the business is part of their identity?	1	2	3	4	5	Or feel very autonomous from the business?
7 Does the family show a high standard of living?	1	2	3	4	5	Or deliberately attempt to understate its wealth?
8 Are policies and rules for family members flexible?	1	2	3	4	5	Or quite formal and precise?
9 Is compensation of family members private?	1	2	3	4	5	Or openly disclosed to family members and to managers?

10	Are there many unspoken topics and issues among family members?	1	2	3	4	5	Or open communications?
11	Is family attendance at family business events voluntary?	1	2	3	4	5	Or expected or required?
12	Does the extended family spend lots of time with each other away from the business?	1	2	3	4	5	Or do folks spend most all of the personal time with their nuclear family?
13	Do family members see the business as creating opportunities for personal freedom?	1	2	3	4	5	Or does it give them more a sense of personal responsibility?
14	Do family members use company resources for personal use?	1	2	3	4	5	Or is use of expense accounts, vehicles or company assets for personal use prohibited?

SCORE FROM PART B: _____

The scoring is completed by totaling the Part A and Part B scores. This score is then compared to the scoring scale below to determine the Family Business Philosophy.

Score on Part A + Score on Part B = TOTAL POINTS

Family Business Philosophy:

Business First	*Family Enterprise*	*Family First*
90+ points	75–90 points	less than 75 points

APPENDIX D: SUCCESSOR'S CAREER ASSESSMENT

Step 1: Explore Your Personal Career Goals

Note: This assessment should be completed by successor generation family members currently employed by the firm or employed somewhere else but considering a family business career.

This exercise will challenge you to think about your career goals and how your family business can contribute to your plans for the future. Rank the following career outcomes by their importance to you and then check if they are achievable at your family business.

Note: Write 'NA' for any outcome that is NOT applicable to your career.

Rank	Career outcomes	Achievable
	Personal growth and development	
	Balanced personal/work life	
	Meaningful personal life	
	Substantial wealth (accumulation)	
	Financial security (comfortable)	
	Personal challenge	
	Opportunity to work with my family	
	Service to others	
	Prestige in the business community	
	Low-risk business venture	
	Base to identify new business opportunities	
	Maintenance of a family tradition	
	Ownership of the family business	
	Personal achievement	
	Opportunity for leadership	
	Other:	

Step 2: Develop Family Business Career Goals

Understanding your career goals is an important step to increasing your personal power in any business organization. Identifying career goals helps individuals to focus their talent and energy on the critical actions and tasks they must success-fully complete to achieve their goal. Identifying and sharing career goals are particularly important in the family system, because other family members may have similar aspirations. Open planning and regular performance reviews can help family members to develop realistic career expectations and minimize unhealthy competition and rivalries.

Using your top three career priorities from Step 1, develop specific and action-able goals. For example, if your first priority was an opportunity for leadership, identify what this means in terms of career positions, the ultimate goal (the presi-dency), and your planned timing.

Priorities	Specific goals	Timing
1		
2		
3		

Step 3: Successor's Assessment and Feedback Form

Understanding your strengths and weaknesses is an important developmental activity for any manager and is particularly critical for family business executives because their career advancement is dependent on their growth within the family firm. This exercise is designed to help you to identify areas for personal growth and to stimulate a constructive dialogue about your family and business compe-tencies. Use the Successor's Assessment and Feedback Form for a self-assessment or as a checklist to inventory your current capabilities for family business leader-ship. Your self-assessment responses will be used in the next activity. **Make at least two extra copies of the form before you complete it to share with others in Step 4: Seek Feedback**.

Successor's Assessment and Feedback Form

Note: Use the 'Other' lines to add skills you feel are critical to your family business.

	Needs work				Strength
	1	2	3	4	5

Personal leadership

Positively influences others

Coaches others

Builds teams

Shares a vision for the business

Other: _____

Family leadership

Balances family and business demands

Communicates effectively

Recognizes individual differences

Addresses conflict positively

Adaptable or compromises

Other: _____

Communication

Gives constructive feedback

States expectations clearly

Addresses conflict positively

Shares ideas and plans

Works at developing consensus

Other: _____

Personal characteristics

Is committed to the business

Demonstrates adaptability

Is determined to achieve success

Has awareness of personal limits

Demonstrates concern for ethics

	Needs work			Strength	
	1	2	3	4	5

Personal characteristics *(cont'd)*

- Is personally motivated
- Is disciplined
- Understands the 'big' picture
- Sets high performance standards
- Other: _____

Marketing competencies

- Sales management
- Market research
- Product development
- Direct mail marketing
- Customer support
- Distribution management
- Bids/proposals
- Other: _____

Operations/production

- Quality management
- Manufacturing management
- Inventory control
- Purchasing
- Cost analysis and control
- Production scheduling
- Other: _____

Finance

- Banking relationships
- Accounting and control
- Budgeting
- Cash flow management
- Credit and collections

	Needs work			Strength	
	1	2	3	4	5

Finance *(cont'd)*

Insurance and risk management

Other: _____

General management

Planning

Problem solving

Decision-making

Persuasion and negotiating

Human resources

Managing professionally

Other: _____

Industry/external relationships

Vendor/supplier relationships

Customer relationships

Product and technology knowledge

Awareness of competition

Other: _____

Family leadership

Is respected by family members

Is trusted by family members

Recognizes the contribution of other family members

Shares his/her business vision

Makes tough decisions

Appreciates family goals/values

Maintains positive relationships with the board and shareholders

Other: _____

Step 4: Seek Feedback

This section is designed to help you to obtain meaningful feedback from your family business system regarding your strengths and weaknesses as an employee or manager. This exercise should stimulate discussion about your management skills and provide a framework for creating your training and development needs.

Give a blank copy of the Successor's Assessment and Feedback Form (Step 3) to two influential people in your family system who can offer meaningful input on your management and family business competencies. Ask them to consider their responses within the context of your family business.

Step 5: Discuss Responses to Successor's Assessment and Feedback Form

After they have completed the Successor's Assessment and Feedback Form, share a copy of your completed self-assessment from Step 3 with each person and ask them to compare their assessment with your self-assessment. Discuss the differences in the results and any other points they feel are important to discuss.

Use the results of the three assessments to reflect on the following questions.

A. How does your assessment of yourself compare with the assessment of others from your family business?
B. Do you feel that your family business' management has an accurate perception of your management strengths and weaknesses? How can you influence and monitor their assessments in the future?
C. Do you have a realistic understanding of the future management skills needed by your family business?
D. What personal development actions do you feel would improve your performance and support the career goals identified in Step 2?
E. What other concerns or issues related to your career in the family firm should be addressed?

APPENDIX E: REARDON FAMILY ENTERPRISE CONTINUITY PLAN

Family Vision

Ten years from now we believe that the Reardon family will own Reardon Technology. The company will be recognized for technological leadership, quality manufacturing and the highly skilled workforce.

Statement of Family Commitment

We are fortunate to have a privately owned business in the Reardon family. The business provides our family with opportunities that are difficult to replicate elsewhere: developing innovative electronic components, earning financial independence, learning the skills of business and leadership, contributing actively to our community, and sharing in common family interests. To work productively is to grow, to respect humility, to know the realities of life. Maintaining the business in the family and seeking to expand and strengthen the business will help to assure that our family will have productive work and future challenges rather than live off the accomplishments of past generations. We are committed to stewardship of our family business for the benefit of our future generations.

Business Values

The business must be professionally managed. In that way, family members will know that they have earned their personal successes; those who work for us will know that their careers and families will be secure. Our Family Agreements confirm that our family business is run like a business. Family members will inevitably have needs and turn to the business to fill them. For that reason, we, as a family, have all agreed to help one another, when one is in need, from our personal resources – not from the business' assets.

We will create a family retirement fund apart from the business to ensure some comfort and security for each family member; we will also pay dividends (based on a board of directors' decision). We hope that family members use prudence by investing the majority of these funds rather than spending them.

Family Values

All family members are welcome in the business. We are fortunate to be a high growth business that creates new job opportunities. As in the past, however, family employment requires a university education and three years' outside work experience. A family employee is reviewed and rewarded like all other employees and may be terminated if their performance does not meet written standards.

We hope that one or more family members will qualify to be able future leaders of the business, a position that will require excellent business skills, exceptional performance and a commitment to the family's values. We want a qualified family member to serve as chief executive and to assume the traditions of our business and family, as well as to ensure by example that it remains a working business for the family – not a passive investment.

Governance

We have established a family council to ensure that the family stays committed and works hard to maintain a shared vision. Six members of the family will be elected as members for two-year terms (at least one member per branch). No family member may serve on the council for more than four consecutive years. The council will plan family meetings, develop family business educational activities and two council members will represent the family on the board of directors. All family members will be encouraged to participate in family meetings and pursue family leadership roles.

Board of Directors

Business decisions will be supported by a board of directors comprising two family council members, four outsiders selected because of demonstrated business knowledge and personal characteristics and the CEO. The outside directors elect the chairperson, make the final decisions on the CEO's compensation, approve dividends and participate in the management succession process. Two outside directors will serve on the Strategic Planning Committee to ensure the board's full support of our business plans and goals. Outside board members will be compensated at above market rates.

Family Council

The family council members will also accept informal roles as family leaders. In that position, they will be available to help any family member in need or to counsel family members on personal, financial or family business matters. The family council may identify investment opportunities for all family members to share in on a voluntary basis. These non-family business investments will provide another form of common family interests. Individual family members are encouraged to suggest any agenda item to the council on a confidential basis.

The family council will also work to examine and resolve family differences or serious conflicts at the request of any family member.

Family Mission

This plan is no stronger than the commitment and love of the entire family. Together we can provide great opportunities for ourselves and our children and even their children. It was done by our parents and surely we can do it again for the future generations.

APPENDIX F: COMPETITOR ANALYSIS WORKSHEET

Describing the Market and Competition

Understanding your competition and their business tactics is an important activity for improving your business performance. An essential outcome of a business plan is to identify how your firm can use its strengths to create an advantage for winning customers in the marketplace. Knowing your competition's strengths and weaknesses enables you to identify actions that create the largest competitive advantage for your firm. For example, if your competition develops a new product line and begins selling against your most profitable product line, it is useful to understand their marketing strategy and capabilities. If you know they lack the customer service staff to support the new line, you can develop a plan that demonstrates your strength in this critical area to protect your position. Before you explore specific competitors, it is useful to know or estimate characteristics about your market.

- How do you describe your market or industry?
- Approximately how large is your current market in dollars?
- What is the annual sales (percentage) growth rate of your market?
- What is the projected 5-year growth rate of your market?
- Do you expect an increase or decrease in competitive pressure? Why?

Competitor's name	Total sales	% of market share
1.		
2.		
3.		

Analyze the Competition

Using the Competitor Profile Worksheet, describe your three most challenging competitors and complete the self-profile of your firm:

Competitor profile worksheet	Competitor
Name	
Location	
Pricing strategy	
Target market	
Market position	
Estimated sales ($)	
Estimated employees	
Products/services offered	
Strengths	
Weaknesses	

Analyze your Firm

Self-profile worksheet	Your firm
Name	
Location	
Pricing strategy	
Target market	
Market position	
Estimated sales ($)	
Estimated employees	
Products/services offered	
Strengths	
Weaknesses	

APPENDIX G: REARDON TECHNOLOGY BUSINESS STRATEGY PLAN

Values

We believe that Reardon Technology has a challenging and rewarding future. During the last 30 years, we have gained the confidence of our suppliers, customers, employees, and community. We have created a competitive advantage based on technology leadership, developing our people, our family's commitment and a long-term investment strategy. Our customers recognize that we are committed to long-term relationships as 'their partners in business.' We assure them fair treatment and a commitment to serve their interests as well as our own.

Our success is in a large part due to the contributions of our employees. We owe them the confidence that our firm will prosper economically and will retain its key values: loyalty; innovation; personal advancement; and a rewards program that shares the results of our success.

We believe that there is an advantage of a family ownership and our shareholders are committed to the long-term perpetuation of the business as a private entity. Private ownership provides us with the freedom to invest in the future and to accommodate short-run variations in the economy without changing our strategy or modifying our valued relationships.

We are also hopeful that capable family members will join the business as employees and shareholders from future generations. Their participation helps assure everyone that our future business will reflect the values of our founder Thomas Reardon.

Business Vision

We are in the business of designing and manufacturing advanced electronic technology for the communications and computing markets. Historically, we have sold domestically achieving a recognized position of market leadership. Our success has demonstrated that we are able to design and market the latest technology in our field on a global basis. We owe our strength to the teamwork of our innovative engineers and quality manufacturing groups. We all know that they significantly affect our success, and we are committed to sharing our successes with them. We must also develop our marketing organization, which comprises customer-oriented people who provide our direct link with our customers.

Internal Assessment

Strengths

1. Reputation as a leading edge technology manufacturer
2. Strong engineering and R&D team

3. Long-term investment strategy
4. Excellent CEO and senior management group
5. Strong balance sheet and additional debt capacity
6. Demonstrated capability in integrating an acquisition

Weakness

1. Limited global marketing experience
2. No business governance function
3. Reliance on internal funding and debt to support expansion
4. Lack of shareholder participation
5. Discontented family members because of employment opportunities for the next generation
6. No family governance or shareholder participation in decisions

External Assessment

Opportunities

1. Global demand for Internet and communication electronics is growing at 30–40% per year
2. Industry consolidation may create acquisition candidates
3. Possibility of alliances with larger manufacturers that lack advanced technology
4. Alliances with suppliers or customers interested in increased integration

Threats

1. Inability to fund expansion internally
2. New technologies that replace existing electronics components
3. Industry-wide shortage of qualified engineering and technical personnel
4. Increased price competition from larger manufacturers
5. Less economies of scale compared to larger manufacturers
6. Accelerated rate of technology change creates lost sales and inventory obsolescence
7. Possible trade barriers from foreign governments to protect local manufacturers

Long-term Goals

Internet electronics products is a high growth global market. We expect to grow at least 30 percent per year in comparable product and market sales. Currently international sales are less than 10 percent of our revenues. Beginning next year will increase that to 20 percent with an increased growth for each of the next five years.

We expect to earn at least 50 percent of our sales from new products introduced within the last two years. We owe our shareholders a fair return on the money invested in the business. We expect to increase the Economic Value of the business by 20 percent per year. We will maintain a high profit margin and tight controls on assets to allow us to finance our growth with internally generated funds and bank debt. Our shareholders will earn a 4 percent dividend yield on their investment as long as the business return exceeds the 15 percent goal.

Our Strategy

The internal and external assessment positions our company with strong internal capabilities and in a highly attractive market. We are a successful company that needs to continue to renew itself. Our Strategic Potential indicates that one of the four basic business strategies in the exploit group would best support our future vision. We evaluated a consolidation strategy based on acquiring others, an aggressive marketing strategy to build market share, expanding our product line and global expansion. Based on the capital available, the family's confidence in management and the family's commitment to the vision we decided to pursue a global strategy. This strategy leverages our technology capabilities, positions us in a high growth market, and best utilizes our available capital.

We believe that the following are critical activities for the next fiscal year:

A. Continued strengthening of our research and development capabilities
B. Invest in manufacturing based on technologically challenging processes
C. Develop marketing programs based on global customer partnerships
D. Maintain investment in employee training and development
E. Develop an employee stock ownership plan
F. Conduct family meetings to ensure family participation and commitment
G. Organize a board of directors with a minimum of two outside members

Our Business Tactics

Product Development

We are a technology driven company. Our growth and profitability depends on our ability to design, manufacture and distribute industry-leading products. New products must have the promise of a profit margin equal or greater than our company goal. The product line will be continuously monitored to ensure that new products comprise 50 percent of our sales. R&D expense will remain at 6.5 percent of sales.

Marketing

We will engage our customers as partners in our research and product design activities. We will grow our domestic position while aggressively increasing our global marketing efforts. Our sales force shall identify a target list of preferred customers whose needs we can fully exceed. The role of our marketing team shall continue to increase as we work to expand our market share in the international marketplace.

Finance

Our company has a strong balance sheet and effective internal controls. We will manage our profit margins and assets to meet our profit and cash flow requirements. Our primary financial goal is to ensure that we can meet our capital expenditure budgets and other investments for strategic innovation projects and R&D.

Manufacturing

The production processes require that manufacturing is involved in all product design and planning. We will invest in the latest technology to ensure that our production is efficient and of the highest quality. Our order production and delivery systems are dedicated to fulfilling customer requests on a timely basis. We promise 7-day fulfillment on standard products and 14 days on special orders. We pledge to our customers a 99.7 percent quality assurance based on the stated product specifications. We will develop and maintain our systems to provide each customer with detailed performance information on every product run.

Employees

Our employees are a scarce resource that must be developed and prepared for increased technological and business responsibilities. We will provide an environment that makes it unnecessary for them to seek outside representation of their interests. All employees are entitled to a minimum of 10 days' training or personal development time per year. All technical, staff and mid-management positions are posted internally before conducting an outside search.

Our people deserve an opportunity to share in the success they help to create. All employees will participate in a company-wide stock-ownership program funded by the corporation.

Planning

We have formed a Strategic Planning Team to review our plans and identify new opportunities for growth or improved performance. The planning team will meet monthly and share with the entire organization an annual summary of the firm's plans. Each department will annually develop plans based on the organization's long-term vision to support our renewed business strategy. A summary of these plans will be distributed to each area before final forecasts, budgets and performance goals are determined.

Organization

Our organization is built on a 'work team' model designed to share the talents and energy of the team in accomplishing our goals. In addition to work teams there are boundary-spanning task forces to ensure the coordination and cooperation of different areas or functions. We are an informal organization that requires delegation of responsibility to assure quick and creative decision-making. Quarterly the operating committee, in preparation for the board of directors meeting, will ask each manager to recap their department's performance and identify accomplishments and challenges. We trust our people but owe them quarterly performance reviews to help them to develop and to learn from their experiences.

Budget and Forecasts

The 2001 Income and Cost Budget and 2001–2005 Sales Forecast and Capital Expenditure Allocations are attachments to this plan.

Notes

Preface

1   Arthur Andersen/MassMutual, *American Family Business Survey* (Springfield, MA: MassMutual, 1997).
2   'In Praise of the Family Firm', *The Economist*, **338** (March 9, 1996) 14.

Chapter 1

1   S. Freud, *Civilization and its Discontents* (London: Hogarth Press, 1955) p. 68.
2   B.S. Hollander, Family-Owned Business as a System: A Case Study of the Interaction of Family, Task, and Marketplace Components, (unpublished doctoral dissertation, School of Education, University of Pittsburgh, 1983); B. Benson, E. Crego and R. Drucker, *Your Family Business: A Guide for Growth and Survival* (New York: Dow Jones-Irwin, 1990).
3   T. Hubler and G. Ayres, 'Family Business Management Course', Graduate School of Business, University of St. Thomas, Minneapolis, MN (1996).
4   Arthur Andersen/MassMutual, *American Family Business Survey*, op. cit.
5   H. Mintzberg, *The Raise and Fall of Strategic Planning* (New York: Free Press, 1994).
6   F. Fukuyama, *Trust: The Social Virtues and the Creation of Prosperity* (New York: Free Press, 1995).
7   R. Mitchell and M. O'Neal, 'Managing by Values: Is Levi Strauss' Approach Visionary or Flaky?', *Business Week*, (August 8, 1995) 61–2.
8   I. Lansberg, 'The Succession Conspiracy', *Family Business Review*, **I**(2)(1988) 119–43.
9   Ibid.
10 Arthur Andersen/MassMutual, *American Family Business Survey*, op cit.
11 J.L. Ward, 'Perpetuating the Family Business'. In C.E. Aronoff, R.B. Good and J.L. Ward (eds), *The Future Of Private Enterprise* (Atlanta, GA: Georgia State University Press, 1986).
12 K. Kaye, 'When Family Business is a Sickness', *Family Business Review*, **IX**(4)(1996) 347–68.
13 L. Danco, *Beyond Survival* (New York: Reston Publishing, a Prentice Hall Company, 1975); N.C. Churchill and V.L. Lewis, 'The Five Stages Of Small Business Development', *Harvard Business Review*, **61**(3)(1983) 30–9; J.L. Ward, *Keeping the Family Business Healthy* (San Francisco: Jossey-Bass, 1987); B. Carter and M. McGoldrick, *The Changing Family Life Cycle: A Framework for Family Therapy*, 2nd edn (Boston: Allyn & Bacon, 1989); and K.E. Gersick, J.A. Davis, M. McCollom Hampton, and I. Lansberg, *Generation to Generation: Life Cycles of the Family Business* (Boston: Harvard Business School Press, 1997).
14 P.M. Senge, *The Fifth Discipline: The Art and Practice of the Learning Organization* (New York: Doubleday Currency, 1990).

15   E.H. Schein, 'The Role of the Founder in Creating Organizational Culture', *Organizational Dynamics*, **12**(1983) 13–28; D. Harris, J.L. Martinez and J.L. Ward, 'Is Strategy Different for Family-Owned Business?' *Family Business Review*, **VII**(2)(1994) 159–76.
16   M. Porter, 'What is Strategy?' *Harvard Business Review*, **72** (November–December, 1996) 61–78.
17   C.K. Prahalad and G. Hamel, 'The Core Competence of the Corporation', *Harvard Business Review*, **90**(3)(May–June, 1990) 79–91.

Chapter 2

1   W.C. Handler, 'Succession Experiences of the Next Generation', *Family Business Review*, **V**(3)(1992) 283–307.
2   L. Danco, *Beyond Survival*, op. cit.
3   N.C. Churchill and K.J. Hatten, 'Non-Market-Based Transfers of Wealth and Power: A Research Framework for Family Business', *Family Business Review*, **X**(1)(1997) 53–67.
4   K.E. Gersick, J.A. Davis, M. McCollom Hampton, and I. Lansberg, *Generation to Generation: Life Cycles of the Family Business*, op.cit.
5   E.S. Browning, 'Heard on the Street: Wharton Study Connects Strengths and Flaws of Directors to Companies' Performance', *Wall Street Journal* (April 25, 1997) 2.
6   J.C. Collins and J.L. Porras, *Built to Last: Successful Habits of Visionary Companies* (New York: HarperBusiness, 1994).
7   A. Morita, *Made in Japan*, (New York: E.P. Dutton, 1986) pp. 147–8.
8   J. C. Collins and J. L. Porras, 'Building Your Company's Vision', *Harvard Business Review*, **74**(5)(September–October, 1996) 65–77.
9   S. Walton and J. Huey, *Made in America* (New York: Doubleday, 1992).
10   P.M. Senge, *The Fifth Discipline*, op. cit.

Chapter 3

1   R.T. Mowday, R.M. Steers and L.W. Porter, 'The Measurement of Organizational Commitment', *Journal of Vocational Behavior*, **14** (1979) 226.
2   C.E. Aronoff and J.L. Ward, *Family Meetings: How to Build a Stronger Family and a Stronger Business* (Marietta, GA: Business Owners Resources, 1992).

Chapter 4

1   V.H. Vroom and A.G. Jago, *The New Leadership: Managing Participation in Organizations* (Upper Saddle River, NJ: Prentice Hall, 1988).
2   M. Hammer and J. Champy, *Reengineering the Corporation: A Manifesto for Business Revolution* (New York: HarperBusiness, 1994).
3   T. Hubler, 'The Ten Most Prevalent Obstacles to Family-Business Succession Planning', *Family Business Review*, **XII**(2)(1999) 117–21.
4   I. Lansberg, 'The Family Side of Family Business: A Conversation with Salvador Minuchin', *Family Business Review*, **V**(3)(1992) 309–21.

5 F. Walsh, 'Healthy Family Functioning: Conceptual and Research Developments', *Family Business Review*, **VII**(2)(1994) 175–98.
6 M.F.R. Kets de Vries, *Family Business: Human Dilemmas in the Family Firm* (London: International Thomson Business Press, 1996) p. 63.
7 M. Bowen, *Family Therapy in Clinical Practice* (New York: Aronson, 1978).
8 M.F.R. Kets de Vries, *Family Business*, op. cit.
9 K. Danco, *From the Other Side of the Bed – a Woman Looks at Life in the Family Business* (Cleveland: University Press, 1981).
10 M.F.R. Kets de Vries, *Family Business*, op. cit., p. 44.
11 For further information on the Ahlström case, see 'Harvard's Praise for Finnish Firm Rips Family Apart', *Wall Street Journal Europe*, (May 18, 2000) 1.
12 R. Chernow, *Titan: The Life of John D. Rockefeller, Sr.* (New York: Vintage Books, 1998) p. 506.
13 C. Blondel and L. Van der Heyden, 'The Next Generation in Large Family Firms', Presentation at the 10th World Conference of the Family Business Network, Stockholm, 1999.
14 W. C. Kim and R. Mauborgne, 'Fair Process: Managing in the Knowledge Economy', *Harvard Business Review*, **75** (July–August, 1997) 69.
15 C.E. Aronoff and J.L. Ward, *Family Meetings: How to Build a Stronger Family and a Stronger Business* (Marietta, GA: Business Owners Resources, 1992).
16 M. McCollom, 'Organizational Stories in a Family-owned Business', *Family Business Review*, **V**(1)(1992) 3–23.
17 M. Bowen, 'The Use of Family Theory in Clinical Practice', *Comprehensive Psychiatry*, **7** (1966) 345–74.
18 K. Danco, *From the Other Side of the Bed*, op. cit.
19 R.S. Carlock, *The Directory: The International Guide to Family Business Education* (Springfield, MA: MassMutual/The Blue Chip Company, 1996).

Chapter 5

1 L. Combrinck-Graham, 'The Developmental Model of Family Systems', *Family Process*, **24** (June, 1985) 139–50.
2 R.S. Carlock, 'Filling Big Shoes at the Carlson Companies: Interviews with Curt Carlson and Marilyn Carlson Nelson', *Family Business Review*, **XII**(1)(1999) 87–93.
3 H. Mintzberg, HBR Classics, 'The Manager's Job: Folklore and Fact', *Harvard Business Review*, **90**(2)(March–April, 1990) 163–78.
4 L. Danco, *Beyond Survival*, op. cit.
5 T. Hirschfeld, *Business Dad: How Great Businessmen Can Make Great Fathers (and Vice Versa)* (Boston: Little, Brown, 1999).
6 T.J. Covin, 'How Young Graduates Rate the Family Business', *Family Business*, **5**(4)(1994) 42–3.
7 J. Timmons, *New Ventures Creation: Entrepreneurship for the 21st Century* (Chicago: Irwin, 1994).
8 M.F.R. Kets de Vries, *Family Business*, op. cit., p. 66.
9 H. Olson, 'Succession and Gender: The Daughter in the Family Business', paper presented at the annual meeting of the Midwest Sociological Society, Minneapolis, MN, (1999, April).
10 M. Bowen, *Family Therapy in Clinical Practice*, op. cit.
11 K. Kaye, 'When Family Business is a Sickness', op. cit.
12 S. Goldberg, 'Research Note: Effective Successors in Family-Owned Businesses: Significant Elements', *Family Business Review*, **IX**(2)(1996) 185–97.

13 J. Zaslow, 'New Nepotism Calls for Junior to Earn Stripes Away from Home', *Wall Street Journal* (January 14, 1986) 35.
14 S. Goldberg, 'Research Note: Effective Successors', op. cit.
15 M.H. Morris, R.O. Williams, J.A. Allen and R.A. Avila, 'Correlates of Success in Family Business Transitions', *Journal of Business Venturing*, **12** (1997) 385–401.
16 G. Swogger, 'Assessing the Successor Generation in Family Businesses', *Family Business Review*, **IV**(4)(1991) 397–410.
17 F. Herz Brown, 'Loss and Continuity in the Family Firm', *Family Business Review*, **VI**(2)(1993) 111–30.
18 L. Danco, *Beyond Survival*, op. cit.

Chapter 6

1 This book proposes an expanded model based on six Ownership Configurations. See Gersick *et al. Generation to Generation: Life Cycles of the Family Business*, op. cit. The authors describe a three-stage model and present cases to demonstrate the impact of life cycle on family firms.
2 J.H. Eggers, K.T. Leahy and N.C. Churchill, 'Stages Of Small Business Growth Revisited: Insights Into Growth Path and Leadership/Management Skills in Low- and High-Growth Companies'. In W.D. Bygrave, S. Birely, N.C. Churchill, E. Gatewood, F. Hoy and W.E. Wetzel (eds), *Frontiers of Entrepreneurship Research*, (Boston: Babson College, 1994) 131–44.
3 A genogram is an expanded family tree that represents the family's structure and relationships across multiple generations. Different types of relationships are designated using a standard notation. Typical relationship patterns include 'close', 'conflicted' and 'cut-off'. Genograms note key family events and dates such as births, adoptions, deaths, marriages and divorces along with demographic information such as health, education or career experiences. For more information on genograms see M. McGoldrick, R. Gerson and S. Shellenberger, *Genograms in Family Assessment and Intervention* (2nd edn) (New York: Norton, 1999).
4 E. Poza, 'Managerial Practices that Support Entrepreneurship and Continued Growth', *Family Business Review*, **I**(4)(1988) 339–58.
5 F. Neubauer and A.G. Lank, *The Family Business: Its Governance and Sustainability* (London: Macmillan – now Palgrave, 1998) p. 247.
6 J. Magretta, 'Governing the family-owned enterprise: An interview with Finland's Krister Ahlström', *Harvard Business Review*, **76**(1)(January–February, 1998) 112–23
7 T. Teal, 'Not a Fool, Not a Saint', *Fortune*, (November 11, 1996) 201.
8 W.G. Dyer, Jr, *Cultural Change in Family Firms: Anticipating and Managing Business and Family Transitions* (San Francisco: Jossey-Bass, 1986).
9 F.M. de Visscher, C.E. Aronoff and J.L. Ward, *Financing Transitions: Managing Capital and Liquidity in the Family Business* (Marietta, GA: Business Owners Resources, 1995).
10 Ownership Agreements are intended to articulate a family's shared understanding of their ownership rights and responsibilities. These agreements should be reviewed by the firm's legal professionals to ensure that family intentions and expectations are consistent with legal requirements.
11 G. Ayres, 'Rough Corporate Justice', *Family Business Review*, **XI**(2)(1998) 91–106.
12 K.M. File and R.A. Prince, 'Attributes for Family Business Failure: The Heir's Perspective', *Family Business Review*, **IX** (1996) 171–84.
13 G. Ayres, 'Rough Corporate Justice', op. cit.
14 F. Herz Brown, 'Loss and Continuity in the Family Firm', op. cit.

15 G. Ayres, 'Rough Family Justice', *Family Business Review*, **III**(1)(1990) 3–23.
16 G. Ayres, 'Rough Corporate Justice', op. cit.

Chapter 7

1 Arthur Andersen/MassMutual, *American Family Business Survey*, op. cit.
2 R.T. Pascale and A.G. Athos, *The Art of Japanese Management* (New York: Warner Books, 1981) p. 125.
3 P.F. Drucker, 'The Future Has Already Happened', *Harvard Business Review*, **75**(5) (1997) 20–4.
4 M. Porter, 'What is Strategy?' *Harvard Business Review*, **72** (November–December, 1996) 61–78.
5 M.E. Porter, *Competitive Strategy* (New York: Free Press, 1980) p. 4.
6 Ibid.

Chapter 9

1 The formulas presented here are to demonstrate the concept of business valuation. All valuation formulas or models used for estate, buy–sell agreements or other business purposes should be reviewed by qualified tax and legal professionals.
2 J.L. Ward, *Keeping the Family Business Healthy*, op. cit.

Chapter 10

1 F. Neubauer and A.G. Lank, *The Family Business: Its Governance and Sustainability*, op.cit.
2 J.L. Ward, *Creating Effective Boards for Private Enterprises* (San Francisco: Jossey-Bass, 1991).

Glossary of Terms

Basic Business Strategies   Twenty-seven specific business actions that determine how the firm will compete.

Business Strategy Plan   Management decisions and actions related to assessing the firm's strategic potential, exploring business strategies and finalizing strategy and investment decisions.

Business Vision   Management's projection of what the business can become in the future.

Family Agreement   The family's shared understanding of the rules that provide consistency in employment, ownership and family participation relationships.

Family Effect   The competitive advantage based on patient family capital created by knowing the risk factors, having liquidity opportunities and sharing a commitment to the business.

Family Enterprise   The overlap between the family and business systems created when multiple generations of a family own or manage a business.

Family Enterprise Continuity Plan   Family planning activities related to family participation, management and leadership, and ownership.

Family Ownership Forces   The three ownership variables that give family ownership groups their changing characteristics (multiple generations, growing numbers and separation of management and ownership roles).

Family Payouts   Cash or financial resources that are used for the family's benefit including bonuses, dividends, funding for ownership transfers, retirement programs or stock repurchases.

Family Reinvestment Decision   The family or ownership group's decision on investing or harvesting the family business.

Family Vision   The family's future expectations for their relationship with each other and the business.

Ownership Configurations   Family businesses can move through six different phases of ownership development each with challenges and characteristics The six phases are Entrepreneurial, Owner-manager, Family Partnership, Sibling Partnership, Cousins' Collaboration and Family Syndicate.

Parallel Planning Process The integration of family and business thinking and action in the formulation of long-term family business plans.

Shared Future Vision An understanding between the family and management that describes future (five or more years) business success and the family's relationship with the business.

Statement of Family Commitment A family's pledge to an active relationship with the business based on the family's willingness to contribute time, talent and capital to support the business' future success.

STEPP Analysis A framework for exploring the general environment in which every organization exists. The analysis identifies environmental factors (social, technology, economic, political and physical) that could affect the organization's future performance.

Strategic Commitment Management beliefs about how they can successfully grow the business.

Strategic Direction Seven broad groups of related business actions that determine how a firm will compete based on Strategic Potential.

Strategic Management A comprehensive model of business management that fully integrates planning and action processes to recognize opportunities (strategic thinking), make decisions (strategic formulation), take action (strategic implementation) and improve performance (strategic reformulation).

Strategic Potential The firm's future prospects based on management's assessment of the firm's internal capabilities and the attractiveness of its external environment.

Strategic Priority Three generic approaches appropriate to a firm based on its Strategic Potential. **Renewal** is maximizing current strategies in existing or related markets. **Reformulation** is improving the existing strategy by moving to a more attractive market or strengthening the firm's capabilities. **Regeneration** is finding a new strategy or opportunity to restore the business' performance.

SWOT Analysis A framework for conducting an internal (strengths and weaknesses) and external (opportunities and threats) assessment of an organization.

Index

Page numbers in *italic* refer to tables, for example 'annuity, family business, 207–8, *208*'.
Page numbers in **bold** refer to entries in the Glossary of Terms, for example 'Business Vision, 31, 40–1, **264**'